Economic Aid and
International Cost Sharing

Economic Aid
and
International
Cost Sharing

By

John Pincus

The RAND Corporation

The Johns Hopkins Press

Baltimore, Maryland

To

ELIZABETH and GREGORY PINCUS

and to our memory of their parents

Preface

This study is the outgrowth of recent work of mine on a variety of subjects, all of which turned out to be related to a common theme. In a sense this study is an effort to demonstrate that relationship by a general review of the factors that determine the nature of international cost-sharing arrangements, with special emphasis on sharing the costs of economic aid to underdeveloped countries. It includes a good deal of empirical material, particularly on the relation between external assistance and economic growth; on the measurement of economic aid costs; and on the relation between commodity policy and economic aid. There is also some discussion of the history of international cost sharing in a number of international organizations.

The primary objectives are to investigate what lies behind the demand for economic aid; what influences the supply and distribution of economic aid costs; to what degree, at present, that supply and distribution meet criteria of adequacy, efficiency, and equity; and what methods can be used to increase "equitably" the flow of resources from rich to poor countries. This task requires some analysis of the application of tax theory to cost sharing in international organizations and in military alliances, where similar problems have arisen.

The study may be of special interest to people working in the field of economic development, particularly those concerned with economic aid, and may also be useful to students of the financing of international organizations.

In reviewing the manuscript for publication there was the perennial temptation to make substantial last-minute amendments, reflecting changes in my own views, as well as to include the most recent data. But it seemed to make more sense to stop revising at a certain point, whatever the imperfections. I hope to be able to return to some of these topics, as they affect the relations among trade, aid, and the economic growth of under-developed countries.

JOHN PINCUS

March, 1965

Acknowledgments

Over the past two years, so many people have collaborated with me in this work that a complete acknowledgment would almost constitute a monograph in itself. I hope this partial list will serve as an earnest of my intentions.

The study was undertaken as part of The RAND Corporation's research program for the office of the Assistant Secretary of Defense, International Security Affairs. Large sections of Chapters 3, 5, and 6 previously appeared as RAND Corporation publications. A condensed version of Chapter 6 appeared in *Foreign Affairs*, January 1964, as "What Policy for Commodities?" Part of Chapter 5 appeared in *The Review of Economics and Statistics*, November 1963, as "The Cost of Foreign Aid." Otto Eckstein, editor of the *Review*, has offered valuable advice. Other colleagues who provided intellectual stimulus and criticism include Doris Iklé of the Stanford Research Institute; Charles Wolf, Jr., of The RAND Corporation, who reviewed the entire manuscript in detail; Dr. Barbara Berman of The Brookings Institution; and Professor Richard Caves of Harvard University. Portions of the manuscript have benefited from the criticism of Horst Mendershausen and Fred Moore of The RAND Corporation. I am also indebted to the staff of the Organization for Economic Cooperation and Development for providing data used in the computations of Chapters 3 and 5.

Professor R. R. Bowie, director of the Harvard University Center for International Affairs, generously allowed me to use the facilities of the Center, where this manuscript was written in the summer of 1963.

A number of the computations in Chapters 3 and 5 are based on real-income estimates prepared by Professor Irving B. Kravis of the University of Pennsylvania. His estimates are shown as the Appendix to Chapter 3 of this study. Sang C. Suh of Harvard University assisted with several of the computations of Chapters 1 and 2.

Finally, among the list of my intellectual creditors, the largest accounts payable are to three friends and colleagues: Professor Carl Kaysen of Harvard University, who originally suggested cost sharing as a research topic; Dr. Charles Zwick of The RAND Corporation, who encouraged me to write this volume; and, although there is assistance for which no acknowledgment is adequate, Professor Edward Mason of Harvard University. The guidance he has given me in this study only adds further to a record of professional encouragement and personal kindness for which I remain indebted.

Contents

xi

Tables

Chapter 4

Chapter 5

Chapter 6

Abbreviations

AID	Agency for International Development
CCC	Commodity Credit Corporation
DAC	Development Assistance Committee of the Organization for Economic Cooperation and Development
ECE	Economic Commission for Europe of the United Nations
EEC	European Economic Community
FAO	Food and Agriculture Organization
GATT	General Agreement on Tariffs and Trade
IBRD	International Bank for Reconstruction and Development
IDA	International Development Association
IFC	International Finance Corporation
IMF	International Monetary Fund
NATO	North Atlantic Treaty Organization
OAS	Organization of American States
OECD	Organization for Economic Cooperation and Development
OEEC	Organization for European Economic Cooperation
SAC	Strategic Air Command
UPU	Universal Postal Union
USDA	United States Department of Agriculture

CHAPTER

1

Some Aspects of the Foreign-trade Impact on Economic Growth

Introduction

This is primarily a study of methods for equitably sharing the costs of international economic assistance to underdeveloped countries. Chapters 1 and 2 discuss the circumstances of requirements for foreign exchange and for external capital that lead to the burden-sharing problem. They set the stage for subsequent chapters, which analyze the theoretical and practical issues involved in sharing the costs of internationally financed activities, and advance proposals for dealing with some of these issues. The reader who is primarily interested in burden-sharing issues, and not in the economic questions of trade and development that lead to the demand for aid, can begin directly with Chapter 3, which also presents fewer technical difficulties for noneconomists than the first two chapters.

There is a considerable literature dealing with the relation between less developed countries' economic growth and their international trade. This chapter makes no attempt to review the field, but limits itself to the points of principal interest for this study:

1. Does the record show that foreign-exchange limitations are likely to be an important barrier to economic growth?

2. How have less developed countries financed their foreign-exchange requirements in the past?

3. What do existing trends suggest about the degree to which trade can finance these requirements in the future?

These questions in turn lead to a discussion of the need for promoting international measures aimed at expanding trade and capital flows, particularly through official channels; and thus to a review of the burden-sharing issue as it affects trade and aid.

Are Foreign-exchange Limitations a Barrier to Economic Growth?

It is generally assumed in the literature that the inability to finance imports limits the rate of economic growth in underdeveloped countries. A country that is moving from static subsistence toward a modern commercial economy with relatively high rates of investment and of output growth is normally considered to have a rapidly growing import demand for consumption and investment, the fulfillment of which often has to be partly financed by foreign borrowing.[1] As the country becomes mature economically, it will tend to run an export surplus in its trade and to become a capital exporter. According to Sombart, with inconclusive empirical verification from Deutsch and Eckstein, the country's trade will then decline as a percentage of gross national product.[2]

It is alleged by Singer, Prebisch, Nurkse, Mehta, and others that in recent years this normal process has been short-circuited by trade-balance problems.[3] Industrial countries' demand for exports is growing relatively slowly, for a number of reasons: low income-elasticities of demand for primary commodities; substitution of synthetics for agricultural raw materials and minerals; and economy in the use of raw materials. Furthermore, if the aggregate demand for underdeveloped countries' exports is

[1] C. P. Kindleberger, *International Trade and the National Economy*, Yale University Press, New Haven, Conn., 1962, Chap. 2. Hilgerdt's well-known study implies a similar process (League of Nations, *Industrialization and Foreign Trade*, Geneva, 1945).

[2] K. W. Deutsch and A. Eckstein, "National Industrialization and the Declining Share of the International Economic Sector," *World Politics*, Vol. 13, January 1961, pp. 267–299. See also H. B. Chenery, "Patterns of Industrial Growth," *American Economic Review*, Vol. 50, September 1960, pp. 624–654.

[3] H. W. Singer, "The Distribution of Gains between Investing and Borrowing Countries," *American Economic Review, Papers and Proceedings*, Vol. 40, May 1950, pp. 473–485; R. Prebisch, "Commercial Policy in Underdeveloped Countries," *American Economic Review, Papers and Proceedings*, Vol. 49, May 1959, pp. 251–269; Ragnar Nurkse, *Patterns of Trade and Development*, Almquist and Wiksell, Stockholm, 1959; F. Mehta, "The Effect of Adverse Income Terms of Trade on the Secular Growth of Underdeveloped Countries," *Indian Economic Journal*, Vol. 4, July 1956, pp. 9–21.

price-inelastic, the terms of trade are likely to move against them when productivity increases shift the aggregate supply functions. This deterioration in terms of trade is apt to be the greater as underdeveloped countries' import demand is more income-elastic and price-inelastic, and as industrial countries' export supply functions shift less to the right with productivity increases.[4]

It is therefore contended that underdeveloped countries must rely primarily on industrialization and expansion of the domestic market as the basis for long-run economic growth, in contrast to the nineteenth-century pattern of export-led growth.[5]

This viewpoint has been disputed on theoretical and empirical grounds by a number of writers, including Haberler, Baldwin, Meier, Morgan, and others.[6] They have claimed that trade is still potentially important as an engine for economic growth in less developed countries; that the data on terms of trade show no sign of long-run deterioration, particularly if single-factor terms of trade are considered; and that the attempt to rely on domestic industrialization at the expense of international specialization and trade is likely to be adverse to long-run welfare.

Kindleberger, Seers, and the United Nations present data tending to support the Singer-Prebisch argument that terms of trade are deteriorating in the long run.[7] Chenery, arguing from cross-sectional data that import substitution has been a vital growth factor, lends support both to the case for growth through domestic industrialization and for the presumption that foreign-exchange shortages are an element in the decision to create

[4] R. E. Caves, *Trade and Economic Structure*, Harvard University Press, Cambridge, Mass., 1960, p. 261; Gerald M. Meier, *International Trade and Development*, Harper and Row, New York, 1963, pp. 56–63.

[5] For discussion of the nineteenth-century pattern, see Kindleberger, *International Trade*, pp. 196–204; R. E. Caves and R. H. Holton, *The Canadian Economy*, Harvard University Press, Cambridge, Mass., 1959, Chaps. 3, 4; and Nurkse, *Patterns of Trade*.

[6] Gottfried Haberler, "Terms of Trade and Economic Development," in H. S. Ellis (ed.), *Economic Development for Latin America*, St. Martin's Press, New York, 1961, pp. 275–297; R. E. Baldwin, "Secular Movements in the Terms of Trade," *American Economic Review, Papers and Proceedings*, Vol. 45, May 1955, pp. 259–269; Meier, Chaps. 3, 7; and T. Morgan, "The Long-run Terms of Trade between Agriculture and Manufacturing," *Economic Development and Cultural Change*, Vol. 8, October 1959, pp. 1–23.

[7] C. P. Kindleberger, "The Terms of Trade and Economic Development," *Review of Economics and Statistics*, Vol. 40, February 1958 (Supplement), pp. 72–85; D. Seers, "A Theory of Inflation and Growth in Underdeveloped Economies Based on the Experience of Latin America," *Oxford Economic Papers*, Vol. 14, June 1962, pp. 173–195; UN, *World Economic Survey 1962*, New York, 1963, pp. 1–5.

import-competing industries.[8] From the Chenery model, one could argue that limitations on import capacity actually stimulate growth, a proposition also implied by Hirschman's formulations concerning import substitution as a basis for industrial development, and subsequently as a basis for growth through backward and forward linkages.[9]

In applying empirical tests to aggregative hypotheses, the data, or at least some of them, can be used to support entirely contradictory views. Thus the views of Haberler and Meier, cited above, gain support from the 1958 General Agreement on Tariffs and Trade (GATT) report on trends in international trade, from the United Nations World Economic Survey for 1958, and from Morgan's study of long-run terms of trade, which indicate that there was an improvement in underdeveloped countries' terms of trade between 1928 and 1957, no decline in their share of world trade during the same period, and no secular decline in their terms of trade over a much longer period.[10]

Supporters of viewpoints that emphasize the declining growth of demand for primary exports, the importance of domestic industrialization and linkages in creating external economies, and dynamic situations favoring growth can point to other data. Thus—

1. Industrial countries' trade has grown much faster than that of under-developed countries since 1957; comparing 1926–1929 with 1960–1962, we find a slower relative growth of underdeveloped countries' trade (Table 1–1).

2. Similarly, with the terms of trade, Kindleberger's data on long-run trends (1870–1952) in industrial Europe's trade with other countries tend to support the case for long-run declines in underdeveloped countries' situations.[11]

---

[8] "Patterns of Industrial Growth," p. 641; A. O. Hirschman, *The Strategy of Economic Development*, Yale University Press, New Haven, Conn., 1958, pp. 182–192.

[9] H. B. Chenery, "Comparative Advantage and Development Policy," *American Economic Review*, Vol. 51, March 1961, pp. 18–51; Hirschman, p. 124.

[10] GATT, *Trends in International Trade*, Geneva, 1958, Appendix Table A; UN, *World Economic Survey 1958*, New York, 1959, p. 18; Morgan, pp. 6–17.

[11] "Terms of Trade," pp. 72–85.

The evidence on both sides of the terms-of-trade argument leaves unanswered the question of whether commodity terms of trade are a good index of welfare. See Meier, Chap. 3; and H. W. Singer, "Comment on 'The Terms of Trade and Economic Development'," *Review of Economics and Statistics*, Vol. 40, February 1958 (Supplement), pp. 85–88. The trend of terms of trade over the past decade has clearly been against under-developed countries; however, this reflects the fact that terms of trade in the early 1950's were very favorable to less developed countries compared with most other periods in this century

TABLE 1–1: DEVELOPED AND UNDERDEVELOPED COUNTRIES' GROWTH OF
AND SHARES IN WORLD EXPORTS, 1928–1962

A. Growth of Exports

Area	Year			
	1928	1938	1948	1962
Developed areas				
Exports ($ billion)	21.4	15.2	36.5	94.7
Value index (1928 = 100)		71	171	443
Underdeveloped areas				
Exports ($ billion)	10.4	5.9	17.1	29.0
Value index (1928 = 100)		57	164	279

B. Share of Exports (% of World Total)

Area	Year					
	1928	1938	1950	1955	1960	1962
Underdeveloped areas	31	31	31	26	21	21
Developed areas	63	62	61	64	67	67
Communist areas	6	7	8	10	12	12

SOURCES: Export values from GATT, *Trends in International Trade 1958*, Appendix Table A; and UN, *Statistical Yearbook 1962*, Table 152. Shares of exports from UN, *World Economic Survey 1962*, p. 102, and *Monthly Bull. Stat.*, June 1963, Table 44; and GATT, *Trends in International Trade*, Appendix Table A.

NOTE: Developed areas here include Western Europe, United States, Canada, Australia, New Zealand, Japan, and South Africa. Underdeveloped areas make up the rest of the world, excluding Communist countries.

3. The industrial countries' trade with each other has risen much faster than their trade with underdeveloped countries in the postwar period; and there is evidence that this may also have been true between 1900 and 1929.[12]

4. Chenery's detailed statistical analysis leads to the argument that import substitution is an important basis for growth.[13]

[12] UN, *Statistical Yearbook 1962*, New York, Table 153; League of Nations, *Industrialization and Foreign Trade*, Chaps. 3, 6. The 1900–1929 evidence is indirect; industrial countries' imports of manufactures grew faster than world imports of primary products.

[13] "Patterns of Industrial Growth," pp. 624–654. Deutsch and Eckstein argue that trade declines in relative importance as the country grows, but their study reveals that the trend is not strong and is interspersed with fluctuations. Therefore, it must be said that the empirical verification for the declining share of trade is quite weak, particularly for countries with population of less than 40 to 50 million.

In general, examination of the aggregate data tends to make one distrust their adequacy for verifying any hypothesis about the optimum course of development. The points that seem clear are that underdeveloped countries have become a relatively smaller factor in world trade (Table 1–1), and that their command over imports has increased slowly over recent years, particularly if petroleum exporters are excluded. Table 1–2 shows the trend of their exports and capital flows since 1956. Table 1–3 shows trends of trade and exports in the past decade.

TABLE 1–2: EXCHANGE RECEIPTS OF LESS DEVELOPED COUNTRIES, 1956–1963
(In $ billion equivalent)

Year	Foods and Beverages	Agricultural Raw Materials and Mineral Ores	Petroleum and Other Fuels	Manufactures	Private Investment (Net)	Foreign Aid (Gross)	Total
1956	8.0	7.0	6.5	3.3	3.0	3.7	31.5
1957	8.3	6.9	7.0	3.2	3.5	4.6	33.5
1958	8.2	6.2	7.4	2.8	2.5	5.2	32.3
1959	7.8	7.2	7.3	3.3	2.3	5.3	33.2
1960	8.1	7.6	7.7	3.7	2.5	5.9	35.5
1961	8.0	7.4	8.1	4.0	2.7	6.5	36.7
1962	8.4	7.4	8.8	4.2	2.4	7.8	39.0
1963	9.4	7.6	9.5	4.8	2.4	7.3	41.0

SOURCES: UN, *Monthly Bull. Stat.*, March 1962–March 1965; OECD, *Flow of Financial Resources to Countries in Course of Economic Development*, 1956–1961 (title varies); and unpublished OECD sources.

The aggregate data appear most consistent with Nurkse's agnostic view that the issue is not whether to support or condemn international specialization as an aspect of development policy, but rather whether the market opportunities are most favorable domestically or internationally. Therefore, it is a matter that will depend largely on production possibilities and demand in each country.[14] He concludes that economic trends in the twentieth century are less favorable to underdeveloped countries' economic growth than they were in the last century, both for reasons discussed above and because many of their twentieth-century industries (coffee, cocoa, petroleum, nonferrous metals) do not create linkages that force a large sector of the economy from subsistence farming to modern agriculture, or from agriculture to industry.

[14] R. Nurkse, *Equilibrium and Growth in the World Economy*, Harvard University Press, Cambridge, Mass., 1961, Chap. 10.

TABLE 1–3: TERMS-OF-TRADE, PRICE, AND VOLUME INDEXES, AND VALUE OF TRADE: 1951–1961

A. Terms of Trade (1953 = 100)

Area	1951	1952	1953	1954	1955	1956	1957	1958	1959	1960	1961
Developed areas	94	97	100	98	98	99	98	102	104	105	106
Underdeveloped areas	112	100	100	106	105	102	98	98	97	97	95
Latin America	107	98	100	112	103	99	94	90	85	86	86
(excluding petroleum)	109	99	100	111	101	98	91	85	80	82	81
Central Africa	108	99	100	113	112	105	95	96	95	94	87
Asia	118	103	100	101	104	101	97	101	107	110	106
Asia (excluding Japan)	118	100	100	97	106	100	97	98	106	104	94
Middle East	114	100	100	107	107	106	108	112	105	104	102
(excluding petroleum)	143	113	100	112	109	111	112	107	102	101	107

B. Price Index and Volume of Trade Index (1953 = 100)

Area		1951 P	1951 V	1952 P	1952 V	1953 P	1953 V	1954 P	1954 V	1955 P	1955 V	1956 P	1956 V	1957 P	1957 V	1958 P	1958 V	1959 P	1959 V	1960 P	1960 V	1961 P	1961 V
Developed areas	Exports	104	95	104	94	100	100	98	106	98	115	101	127	104	136	101	132	99	143	100	160	101	168
	Imports	110	95	108	95	100	100	99	105	100	119	102	128	105	135	99	135	96	150	97	169	96	178
Underdeveloped areas	Exports	118	97	107	93	100	100	102	102	102	110	102	117	101	120	97	120	94	130	95	136	92	140
	Imports	105	106	107	106	100	100	96	109	97	117	99	124	103	135	99	130	97	130	98	140	97	142
Latin America	Exports	108	95	103	90	100	100	107	97	99	105	99	115	96	118	90	120	84	130	84	133	83	134
	Imports	101	118	105	112	100	100	95	119	97	119	99	122	103	139	98	130	99	121	98	127	98	132
Africa	Exports	114	89	110	89	100	100	103	105	102	112	103	117	101	121	100	121	93	134	93	146	89	155
	Imports	98	104	107	100	100	100	97	107	96	119	99	119	102	127	95	131	96	128	97	140	97	137
Asia	Exports	138	103	113	97	100	100	96	108	100	121	97	132	98	139	94	133	98	148	103	160	97	172
	Imports	117	94	110	97	100	100	95	101	96	109	96	128	101	145	93	127	92	137	94	154	92	170
Asia (excluding Japan)	Exports	129	98	108	95	100	100	93	104	99	107	93	112	94	121	95	108	98	116	97	119	89	129
	Imports	110	79	109	93	100	100	95	95	93	105	93	116	97	122	111	106	93	100	94	115	95	127
Middle East	Exports	115	90	107	84	100	100	104	110	104	126	108	129	112	134	111	149	103	161	101	179	100	185
	Imports	101	103	107	99	100	100	97	108	98	125	101	129	104	139	99	154	97	162	98	172	98	180

TABLE 1-3—continued

Area		1951	1952	1953	1954	1955	1956	1957	1958	1959	1960	1961
C. Value of Trade (in $ million)												
Developed areas	Exports	52,000	52,100	53,100	54,800	60,000	68,100	74,400	70,500	75,000	85,400	90,200
	Imports	56,900	55,300	54,400	56,700	64,300	71,100	77,400	72,200	78,100	88,900	93,100
Underdeveloped areas	Exports	24,100	20,900	21,000	22,100	23,700	24,800	25,400	24,600	25,600	27,300	27,600
	Imports	24,000	24,300	21,500	22,500	24,300	26,300	29,800	27,800	27,000	29,900	30,700
Latin America	Exports	7,790	7,050	7,620	7,880	7,960	8,640	8,650	8,190	8,270	8,240	8,650
	Imports	7,800	7,660	6,530	7,400	7,550	7,940	9,330	8,530	7,790	8,600	8,560
Africa	Exports	3,110	3,270	3,290	3,610	3,710	3,890	3,790	3,840	3,930	4,350	4,520
	Imports	3,650	4,090	3,790	4,020	4,420	4,620	5,040	4,900	4,780	5,260	5,240
Asia (excluding Japan)	Exports	9,050	6,700	6,040	5,980	6,840	6,870	7,080	6,370	7,170	7,650	7,500
	Imports	8,300	8,120	7,040	6,690	6,920	8,390	9,510	8,230	8,230	9,830	10,010
Japan	Exports	1,355	1,273	2,410	1,629	2,011	2,501	2,858	2,877	3,457	4,055	4,236
	Imports	2,044	2,028	2,830	2,399	2,471	3,230	4,284	3,033	3,600	4,491	5,810
Middle East	Exports	2,990	2,560	2,830	3,220	3,720	3,940	4,230	4,670	4,700	5,140	5,220
	Imports	2,620	2,680	2,520	2,650	3,080	3,280	3,620	3,850	3,970	4,390	4,600
D. Terms of Trade: Developed Countries by Region (1953 = 100)												
Western Europe		93	98	100	100	99	99	99	104	104	105	106
U.S. and Canada		91	98	100	96	98	100	100	103	106	106	108
Australia, New Zealand, and Union of South Africa		116	90	100	94	89	88	88	74	79	77	75

SOURCES: For 1951–1959, UN, *Statistical Yearbook 1960*, for 1960–1961, UN, *Statistical Yearbook 1962*.

Thus, the development of the grain-export economies in the last century (Canada, Argentina, Australia) required the development of efficient transportation and distribution systems throughout large areas, and imposed the national and international propagation of improved techniques and machinery use. Canada early became a leading producer of agricultural machinery, and more recently of chemical fertilizers.

On the other hand, many of the major exports of underdeveloped countries today, such as coffee and cocoa, do not require techniques that promote modernizing impulses for the whole economy. Even petroleum production and refining, capital-intensive and technology-creating as they are, can easily be carried on as a relatively independent sector in underdeveloped countries. This is not an argument against producing either coffee or petroleum for export. Clearly, the resulting increases in income can be devoted to modernizing the economy and fostering the growth of output; however, there is very little in the production and export of petroleum to *force* this process.

In some sort of aggregate terms, then, as borne out by the data of Tables 1–1 and 1–2, the typical underdeveloped country is probably less able to develop on the basis of international markets than it once may have been. It has often been pointed out that rapid economic development in the last century was generally based either on commodity trade, in the regions of new settlement; or, in Europe, on manufactures both for domestic markets and for a relatively free world market. Today, most underdeveloped countries have a very different social and cultural tradition from that of the nineteenth-century regions of new settlement. Furthermore, they have been entering the world scene at a time when world markets for "low-wage" manufactured exports and for agricultural products that compete with temperate-zone crops are often highly restricted. These facts probably work in the same direction as do the sluggish growth of demand for primary products and the limited integration of export and domestic sectors of the economy, although Japan's economic growth shows that a country can develop rapidly on the basis of manufactured exports despite social and cultural differences from its markets and despite a number of restrictions on "low-wage" imports.

When we turn to disaggregated data, we see why general hypotheses about the relations between trade and growth are difficult to reject or affirm conclusively. As Table 1–4 shows, some countries have had a rapid growth of output with slow growth of imports, and some have had a slow growth of output and rapid growth of imports. There are virtually no cases in which output grew while imports declined over any substantial period of time (Brazil in the period 1952–1958 is perhaps the only modern example); but almost any other relationship between income growth and import growth can be found during the past decade.

The correlation between import growth and GNP growth for the 26 underdeveloped countries shown in Table 1–4 was −0.151, not significant. (These were the only countries for which data were available—generally,

TABLE 1–4: PERCENTAGE GROWTH OF REAL GNP AND IMPORTS IN
UNDERDEVELOPED COUNTRIES, 1951–1952 TO 1959–1960

Country	Rate of GNP Growth (Annual)	Rate of Import Growth (Annual)	Ratio of Import Growth to GNP Growth
Asia			
Taiwan	6.2	4.8	0.77
Burma	6.0	5.1	0.85
Philippines	5.9	3.5	0.53
Thailand	3.6	7.3	2.03
Ceylon	3.5	2.8	0.80
India	3.5	5.0	1.43
Middle East			
Israel	10.7	4.1	0.38
Malta	4.8	5.2	1.08
Sudan	3.7	6.0	1.62
Cyprus	2.1	12.2	5.81
Latin America			
Colombia	9.5	1.0	0.11
Venezuela	8.5	6.5	0.76
Jamaica	8.3	7.9	0.95
Panama	8.3	7.9	0.95
Dominican Republic	7.5	13.6	1.81
Costa Rica	5.1	2.5	0.49
Ecuador	5.1	3.3	0.65
Chile	3.8	4.3	1.13
Peru	3.7	5.1	1.38
Brazil	2.7	−0.002	−0.08
Argentina	2.0	2.8	1.40
Africa			
Rhodesia-Nyasaland	9.3	1.8	0.19
Ghana	7.1	9.8	1.38
Nigeria	3.4	13.9	4.09
Mauritius	2.8	7.3	2.61

SOURCES: UN, *Statistical Yearbook* and *Yearbook of National Income Accounts*. Data for some countries use 1957–1959 as terminal years, or 1951–1953 as initial years.

for the period 1950–1951 to 1959–1960.) The ratio of import-growth rate to GNP growth for these countries was typically between 0.5 and 1.5; the range was from −0.08 (Brazil) to 5.81 (Cyprus). The unweighted average was 1.25 (1.11 excluding Cyprus). For countries with rapid rates of growth (over 5 per cent annually), however, GNP normally grew faster than imports. By definition, a country whose production grows faster than imports is growing partly by import substitution (a larger proportion of total demand is being met from domestic production); but it is not clear from the available data whether import substitution in these cases took the form of domestic industrialization. In any event, the tendency for GNP growth in fast-growing underdeveloped countries to outpace import growth bolsters Nurkse's contention that trade is less likely to be an engine of growth for underdeveloped countries than it once was.[15]

Interestingly enough, during the same period (1950–1951 to 1959–1960), the import volume of *every* developed country except primary-exporting New Zealand, Australia, and South Africa, grew faster than GNP. This is an aspect of the fact noted earlier that developed countries' trade has risen much faster than that of underdeveloped countries in the past decade.

Several studies of Latin American countries have emphasized the effect of economic structure on the trade-growth relationship, in showing how stagnation of exports may lead to distortions and inhibitions in the growth pattern, arising from the nature of the national economy.[16] This kind of investigation, conceptually consistent with some of the theoretical views expressed by Nurkse, Chenery, and Hirschman, would allow more meaningful generalizations about the effects of import restrictions.

Meanwhile, we are left with one obvious theoretical point, which is implicit in Seers' model. If a country's imports are restricted, it will have to use its own resources to produce the import substitutes required for development. This predicament may be entirely consistent with faster rates of growth than those that prevailed before import restrictions were necessary. But growth itself will produce a further demand for imports both because the industrialization process requires linkages, including

[15] This is not to deny that trade can be an important catalyst in economic development, even if it does grow more slowly than total output.

[16] For such a structural model (although not tested statistically by empirical findings), see Seers. See also Richard Mallon, "Economic Development and Foreign Trade of Pakistan," unpublished Ph.D. thesis, Harvard University, Cambridge, Mass., June 1963, particularly Chap. 3.

import linkages, and because the attendant urbanization increases the demand for manufactured goods.[17]

This process is likely to result in bottlenecks in various industrial sectors and in factor supplies (skilled labor and capital); moreover, an inflationary process, which is simultaneously a cost inflation and a demand inflation, is likely to set in. A consequence will be pressure on foreign-exchange rates, which may lead either to devaluation or to overvalued exchanges, discouragement of exports, and the same pressure on imports. Depending on our assumptions about initial conditions, supply and demand elasticities, and the behavior of government and individuals, we can in theory emerge with almost any long-run results. But under reasonable assumptions about the elasticity of transformation, efficiency of government, and the strength of political forces favoring inflation and opposing devaluation, it seems likely that forced import-substitution policies can have unfortunate consequences in a number of underdeveloped countries, particularly if the process is pushed very far, as it has been in Argentina and Brazil.[18]

Even if we accept this view of the effects of import restrictions on growth, it still gives us no quantitative measure of the price the economy pays for inadequate foreign-exchange earnings.

In static terms, theoretically, the real cost of growth achieved by import substitution is measured by the difference between the point on the utility-possibility function that is actually reached and the one that could be achieved if the factors engaged in import substitution were, directly or through factor substitution, engaged in export industries. Now, clearly, if we assume a free and flexible economy, this cost should be zero. If not, factors would move from import substituting to export lines. Therefore, for import substitution to have a cost, we must assume institutional or monetary restrictions that inhibit exports or subsidize import replacement; or factor immobilities or rigidities or divergence between private and social cost with a similar effect. All of these conditions can and do arise, but they may work in either direction, as can external and internal economies, both being related to the network of demand-supply relations described by Nurkse and others.

[17] This tendency has been prevalent in Latin America. See, for example, UN, Economic Commission for Latin America, *Economic Survey of Latin America 1956*, New York, 1957; and Seers.

[18] Seers, pp. 186–189; and International Bank for Reconstruction and Development, Economic Staff, "Imports and Economic Growth," Washington, D.C., January 3, 1963 (mimeographed), pp. 15–19.

There is no *a priori* reason to believe that the economic factors promoting import substitution are stronger than those promoting export trade. If institutional pressures do in fact promote import substitution, it may be in part because of factor immobilities that must be overcome by policy pressures.

In short, one could argue that countries that impose import restrictions do so because they have no way of increasing exports except at substantial opportunity cost. The alternative to inflationary growth and constant pressure on foreign exchange may be slower growth or stagnation.

This conclusion, however, gives us no valid guide to the optimum level of imports required for a given rate of growth. Determining appropriate import levels requires a judgment about the optimum progress of import substitution. Rational decisionmaking presumably should include consideration not only of the import effect of the new industries, but also of comparative advantage. Yet factor prices in underdeveloped countries are not likely to reflect opportunity costs; even if they did, the existence of economies of scale, of complementarity, and of dynamic changes in factor supply conditions would all tend to undermine the significance of opportunity cost calculations for import substitution. In practice, assuming a significant import barrier to development, we may have to resort to estimating the direct and indirect effects of import substitution (including the export potential of the factors used in import substitution) on import requirements of the economy. This recourse somewhat simplifies the problem of estimating import requirements, but at the cost of ignoring the difficulties listed above.

Furthermore, the problem of estimating appropriate import levels is complicated by the fact that import substitution may be undertaken to prevent dependence on imported materials and manufacture in periods of cyclical or secular decreases in demand for exports. Thus, one of the benefits to be written off against the costs of import substitution is the assurance of supply availability. This is hard to quantify, but it cannot be ignored in arriving at policy choices, unless the country is assured of some sort of compensatory finance against export declines (see Chapter 6).

Therefore, both for deciding if there are potential gains from increased trade, and for deciding the dynamic analogue, the practical problem comes down to a country-by-country analysis of whether import limitations impose a barrier to acceptable rates of growth. Cases like those of Argentina on the one hand and Iraq on the other are clear enough. Argentina's development has suffered from postwar trade stagnation; import substitution at the cost of exports has probably gone too far in the short run, and economic growth has been arrested. Iraq's development difficulties have nothing to do with inadequate command over imports, but primarily with problems of political instability, inadequate domestic savings and investment, quality and quantity of factor supply, and market size, including income distribution effects on market size. The following sections often treat major petroleum exporters separately, on the assumption that they need not be considered a significant element in foreign-aid burden sharing, although some of them—notably Iran—have received sizable economic aid.

For the other countries, we would simply have to make heroic assumptions derived from capital-output ratios and/or import propensities to reach some notion of the value of exports required to maintain import levels consistent with acceptable growth rates. A more detailed analysis, not attempted here, would try to work out these factors country by country, in some sort of a general equilibrium model with trade.

How Have Underdeveloped Countries Financed Their Import Requirements?

Table 1–2 above showed the sources from which underdeveloped countries have financed their imports in recent years. Table 1–5 compares total exchange receipts from Table 1–2 (after subtracting debt-service obligations) with imports and changes in reserves. The typical surplus of exchange receipts over imports reflects passive balance on service account, net payments of royalties and dividends abroad, and capital outflow. During the period 1956–1962 there was a reduction of 15 per cent in underdeveloped countries' official gold and foreign-exchange holdings, while those of industrial countries rose by 17 per cent.

As is clear from Tables 1–2 and 1–5, export earnings have been sluggish. Almost 60 per cent of the value of exports is accounted for by the traditional primary products: food and beverage crops, agricultural raw materials, and mineral ores. The value of these exports has remained essentially unchanged since 1956. Two export categories were more buoyant: The value of petroleum exports increased by about 45 per cent between 1956 and 1963, and manufactured exports grew by about the same percentage from a much smaller base.

TABLE 1–5: LESS DEVELOPED COUNTRIES' FOREIGN-EXCHANGE
USE COMPARED WITH IMPORTS, 1956–1963
(In $ billion)

Year	Exports	Net Aid and Investment Flow	Changes in Official Reserves	Total Exchange Receipts	Imports	Other Foreign-exchange Use
1956	24.8	5.7	−1.0	31.5	26.3	5.2
1957	25.2	7.0	−0.9	33.1	29.8	3.8
1958	24.6	6.4	−1.0	32.0	27.8	4.2
1959	25.6	5.9	+0.6	30.9	27.3	3.6
1960	26.7	6.3	−0.1	33.1	29.9	3.2
1961	27.5	6.7	−0.4	34.6	30.8	3.8
1962	29.0	(7.5)	−0.3	36.8	31.3	5.5
1963	31.5	(7.4)	—	38.9	32.3	—

SOURCES: Exports and imports: UN, *Monthly Bull. Stat.* Net aid and investment flow: Table 1–2. Changes in official gold and foreign-exchange holdings: IMF, *Intern. Financ. Stat.*, July 1963. Other foreign-exchange uses (capital outflow, dividend and royalty payments, net payments for services, etc.) calculated as residual. There are undoubtedly unrecorded inflows also, and this table is not comprehensive enough to serve as a balance of payments record for the less developed countries.

The value of exports (excluding petroleum) grew by about $1.7 billion (9 per cent) between 1956 and 1962, while imports grew by $5 billion (20 per cent).[19] The growth in imports (and in debt service, interest, and dividend payments) was presumably financed by increases in foreign aid and reductions in holdings of gold and foreign exchange.

Increases in foreign aid were the most important incremental source of revenue for countries not exporting petroleum. Gross Western aid commitments rose from $3.7 billion in 1956 to $7.8 billion in 1962 (Table 1–2). In 1962 they were equivalent to 25 per cent of the value of underdeveloped countries' imports; however, in view of the steadily increasing debt-service burden (Table 1–6), the real increase in commitments was somewhat less: from an estimated $2.7 billion in 1956 to about $5.1 billion in 1962, equivalent in the latter year to about one-sixth of the value of imports. The actual net flow of aid was smaller, reflecting delays in shipments.

The traditional exports—foods and raw materials—stayed relatively stable. This stability, as Table 6–11 reveals, covers rises in export values of some products (sugar, cotton, rubber, tobacco) and decreases in others (coffee, cocoa, tea, rice) between 1956 and 1962.

[19] Assuming that imports of petroleum-exporting countries grew by the same amount as their exports. The value of commodity exports rose sharply in 1963, but this rise may have been temporary (see p. 24 below).

TABLE 1–6: WESTERN ECONOMIC AID COMMITMENTS AND
DEVELOPING COUNTRIES' DEBT SERVICE,
1956–1963
(In $ billion)

Year	Aid	Debt Service
1956	3.7	1.0
1957	4.6	1.1
1958	5.2	1.3
1959	5.3	1.7
1960	5.9	2.1
1961	6.5	2.5
1962	7.8	2.7
1963	7.3	2.9

SOURCES: Table 1–2 and unofficial estimates.

Exports of manufactures rose fairly steadily but the total six-year increase amounted to only $700 million, less than one-sixth of the increase in imports during the period.

Foreign private investment was stable, ranging only between $2.5 and $3 billion. No data were available on the return flow of interest, on dividend and royalty payments, nor on capital flight, although the final column of Table 1–5 gives some indication of the magnitudes.

The last decade's pattern of imports and exports (1953–1962) corresponds to a reasonably normal period. Although it does not give us an index of the appropriate import level, it has been sufficient to support GNP growth of about 4.6 per cent annually in underdeveloped countries.[20]

The rate of growth of aggregate imports during the past decade was almost identical (4.6 per cent) to the rate of growth of aggregate GNP, indicating a constant marginal propensity to import, a finding consistent with Chenery's results. Import growth was partly limited by slow export growth. Since the income elasticity of demand for food and raw materials is higher in underdeveloped than in developed countries, the slow growth of certain commodity exports (for example, rice, fats, and oils) may reflect restrictions in export availabilities as domestic incomes rise (and, in the event, as inflation renders the home market more attractive). In other words, income elasticity of export supply may be low or even negative for certain products.

[20] UN, *World Economic Survey 1962*, p. 5.

What Are Future Import Requirements and How Can They Be Met?

Barring striking changes in economic aid policies, future import increases will have to be financed primarily by exports. It was stressed early in this chapter that we have no clear indication of the amount of the import increases required. Even if there were some single functional relation over time between income change and import change for each country, a number of countries have been consistently handicapped by foreign-exchange limitations that have led them to adopt perhaps less than optimal import-substitution policies. Although analysis of the statistical data gives us some general indications, they are not very useful for predicting aggregate import requirements. We know there is almost no association between income *levels* and the ratio of imports to income.[21] We also know that countries with small populations have higher import ratios than do those with large populations. The historical evidence indicates that the long-run tendency for trade to decline as a proportion of GNP is slight:[22] The United States and Russia are the principal examples. Smaller countries offer no general pattern, although historically the import ratio often rises in the early stages of development. Historical data indicate that capital-goods imports tend to rise in relation to total imports, but this trend is not borne out by recent cross-sectional data for underdeveloped countries because capital-goods imports are now a much higher proportion of total imports at all income levels than they were historically at comparable stages of development.

Adams has pointed out that the tendency for large countries to have a small foreign-trade ratio means that they may be forced to produce capital goods even at high cost. If imports are 10 per cent of GNP, as they often are in countries of over 40 million population, and the intended level of investment is 15 per cent of GNP, then, assuming a 30 per cent import component of investment, 45 per cent of a country's imports must be devoted to capital goods. A small country with an import ratio of 25 per cent can achieve the same relative level of investment by allotting to capital goods only 18 per cent of its imports. In view of the evidence cited above

[21] N. Adams, "Economic Growth and the Structure of Foreign Trade," unpublished Ph.D. thesis, Harvard University, Cambridge, Mass., 1962, p. 64; Simon Kuznets, *Six Lectures on Economic Growth*, The Free Press, Glencoe, Ill., 1959, Chap. 5.

[22] Deutsch and Eckstein; Adams, Chap. 3.

("Are Foreign-exchange Limitations a Barrier to Economic Growth?"),
this fact implies that large underdeveloped countries (India, Brazil,
Pakistan) may have to reduce their growth rates below an acceptable
minimum because of the high costs of import substitution. They may be
forced into high-cost capital-goods production because the alternative—
increasing the already high ratio of capital-goods imports to total imports—may prevent them from obtaining imported raw materials when
export receipts fall or when productive capacity increases. Increased
production of consumer goods instead of capital goods is not necessarily
a solution of this difficulty, because the consumer-goods industries may
have a high import component.[23]

Taking the results of time-series and cross-sectional data, in addition to
population trends, it seems clear that the pressure of import demand will
continue to be severe for many countries in the next decade or two.
Countries now facing foreign-exchange stringencies will generally have to
turn, as in the past, to more rapid growth of exports of commodities and
manufactures, to an accelerated pace of import substitution, or to increased
capital flows from abroad.

Let us look at each of these in turn, reserving a more detailed discussion
of capital flows for Chapter 2. The prospects are generally unfavorable.

Exports of Manufactures

Manufactured exports today account for about 15 per cent of underdeveloped countries' exports, compared with about 13 per cent in 1956
(Table 1–2). Nearly one-third of total manufactured exports are simply
refined metals. In the long run, an increasing portion of GNP will originate
in manufacturing, and there will be a tendency, particularly in heavily
populated countries, for manufactured exports to account for a larger
share of total exports. But this is a long-term process. It typically takes
several decades, even in a rapidly industrializing country that starts out
from an agricultural base, for manufacturing production to equal agricultural output in value[24] at a level where each is from 20 to 30 per cent
of the GNP. During the early industrializing period, manufactured exports
may be important, particularly for labor-intensive industries in heavily

[23] Mallon, Chap. 2.
[24] Simon Kuznets, "Quantitative Aspects of the Economic Growth of Nations:
II. Industrial Distribution of National Products and Labour Force," *Economic Development and Cultural Change*, Vol. 5, July 1957 (Supplement), Appendix Table 2.

populated countries (Japan, India, Netherlands), or in countries having easy access to large foreign markets (a number of Western European countries in the nineteenth century, Canada in the early twentieth century). More typically, semi-industrialized countries are not large exporters of manufactured goods; they continue to rely on exports of primary products. Some thinly populated countries with large agricultural or mineral resources show no important trend toward manufactured exports, even though manufacturing is important in the national economy (Australia, New Zealand, South Africa).

Because only a few underdeveloped countries are even at the semi-industrialized stage today (India, Brazil, Mexico, Argentina, Israel, Chile), the prospects for dramatic increases in manufactured exports over the next decade must be considered slight. On the supply side, it is possible that manufacturing production will increase rapidly in a number of underdeveloped countries, particularly in those where import substitution is considered necessary (Pakistan, Turkey) or where countries are starting from a very low level of industrial development (South Korea, Honduras, Syria). In general, an efficient manufacturing industry and the supporting financial and distribution systems remain to be organized and built; and even the semi-industrialized countries listed above, with about 20 per cent of GNP originating in manufacturing, cater primarily to the protected domestic market. Furthermore, supply for the world market is limited by inadequate demand in the home market, to the extent that economies of scale are significant.

On the demand side, tariff reduction, tariff preferences in industrial countries, and removal of quantitative restrictions on "low-wage" imports could offer some immediate benefits to the semi-industrialized countries' exports.

Generally speaking, developed countries' tariffs are highest on light manufactures, such as textiles, clothing, and footwear, items for which underdeveloped countries may often enjoy a comparative advantage. Furthermore, developed countries' tariffs rise with the degree of processing of primary products. Thus oilseeds may enter duty free; vegetable oils pay a duty. Copper ore is generally free; refined copper pays a small duty, and copper rollings pay a higher one, etc. The tariff structures of industrial countries thus inhibit the traditional process of using the primary export base as a source of expanding manufactured exports.

In addition to tariff barriers, quota restrictions on a number of underdeveloped countries' products (primarily textiles, but also bicycles, motors, jute and coir manufactures, etc.) limit the export potential. Measures to remove these restrictions and even to offer preferential tariff treatment to underdeveloped nations have often been proposed, but no significant steps have yet been taken by developed countries.

Even if we assume that industrial countries immediately adopt favorable commercial policies toward the import of manufactures from underdeveloped countries, it would be unrealistic to expect a resultant major increase in foreign exchange over the next decade—particularly where export supply problems are intensified by the growth of domestic demand. From 1956 to 1963, underdeveloped countries' industrial exports increased by slightly more than 5 per cent a year. If this rate doubled over the next decade, it would add $5 billion to the present annual level of export receipts by 1972. Against this sum in the trade balance, we would have to offset the increased import requirements for capital and raw materials generated by increased production. The lower the proportion of domestic value added, the smaller the net impact on foreign-exchange shortages. Naturally, this dictum need not imply that underdeveloped countries should avoid industries with a high import component for that reason alone.

Commodity Exports

Primary commodities account for 85 to 88 per cent of the exports of underdeveloped countries. If, over the next decade, these countries are going to rely on trade as the principal method of improving their ability to pay for imports, their success will largely depend on increases in the value of primary commodity exports. The prospects for this expansion are on the whole not encouraging. The aggregate exports of commodities excluding petroleum have averaged $15 to $17 billion annually since 1956. This aggregate stability covers up declines for some products and increases for others (see Chapter 6 for details). It is well known that developed countries' demand for primary commodities is generally income-inelastic and, at least in the short run, price-inelastic. Therefore, revenues could increase steadily if (1) with stable demand, supply curves shifted to the left (weather, disease, increased domestic consumption, or increased factor costs); (2) or with stable supply, demand shifted to the right (population and income increases in importing countries, war or other special situations, increases in prices of substitutes, decreases in price of complementary goods); (3) or with both demand and supply shifting to the right, demand shifts outpace supply (the Ricardian model).

In the postwar period, supply increases have been at least equal to demand shifts, and have exceeded them in the past decade (see unit-value data in Table 1–3). In some cases, it is arguable that the failure of supply to increase rapidly enough is responsible for the failure of demand to shift; industrialization in semi-industrialized countries, and increases in domestic demand, may have meant that prices of primary exports rose rather rapidly compared to manufactured exports, thereby encouraging substitution or domestic production in importing countries.[25] Although this argument cannot be rejected entirely (it may help explain the growth of import-competing rice production in Asia), Maizels' statistical analysis shows that lagging growth of semi-industrial countries' primary exports probably reflects slow growth of demand more than it reflects supply decreases.[26]

To the extent that long-run demand is elastic, declining relative prices brought about by supply shifts help prevent sharp increases in import-substituting production in importing countries. But this is cold comfort for commodity exporters, who are generally not interested in how much worse things might have been, but in how much better they should be.

In the next decade, we can be reasonably confident only that demand will increase rapidly for petroleum and aluminum exports by under-developed countries. Among products that are now of lesser importance, iron ore, citrus fruits, fish meal, and possibly tobacco face reasonably favorable demand prospects. In general, countries relying on other commodities cannot count on rapid demand increases; aggregate supply seems likely to grow just as fast—a good deal faster in cases in which supply is being augmented by synthetic substitution or rapidly growing domestic production in importing countries. In unsheltered markets, prices therefore will probably remain relatively low and exports will not increase much faster than population growth in importing countries.[27]

[25] A. K. Cairncross, "International Trade and Economic Development," *Kyklos*, Vol. 13, No. 4, 1960.
[26] A. Maizels, "Effects of Industrialization on Exports of Primary-Producing Countries," *Kyklos*, Vol. 14, 1961, pp. 18–46.
[27] Food and Agriculture Organization, "Agricultural Commodities: Projections for 1970," Special Supplement to *FAO Commodity Review 1962*, UN, Rome, 1962; United Nations, Economic and Social Council, "Prospective Demand for Non-Agricultural Commodities: Problems of Definition and Methodology," New York, May 23, 1962 (mimeographed). Of course, individual countries can still benefit at the expense of others if their productivity increase outstrips the world average.

It is often stated that faster rates of income growth in importing countries would greatly increase the revenues of commodity exporters. This is undoubtedly true, but the potential effects should not be exaggerated. If income elasticities of demand are low, a doubling of income growth rates in importing countries does not mean a 100 per cent increase in growth of demand, but one of perhaps only 20 per cent. In practice, if the industrial countries' growth rates were to increase by one-third over the next decade, let us say from an average of 3 per cent to one of 4 per cent annually, the achievement would be considered substantial. Yet the import demand effects of such an increase could be largely offset by simultaneous decline in income elasticities of demand with income growth.

Further difficulties that will hamper prospects for rapid growth of commodity exports include protection for agriculture and mining in developed countries; the agricultural policy of the European Economic Community, for example, is likely to bring Western Europe closer to agricultural self-sufficiency over the next decade. Furthermore, demand is more price-elastic in the long run than in the short run. This fact tends to make price-fixing policies risky, although they are feasible for a limited number of products (see Chapter 6).

Capital Flows

Foreign private investment can be a major source of import finance; historically, it financed the trade deficits of developing countries before 1914. It still finances those of countries like Canada, Puerto Rico, Jamaica, and other areas considered both safe and profitable. In recent years, however, aggregate private investment in underdeveloped countries has not increased (Table 1–2); and there is some evidence that a good part of it is offset by dividends, royalties, interest payments, and capital flight. There has been a great deal of discussion, and some action in the form of favorable investment laws, tax concessions, guarantees against expropriation, etc., all aimed at stimulating the flow of private capital to underdeveloped countries, but the results are meager. Furthermore, if the above prognosis for commodity trade is correct, private investment in the commodity export sector is more likely to decline than to rise. Finally, because investment in industrial countries is generally profitable and safer, many underdeveloped countries can offer no irresistible economic inducement to compensate for the risk.

For two reasons, foreign aid is unlikely to grow as rapidly in the future as it has over the past decade. First, the U.S. aid program, which has been the principal source of funds, is unlikely to increase substantially, barring major policy changes. Western aid commitments to underdeveloped countries rose steadily until 1962, and declined somewhat in 1963 and 1964. Second, most aid is in the form of loans, which impose an increasing debt-service burden. Therefore, unless aid increases faster than the debt service, the net value of aid does not increase. Chapter 2 discusses capital flows in more detail.

Import Substitution

Countries finding themselves short of foreign exchange for consumption and investment needs will continue to turn to import substitution; as pointed out above, investment in import-substituting industries may often be a rational aspect of development policy, independent of trade problems. The relevant question here is how big a contribution this process can make over the next decade or so toward reducing the import gap.

Chenery has estimated that 50 per cent of industrial growth is accounted for by import substitution, defined as the increased share of domestic production in total supply. Industry is a small part of the economy in underdeveloped countries, however, typically ranging from 5 to 15 per cent of gross domestic product. Thus, if 50 per cent of industrial growth is import-replacing and if industry, accounting originally for 10 per cent of GNP, grows at 5 per cent a year, we are dealing with a magnitude of one-half of one per cent of GNP, of which only one-half is an increase in the share of domestic production in total supply. This amount of increase may well be significant compared to a country's import gap, but it is often "paid for" by increases in capital imports, as well as in imports of goods and services for other sectors of the economy. Aggregate income elasticities of demand for imports are generally estimated to be close to 1; and most estimates of import requirements to achieve GNP growth of about 5 per cent annually project that imports will increase somewhat faster than national product.

This assumption, used in the UN estimates discussed below, is open to some question. In certain countries, as can be seen in Table 1–4, income has grown faster than imports, and it is certainly not clear that imports will have to increase faster than GNP to maintain current growth rates.

It is possible, up to a point, to plan investments that have a relatively large domestic component. At the present stage of knowledge, all we can say about import substitution in the future is that it will presumably reduce the import gap below what it would have been if output growth were proportional to demand growth.[28] We cannot project a likely rate of import substitution with attendant effects on import needs because import requirements seem to be primarily determined by income, market size, export earnings, and capital flows.

Whenever there are sharp increases in the prices of developing countries' exports, as during the Korean crisis, or more recently in 1963–1964, the question of import substitution naturally becomes somewhat less urgent in the eyes of many developing countries. Thus, in 1963, the prices of several major tropical crops, notably sugar and coffee, rose sharply. As Table 1–2 shows, this had substantial effects on the 1963 foreign exchange earnings of countries that export foodstuffs. However, during 1964 prices of these crops declined toward previous levels. Therefore it seems unlikely that the record increases in export earnings registered between 1962 and 1963 could be long sustained. The most probable contingency is a return towards the preceding decade's slower rate of trade growth, with its somewhat discouraging implications for developing countries' capacity to import. To the extent that industrial countries, particularly the United States, continue the rapid income growth of recent years, developing countries' export earnings may grow somewhat faster than they did in the decade 1953–1962. However, if tropical crop producers follow the traditional supply response, a period of depressed prices is likely to result as the growth of supply outpaces demand. In other words, the pressures that induce import substitution may vary in intensity, but the long run prospect is for steady increase in import substituting industry, both as a hedge against foreign-exchange uncertainties and as a potential source of domestic economic growth.

---

[28] Chenery's work shows that although industrial output increases at a faster rate than domestic demand, imports increase at about the same rate. Both he and Kuznets point out that population (as an indication of market size) has much more effect than does income in reducing imports as a percentage of national product. Small countries maintain high foreign-trade ratios even when per capita GNP is high.

2

Future Import and Capital Requirements

Projections of Import Gap

We have seen that there will probably be an import gap not covered by trade, particularly if we think in terms of target growth rates that will perceptibly raise per capita income (for example, an increase of 2¾ per cent annually will double per capita income every 25 years). The size of that gap over the next decade cannot be predicted with any accuracy. Income partly depends on trade levels, and they, in turn, partly depend on income; and growth of income in industrial countries seems to be less of a propulsive force for underdeveloped countries than in the past, so that estimating exports from developed countries' income projections is probably less safe now than it may once have been. Furthermore, much depends on the commercial policies and domestic farm policies of industrial countries, neither of which can be reliably forecast. Also, capital-goods import projections will vary greatly depending on the capital-output ratio assumed and its import content. More generally, long-term forecasts of the structure of investment and consumption are necessarily based on assumptions about factor and product prices and supply elasticities that are subject to substantial margins of error.

Finally, the import gap is a residual of relatively large numbers. In 1962 underdeveloped countries' exports were $29.0 billion, imports were $31.3 billion, and total foreign-exchange spending $36.0 billion. If imports had been 5 per cent smaller and exports 5 per cent larger, there would have been no aggregate foreign-trade gap, although many countries would still have had passive trade balances. For the structural reasons discussed above, however, it is extremely unlikely that aggregate export increases of this magnitude could be achieved without also increasing imports. In a sense, the apparent narrowness of the import gap simply reflects the under-developed countries' inability to mobilize foreign capital. If capital inflows were greater, the trade gap would be bigger.

Despite these difficulties, if we make "reasonable" assumptions about population growth, export trends, propensities to import, and per capita income growth, we can arrive at trade projections that may be of the right order of magnitude in light of the projected income increases. A number of such projections have been made in recent years; Table 2–1 summarizes three, made by the Economic Commission for Europe (ECE), the General Agreement on Tariffs and Trade (GATT), and the United Nations' Department of Economic and Social Affairs.[1]

Shifting the estimates shown in Table 2–1 to a 1970 terminal date, we arrive at the results of Table 2–2. The differences in trade gap shown in Table 2–1—Col. (7) minus Col. (6)—reflects not only differences in income

TABLE 2–1: UNDERDEVELOPED COUNTRIES' PROJECTED GROWTH OF
INCOME, TRADE, AND POPULATION, 1958–1980

Agency		Period	Projected Growth Rates (%)				Terminal Year Values ($ billion)		
			Popu-lation	In-come	Ex-ports	Im-ports	In-come	Ex-ports	Im-ports
			(1)	(2)	(3)	(4)	(5)	(6)	(7)
ECE	(A)	1958–80	2.2	5.4	4.7	4.6	463	71.7	79.4
	(B)	1958–80	2.2	5.4	4.5	4.5	416	50.3	60.0
GATT	(A)	1960–69	2.0	5.2	—	7.3	236	—	51
	(B)	1960–69	2.0	3.8	—	5.3	218	—	43
UN		1959–70[a]	—	4.9	3.4	6.3	304	29	41

SOURCES: Computed from sources listed in footnote 1, below.

NOTE: ECE version (B) excludes petroleum-exporting countries. GATT (A) assumes a 5.2 per cent and GATT (B) a 3.8 per cent growth rate of product.
[a] Exports and imports among underdeveloped countries are excluded.

[1] UN, ECE, *Economic Survey of Europe in 1960*, Geneva, 1961, Chap. 5; GATT, *International Trade 1959*, pp. 40–56; UN, *World Economic Survey 1962*, Chap. 1. A useful summary of these and other estimates is found in Goran Ohlin's recent mono-graph, *Reappraisals of Foreign Aid Policies* (OECD, Paris, December 1964), pp. 91–97.

TABLE 2–2: PROJECTIONS OF UNDERDEVELOPED
COUNTRIES' TRADE GAP IN 1970
(In $ billion; 1959 prices)

Source		GNP	Imports	Exports	Trade Gap
ECE	(A)	259	50.3	45.2	5.1
	(B)	235	38.2	32.2	6.0
GATT	(A)	249	54.6	—	—
	(B)	217	45.2	—	—
UN[a,b]		253	41.0	29	12.0
			(44.0)[c]	(32.0)[c]	(12.0)[c]

SOURCE: Table 2–1.

[a] Excludes underdeveloped countries' trade with each other, averaging about $5.5 billion for 1955–1960; estimated value 1970, $7.5 to $8 billion.

[b] 1959 GNP base adjusted for comparability to ECE and GATT estimates.

[c] Includes underdeveloped countries' trade with each other.

projections and estimates of export prospects and import projections, but also different time spans. Table 2–2, expressing all projections for the year 1970, therefore gives us a better idea of the possible range of the projected gap. Columns (1) to (4) of Table 2–1 are not repeated because the same growth rates apply.

The large gap in the UN estimate is increased in its original projection by an additional $8 billion for service-trade deficit and investment-income payments. Of this larger total gap of $20 billion, $9 billion (net) is assumed to come from long-term capital inflows; the financing of the remaining $11 billion is about equally divided among various "adjustments": import substitution; export increases on trade and service accounts; and more liberal trade policies and more rapid growth in industrial countries.[2]

The ECE estimates are probably much too optimistic on the export side, at least in terms of 1970 potential. The projection calls for a 4.5 per cent annual growth rate in exports, compared to 3.1 per cent for 1952–1961 (2.7 per cent in purchasing power, correcting for terms-of-trade changes). Such growth would require, among other things, an increase in manufactured exports of about 200 per cent above 1960 levels by 1970 (and of

[2] These UN estimates of the trade gap have been used by the Secretariat of the United Nations Conference on Trade and Development (1964) as a basis for supporting higher prices for tropical commodities, and for urging tariff preferences for underdeveloped countries' manufactured exports.

400 per cent by 1980). Nothing in the prospects for the years between now and 1970 justifies projecting an increase of even half this amount.

On the import side, ECE has assumed an income elasticity of demand of 0.85. Both the UN and GATT assume that imports will increase faster than income. The GATT method includes forecasting a rate of import-demand growth based on the last decade's results and adding to it, in GATT (A), the capital import requirements needed to raise the output growth rate to 5.2 per cent annually. The UN method is based on esti-mating, from 1953–1960 data, the less developed countries' income elasticities of demand for imports by Standard International Trade Classification, and applying these coefficients to the projected pattern of consumption and investment. Because investment would have to increase relatively to achieve the growth rate specified, and because investment has a high import coefficient, the net effect will be to increase imports faster than income.[3] The two have increased at approximately equal rates (4.6 per cent) since 1950, according to the UN survey (although GATT figures cite an income growth rate of 3.8 per cent). At any rate, for what the figures are worth, underdeveloped countries' GNP is probably growing faster than that of industrial countries;[4] but their population is also grow-ing faster, so that the net percentage effect per capita is uncertain. In any event the absolute size of the income gap between rich and poor countries is obviously increasing.

All three projections imply a large increase in net capital flows. The UN projects an increase to $10 billion annually by 1970, even after allowing for a shortfall of $4 billion in the projections. GATT estimates that even at current growth rates (3.8 per cent), and allowing for $5 to $6 billion in capital inflows, 1970 import demand cannot be financed by trade unless there is a dramatic increase in manufactured exports. At the higher growth rate (5.2 per cent), capital-flow and import requirements would increase by much larger amounts.[5]

The ECE estimate, adjusted to 1970, implies a trade deficit of about $5 billion. With more realistic estimates of export possibilities for manu-

[3] However, this assumption does not allow for the possibility of lowering the import component of investment by emphasizing greater use of domestic resources in investment.

[4] Actually, over the past decade, faster than that of North America; slower than that of Europe, Japan, and Communist countries. Since 1961, the per capita growth rate of underdeveloped countries has lagged behind that of industrial countries, largely as a consequence of more rapid growth rates in the United States.

[5] GATT, *International Trade 1959*, pp. 50–53.

factures, and of import elasticities (0.95 appears to be much closer to the mark than the coefficient of 0.85 used by ECE), the gap would be close to the $12 billion figure cited by the UN.

A more recent estimate of the foreign-trade deficit has been published in a U.S. Government-financed study, written by Bela Balassa. His study, which analyzes individual import and export sectors in some detail, assumes that underdeveloped countries' exports will largely be determined by the growth of demand in industrial countries. The underdeveloped countries' import requirements are estimated primarily as a function of time-series observations that yield apparent income elasticities of demand. Thus, specifying GNP growth of 3.9 per cent annually in the United States and about 4.1 per cent in the Common Market countries (in conjunction with a 4.2 per cent growth projection for underdeveloped countries), Belassa arrives at import requirements of $35 billion to $36 billion, as compared to an export total of $31 billion by 1970. Combining the trade gap of about $4.5 billion with a service account gap of about $5 billion gives a "most likely" total foreign-exchange gap of $9.4 billion in that year, rising to $11.3 billion by 1975.[6]

After allowing for manifold uncertainties, as demonstrated by the considerable differences among these projections, it is still certain that import demand in underdeveloped countries is generally mounting faster than export revenues, except in petroleum-exporting countries, and that the process of domestic industrialization will probably increase that demand faster than the growth of exports can finance it.

Depending on one's assumptions, therefore, the import gap may decrease, remain the same, or increase. There can be little doubt, however, that a significant gap will remain if annual growth rates of 4.5 to 5.5 per cent are to be maintained. This study is primarily concerned with discussing the gap in relation to burden sharing. Whether the actual gap in 1970 is $5 to $6 billion, as projected by the ECE estimates, or nearer to the higher figures advanced by Balassa and the UN (and also implied by the GATT study), it seems clear that it will be large enough to pose significant questions for burden sharing over the next decade, at least. In some of the following chapters, the lower figure of $5 billion is used for illustrative purposes; but it should be kept in mind that attempts to determine the "true" value of the import gap are inherently no more than exercises,

[6] Bela A. Balassa, *Trade Prospects for Developing Countries*, Richard D. Irwin, Homewood, Ill., 1964, p. 104.

because the nature of the functional relations that determine the gap (that is, the nature of the trade-development relationship) is not fully understood.

Fortunately, it is unnecessary that we accept any specific projection of the import gap. It is sufficient to note, after allowing for the effects of import substitution, that to maintain reasonable growth rates many countries will experience continuing and perhaps intensifying pressure on foreign exchange. It is not our task here—important as it may be in other contexts—either to identify the countries or to make detailed quantitative estimates of the effects of foreign-exchange shortages on growth and stability.

Capital Flows and Burden Sharing

The last section discussed capital flows as one way of financing the import gap. Capital flows were treated as a residual that would pay for import "requirements" not covered by export proceeds. Some discussions of capital flows treat the import gap primarily as an aspect of total savings, thereby determining investment levels and growth of national product.

In theory, under equilibrium conditions, this savings gap will be identical to the import gap; that is, if savings equals investment, imports necessarily equal exports. If there is a persistent tendency *ex ante* for imports minus exports to exceed investment minus savings, it must theoretically reflect some such imbalance as overvalued exchange rates, expansionary monetary policies, or government deficits. Some combination of anti-inflationary policies with or without exchange-rate adjustments will normally restore equilibrium. And, by definition, $I - S$ will always equal imports minus exports, in an accounting sense.

In practice, of course, one or more of these imbalances tend to be present, and the effective constraints on growth include not only the inadequacy of domestic savings, but also foreign-exchange shortages. That is, the equality

$$\text{Investment} - \text{Savings} = \text{Imports} - \text{Exports}$$

will seldom apply in the *ex ante* sense. If it does not apply, then estimates of capital-inflow requirements to attain a given growth rate will often be much larger than if we assume that inadequate domestic savings are the only constraint. The UN, GATT, and ECE projections summarized above assume both a "savings gap" and an "import gap."[7] Rosenstein-Rodan's estimates, discussed below, assume that the policy measures required to achieve external balance have been adopted; his capital-inflow projections are therefore much lower than those cited above.

In practice, it seems safer to assume that these adjustments will not be made readily. They may seem to conflict with growth objectives; or demand elasticities for imports and exports may be perverse; or political considerations may make it unwise to adopt the "appropriate" balancing measures. Thus, for example, the United States has chosen not to devalue the dollar when faced with persistent payments deficits.

Furthermore, one of the well-known barriers to growth in underdeveloped countries is the inability to transform resources (inelastic supply functions); consequently, it seems unrealistic to assume that the transfer of resources to import-substituting or export industries, as required for balance-of-payments equilibrium, will in fact take place smoothly.

In discussing burden sharing, we will therefore assume that the gap to be met by foreign capital inflows includes both that part required to finance investment and that required to finance desired imports not paid for by the sum of exports plus the net investment inflow. However, this section does review two estimates based on the assumption that the economy can transform its product-mix in such a way as to keep its external accounts in balance.

Domestic Savings and Capital Inflows as Source of Growth

As we saw above, trade, no matter how unsatisfactory its growth prospects, will as a practical matter have to be the principal source of

---

[7] In the literature of the subject those two gaps are often referred to as "resources gap" and "foreign-exchange gap," respectively. The reader who is accustomed to that terminology can think of my usage, "savings gap" and "import gap," as being synonymous for the more familiar expressions. The point is that a given country may want to invest more than it can save; or it may want to import more than it can export. In the first case it is short of resources; in the second case, short of claims on foreign resources. The two gaps are related; indeed, as pointed out above, the two gaps are always equal in an accounting sense. The adjustment between possible divergencies in intended levels and equality in actual ones is typically accomplished (where the savings gap dominates) by reduced investment, increased imports (externally financed), or a combination; where the import gap dominates, the adjustment would normally take place via import reduction, increased domestic consumption, or a combination. In both cases, the adjustment (unless it is externally financed) implies a slower growth of income than would have taken place without the constraint.

foreign exchange for almost all underdeveloped countries. In the same manner, domestic savings will generally be the principal source of their capital formation. Given the state of data on national accounts and on capital movements, we cannot make even reasonably accurate annual estimates of the relation between savings and foreign capital inflows. Rosenstein-Rodan has made an avowedly rough estimate for the year 1961,[8] reproduced here as Table 2–3.

TABLE 2–3: GNP, INVESTMENT, AND SAVINGS IN UNDERDEVELOPED COUNTRIES, 1961
(In $ billion)

Area	GNP	Net Investment	Domestic Savings	Net Capital Inflow (Residual)
Africa	20.6	1.7	1.2	0.5
Latin America	65.3	6.8	5.9	0.9
Asia	65.3	6.0	4.6	1.4
Middle East	19.9	1.8	1.6	0.2
Total	171.1	16.3	13.3	3.0

SOURCE: Rosenstein-Rodan, pp. 118, 131.

Whether we assume that net capital inflows are $3 billion—the total of residuals between estimated net investment and domestic savings in Table 2–3, or $5 to $6 billion—arrived at by subtracting an allowance for interest, dividends, royalties, and capital flight from the capital-outflow estimates of the Organization for Economic Cooperation and Development (OECD) (Table 2–4, p. 33), it is clear that foreign capital is an important and growing element in meeting investment needs. Nevertheless, it is and will presumably remain a smaller element than domestic savings in financing most countries' investments (a few countries that receive relatively large amounts of economic aid—Taiwan, South Korea, Israel—are exceptions).

Net investment apparently amounts to about 10 per cent of combined GNP. If we assume a capital-output ratio of 2.3:1, we arrive at a growth rate consistent with the UN estimate of growth over the past decade. Higher ratios, such as 2.6:1, give growth rates consistent with the GATT estimates. If we further assume that the productivity of foreign capital is

[8] P. N. Rosenstein-Rodan, "International Aid for Underdeveloped Countries," *Review of Economics and Statistics*, Vol. 43, May 1961, p. 131.

equal to the average productivity of investment, then foreign capital inflows account for somewhere between 17 and 30 per cent of the increase in output, if Rosenstein-Rodan's 1961 estimates are typical of recent experience.

Kuznets' data for the post-World War II period indicate that foreign financing accounted for a substantial percentage of gross domestic capital formation in less developed countries.[9]

The pattern is very erratic, with "dependent areas" such as Israel, Puerto Rico, and South Korea receiving very large inflows. In the poorer countries, the modal values are from 10 to 30 per cent of gross domestic capital formation, averaging 18 per cent in countries of less than $150 per capita GNP, and smaller percentages at higher income levels.

TABLE 2–4: TOTAL FLOW OF FINANCIAL RE-
SOURCES TO UNDERDEVELOPED COUNTRIES,
1956–1963[a]
(In $ billion)

Year	Official Aid	Private Investment	Total
1956	3.2	2.4	5.6
1957	3.8	3.4	7.2
1958	4.3	2.7	7.0
1959	4.2	2.2	6.4
1960	4.8	2.6	7.4
1961	6.0	2.6	8.6
1962	6.0	2.4	8.4
1963	6.0	2.4	8.4

SOURCE: Compiled by author from OECD sources.

[a] Excludes Soviet Bloc aid.

Table 2–4 shows the OECD estimate of the capital flow to underdeveloped countries since 1956, net of amortization and disinvestment, but including interest, dividends, royalties, and capital flight.

It is doubtful if any country except the USSR, United Kingdom, and perhaps Japan, has ever achieved long-term economic development without passing through a long stage as a net importer on current account and a net debtor on capital account. In the nineteenth century and in the first

[9] Simon Kuznets, "Quantitative Aspects of the Economic Growth of Nations: V. Capital Formation Proportions: International Comparisons for Recent Years," *Economic Development and Cultural Change*, Vol. 8, July 1960 (Supplement), Table 18, p. 70.

quarter of this century, most foreign capital was transferred to developing countries by (1) private purchases of government bonds or utility and railway securities; and (2) to a lesser extent, by direct investment in plantations and extractive industries. Official grants and loans were negligible except in wartime. As can be seen from Table 2–4, that pattern has changed radically since World War II. Official loans and grants have dominated private investment, and private investment has been predominantly direct investment (except for purchase of World Bank bonds). At the same time, total capital flows have increased greatly over the levels of the 1920's.[10]

This transformation of the pattern of capital flows emphasizes the continuing importance of foreign investment in the development process. In the past, external capital flowed in because interest rates or profits abroad appeared more attractive than home investment; but in recent years, the countries seeking foreign capital are no longer the old "safe" underdeveloped areas—colonies or regions of recent settlement by European population. Instead, they are independent, politically unstable, and— however attractive the potential return—unfamiliar to the Western investor, commercially, legally, socially, and politically.

Nonetheless, the need for capital has persisted. In the absence of the necessary flow of private capital, and often in the presence of some hostility toward it, developing countries have turned to Western governments (and to a lesser extent to the USSR) for external capital.

This transformation of capital sources potentially implied a reduction of debt-service burdens. Unlike private investors, governments are free to tax citizens to subsidize other countries. In the period 1946–1952, when the volume of official aid to underdeveloped areas was relatively small, most of it was in the form of grants. Since then, the amount of official lending has increased sharply, and debt-service payments have accounted for an increasing proportion of export earnings.[11] As of 1958, private service payments (including interest, amortization and dividends, and retained earnings) were considerably larger than official service payments. The total amount of private capital, particularly in Latin America and in petroleum-exporting countries, was far greater (and the return generally higher) than the outstanding amount of official loans. In more recent years,

[10] D. G. R. Avramovic and R. Gulhati, *Debt Servicing Capacity and Postwar Growth in International Indebtedness*, The Johns Hopkins Press, Baltimore, Md., 1958, p. 16.

[11] *Ibid.*, pp. 6, 97.

however, official debt service may have become a relatively more important element in the balance of payments, for two reasons: (1) Official loans have grown relative to private investment. (2) A proportion of private-investment service payments are either reinvested or retained in the country and do not create an immediate demand for foreign exchange.

Up to 1955 income, savings, and exports grew rapidly enough to allow underdeveloped countries to meet their service commitments without making too deep inroads either on domestic income and savings or on foreign-exchange resources.[12] Since 1956, with the rapid rise of capital inflows (see Table 2–4) and the stagnation of export earnings, conclusions from the experience of the first postwar decade are no longer valid. In 1955 underdeveloped countries' public debt service amounted to about $800 million annually; in 1961 it was estimated at $2.5 billion, and in 1963 at $2.9 billion.

Obviously, there is no necessary short-run connection between private investment or investment financed by foreign aid and the ability to meet debt-service requirements; the connection is established over time by transformation. Debt-service capacity must therefore be analyzed in terms of both domestic savings and foreign-exchange earning capacity.

Because underdeveloped countries have low domestic savings ratios that grow slowly, they are more sensitive to the pressures of service obligations than are developed countries. Avramovic lists, for 40 countries, the ratio of debt-service payments to gross savings in 1954. Of the 15 countries with ratios above 10 per cent, only Australia was a developed country.

Similarly, underdeveloped countries' debt-service payments tend to take a larger proportion of their export earnings than do those of developed countries. In 1955 no industrial country's service payments reached 10 per cent of export earnings, while a number of underdeveloped countries' payments exceeded 20 per cent.[13]

As noted above, given the capacity to transform resources, developing countries can in the long run sufficiently increase exports and decrease imports to finance service payments (unless the productivity of investment is very low). Given the difficulties of transformation in many under-developed countries, however, the long run may stretch to a grueling

[12] *Ibid.*, Chap 11.
[13] Apparently, as of 1956, the ratio of service payments to export receipts was somewhat lower than in the nineteenth and early twentieth centuries. *Ibid.*, p. 192.

length. We can expect a continuing pressure for more capital inflows for a number of years, partly to help finance service payments.

On the assumption that the appeal for official capital will continue to be a central element of development strategy, burden-sharing questions can be seen as an integral part of developed countries' long-range economic policy. The West is not forced to spend public funds in the interest of less developed countries, but it has made a political decision to do so. Unless it is much more successful than it has been so far in persuading private investors to substitute their funds for official contributions, it will have to carry this burden until the political decision is reversed or the need for external capital passes. The questions that will occupy us for the rest of this study revolve around the burden-sharing issue, broadly defined.

Capital-flow Projections

Before turning to this theme, we should conclude one task begun in Chapter 1: reviewing estimates of the level of future foreign-aid and investment requirements. In Chapter 1 we reviewed projections based on the import gap. In this section we will look at methods based on the deficiency of domestic savings, assuming that the current account is in balance at the assumed level of savings.

Rosenstein-Rodan has estimated underdeveloped countries' capital requirements by this method for the period 1961–1976. His assumed growth rates are based on each country's estimated absorptive capacity for using capital productively, as reflected in recent growth of investments and savings, and on a subjective valuation of each country's development potential. These estimates result in growth rates that seem low, particularly for the period 1961–1966. He has estimated capital-inflow requirements by five-year periods, using the following formula:

$$ F = (k\Gamma - b) \sum_{i=1}^{5} Y_i + 5Y_0 \ (b - S_0/Y_0), $$

where F = capital inflow for a five-year period; k = capital-output ratio, assumed to be $3:1$; Γ = absorptive capacity (rate of sustainable growth, varying with the country); b = marginal domestic savings rate, varying with the country; Y_0 = initial year's GNP; and S_0/Y_0 = initial year's average savings rate.

The first term expresses the difference between marginal savings rates and the investment level needed at the given absorptive capacity; the second term reflects the fact that marginal savings rates are normally higher than average rates. It permits the required investment rate, as determined by marginal savings, to be maintained through a capital inflow that covers the discrepancy between marginal and average savings at the initial GNP level.

TABLE 2–5: EXTERNAL CAPITAL REQUIREMENTS
OF UNDERDEVELOPED COUNTRIES, 1961–1976
(In $ billion)

Area	Period		
	1961–66	1966–71	1971–76
Africa	0.4	0.6	0.7
Latin America	1.6	1.5	1.0
Asia	2.7	2.4	1.3
Middle East	0.6	0.8	0.4
Total	5.3	5.3	3.4

SOURCE: Rodenstein-Rodan, p. 127.

NOTE: In the three periods, private investment is assumed to provide 25, 33, and 50 per cent of the capital, respectively.

The equation makes no direct provision for balance-of-payments effects of growth; therefore Rosenstein-Rodan's estimates are unlikely to cover the capital requirements as discussed above under "Projections of Import Gap." Table 2–5, summarizing his results, confirms this inference. The capital flows are much smaller than those implied by Tables 2–1 and 2–2; furthermore they decline with time, while the estimates of Tables 2–1 and 2–2 show an increasing gap. This result stems partly from the nature of the estimating equation. The second term is always positive, because the savings function is assumed to be of the form

$$S = a + bY,$$

where a is less than zero (dissaving at low levels of income); therefore $(b - S_0/Y_0)Y_0$ will be greater than zero, but the first term is likely to be negative, and will be a larger negative number as Y increases. Typical values used by Rosenstein-Rodan for k, Γ, and b are 3.0, 0.02, and 0.10, respectively. Thus within a given five-year period, F will tend to decrease unless $(k\Gamma - b)$ is positive. From period to period, F will tend to decrease, because increases in b diminish the first term more than they increase the second. S_0/Y_0 has to increase from period to period (unless b stays constant) and tends to approach b; thus the second term declines when the parameters change. For the first term to increase from period to period, $k\Gamma$ must increase more than b. For the two terms combined to increase from period to period, the first term must rise more than the second term declines. It can do this only if the absorptive capacity and the capital-output ratio rise substantially from period to period, or if increasing income brings little or no change in marginal savings from period to period. It should be noted that in the latter case, an increase in marginal savings may be accompanied by increased requirements for external capital. This could happen if growth in the first period removed bottlenecks and thereby allowed a substantial increase in absorptive capacity.

We put together an optimistic and reassuring vision of the future when we assume away foreign-exchange problems and use an estimating equation that tends to yield declining values from period to period. The resulting magnitudes, on the face of it, indicate that the present normal flow of economic aid is adequate to meet underdeveloped countries' requirements as determined by their absorptive capacity and ability to mobilize domestic capital.

Table 2–4 listed the official figures for the flow of long-term financial resources to underdeveloped countries since 1956.[14] The totals well exceed Rosenstein-Rodan's estimated requirements, even if we follow his proposal and allow a deduction from the totals (of $600 million annually) for overvaluation of U.S. food and aid under Public Law 480 and for private investment directed to petroleum and other extractive industries, and another deduction for short- and medium-term official loans (up to 10 years).[15] He has also suggested deducting a portion of so-called defense-support expenditures, which are aimed at allowing certain countries to finance large military budgets without increasing taxes.

Another estimate, however, made by the Netherlands Economic Institute, assumes that poor countries' per capita income is now increasing by

[14] As estimated by the Development Assistance Committee of the OECD. Soviet Bloc aid excluded.

[15] The actual flow of short- and medium-term credits is difficult to determine, because the data on private sector short-term export financing is incomplete. Rosenstein-Rodan has estimated combined public and private lending of less than ten years' duration at about $2 billion annually in 1961.

1.5 per cent annually, a figure that could be raised to 3.5 per cent by a $7 to $8 billion increase in annual investment, most of which would obviously have to come from abroad in the short run.[16] This estimate, like Rosenstein-Rodan's, is based on capital-output relations, and does not deal with balance-of-payments problems. If we assume that $5 billion of this incremental investment comes from developed countries, it would represent a doubling of the present net aid flow (or an increase of 60 per cent, if we use the estimates of Table 2–4, which include interest, dividends, and certain other return-flow elements).

This review, as well as that discussed above under "Projections of Import Gap," makes it clear that projections of external capital and exchange requirements are wildly uncertain. The salient point emerging from all such exercises is that if underdeveloped countries' income is to increase by 4.5 to 5.5 per cent annually (2.5 to 3.5 per cent per capita), there will have to be a larger resource flow from developed countries, in the absence of draconian measures to increase domestic savings. We are surely not guilty of exaggeration if we say that, to meet these goals over the next ten years, the annual flow will have to increase by at least $5 billion net by the end of the period. Furthermore, with the steady growth of debt-service obligations, a net increase of $5 billion implies a much larger gross increase, unless all the transfers are in the forms of grants.

[16] Netherlands Economic Institute, "The European Community and Underdeveloped Countries," Rotterdam, May 1959 (mimeographed), quoted in Jan Tinbergen, *Shaping the World Economy*, The Twentieth Century Fund, New York, 1962, p. 120.

3

Reflections on the Meaning of Burden Sharing

Demand for and Supply of Foreign Aid

Demand for Aid

Chapter 1 concluded that there can be no general and rigorous theoretical demonstration that underdeveloped countries' growth is hampered by inadequate foreign-exchange earnings or inadequate capital inflows. At the same time, it is clear from the historical record that most countries (except England and the USSR) have in fact financed part of their growth with import surpluses and increasing foreign trade. Today there are some countries (oil exporters and countries at a very low level of development) for whom lack of purchasing power over imports and inadequate domestic savings are presumably not primary barriers to growth now.

In general, however, the demand for foreign aid can be justified on "objective" grounds by its importance in helping to maintain acceptable domestic growth rates, a benefit that may reduce the likelihood of serious political and social disorder. Or if we think of growth as a goal in itself— as an aspect of the good life—then the persistence of the import gap discussed in Chapter 1 justifies the demand for foreign aid.

From the viewpoint of the underdeveloped countries, of course, the justification is simple enough: it is cheaper to let others pay for your development than to pay for it yourself. If foreign aid is beneficial and costs nothing, clearly the more of it the better.

Although it is ordinarily true from the recipients' viewpoint that the benefits of aid greatly outweigh its costs, it should be remembered that there are costs, nonetheless, over and above the obvious ones of loan amortization, matching contribution requirements for development projects, and the like. Sometimes these costs—such as political strings attached to aid, or threatened prestige—may be high enough to impel a country to forgo aid entirely. Portugal, for example, with relatively low per capita income, prefers for various reasons to give aid rather than to receive it. Burma, Indonesia, and Cambodia have renounced U.S. aid to maintain their nonaligned status. Presumably, in view of potential Chinese domination of Southeast Asia, the costs of dependence on the United States seem too great to compensate for its benefits. In 1963, however, Cambodia sought French aid as a substitute for U.S. aid, the implication being that it would be less provocative to depend on a lesser Western power than on a major power hostile to China.

If there were some clear connection between income growth and the cost-benefit balance in the demand for aid, each country would tend to find aid less and less attractive as its income rose. But such connections are not palpable and dominant. Low-income countries have renounced aid, and countries with relatively high incomes have protested bitterly against aid reductions. Normally, the decision to forgo aid is not based on economic costs, although they may play a part (for example, if aid in the form of food grants reduces domestic farm prices below remunerative levels).

Supply of Aid: Military Considerations

It is easy enough to see why underdeveloped countries should want foreign aid, but it is less clear why industrial countries should offer it. The reason normally advanced—in the United States, at least—is national security. But this term is too broad to have any intrinsic operational content. In the narrowest sense of the term—military defense of the country against hostile powers—the underdeveloped countries have little importance for North America and Western Europe (or for the USSR) and will have still less as long-range nuclear missiles become more effective.

Such a narrow definition of national security, however, clearly fails to cover the range of national security interests. Issues of power and prestige, although linked only indirectly to the military defense of the United

States, are nonetheless of substantial importance in shaping our foreign policy. Thus we might want to extend foreign aid to help prevent the spread of Communism, or to help build societies that accept U.S. values and follow our political lead.

Presumably, these broader goals assume that Western society will prosper more in a world where non-Communist regimes predominate; conversely, the USSR might be expected to benefit from the growth of Communist ones. But the history of U.S. experience with Nationalist China and Vietnam, and that of the USSR with Yugoslavia, Albania, and Communist China, cast at least some doubt on this simple hypothesis.

It is convenient to begin by analyzing the U.S. national security motive in terms of two opposed and extreme viewpoints, both of which have been expressed in discussing aid policy.

The first is the "square mile" hypothesis. According to this view, the United States cannot afford to surrender even one square mile to Communism. The rationale is that any Communist gain propels a dynamic sequence of future gains, as our allies become demoralized by our inability to defend free-world territory. Furthermore, it is argued, these territorial gains offer a military basis for further advances, setting in motion the often discussed "falling dominoes" sequence. The best way, then, to convince both allies and adversaries of your determination is to relinquish nothing.

Variations of the square mile viewpoint have been advanced by U.S. official witnesses before Congressional committees. This viewpoint can be defended by correctly pointing out that the costs of protecting Country B (for example, Vietnam) increase substantially as Country A (Laos) comes under Communist control. This argument, however, evades the question of how important Countries B through X are to U.S. security in the first place. In other words, although it is true that the loss of one country is almost sure to make it more expensive to defend some other country, this does not tell us whether either country has military value for U.S. security.[1] Perhaps more important in practice, it does not make it explicit that the square mile policy, if rigorously pursued, may have very high costs—in some cases, higher than we may want to pay. For example, it is perfectly

[1] Of course, Countries B, C, D, . . . may really be important to U.S. military security, in which case the square mile theory is valid for the particular countries in question. Or even if they are not important to U.S. military security, we may fear a loss of U.S. prestige and a consequent reduction in our ability to influence the direction of world affairs.

clear that there are prices that the United States is not willing to pay to prevent a Communist take-over in, say, Ghana or Indonesia. There was also a price we were unwilling to pay to overthrow Communist advances in Cuba.

In other words, even the proponents of the square mile thesis do not accept it absolutely. The recognition that there are exceptions is, after all, nothing more than an acknowledgment of reality, because in its extreme form the square mile hypothesis is as vulnerable as its opposite, which we will discuss below. We know from experience that the square mile sequence has not in fact taken place. Communist take-over in Czechoslovakia did not spread to Western Europe; nor has Communism in Cuba ignited a further sequence of revolution in the Caribbean. Whatever the merits of this view, then, it is clear that it cannot be accepted in its extreme form; nor is U.S. policy based on the extreme assumption. On the other hand, in assessing its weaknesses, we should also remember its virtues. For one thing, it is easy for friend and enemy to understand. Furthermore, it has important domestic political advantages, because it shows a suitable toughness toward Communism.

The second and opposite hypothesis can be epitomized in the blunt question, "Who needs them?" If the paramount objective is U.S. military security, underdeveloped countries are clearly of diminishing importance—either as friends or as enemies—particularly as long-range nuclear missiles and space satellites become more effective. Thus, Cuba may be important to us today as a possible base for surprise Soviet missile attack; ten years from now, our nuclear strength and advanced detection methods may make Cuba a trifling concern. Furthermore, it is at least arguable that African and Asian territory is important to us mainly as bases for intelligence and communications. In the future, facilities based in space satellites or on the oceans or in other continents may replace these with equal effectiveness and at comparable cost. If so, we can—at least for military purposes—dismiss the underdeveloped countries from consideration.

Just as we can observe that dogmatic devotion to square mile views is untenable, so can we state that "Who needs them?" extremism is also off the mark.

So far, at least, technology has not progressed to the point where we can safely contemplate abandoning all bases in underdeveloped countries—at least not without substantial increases in the military budget. In theory, one could estimate the cost, under static assumptions, of providing equivalent protection to the United States from other bases, and compare this cost with that of foreign military and economic aid.[2] Such an estimate is certainly feasible, as an approximation, but preparing it would itself require a full-length study. The report of the 1963 Clay Committee on foreign aid implies such analysis: "Dollar for dollar, these programs contribute more to the security of the free world than corresponding expenditures in our defense appropriations."[3] Unfortunately, the Committee offers no evidence of analysis to support its conclusion that an additional dollar of aid buys more free-world security than does an additional dollar of domestic defense expenditure. In fact, the Committee's conclusions, looking forward to reductions in aid, do not follow from the statement quoted above. If they believed that statement to be true, they should logically have called for transfer of additional funds from the U.S. defense budget to the foreign-aid budget, because in that way, according to their contention, we would be buying more security for the same amount of money.

Our conclusions on the role of foreign aid in U.S. security must therefore remain agnostic in the absence of the appropriate analysis. It is not surprising that the research that would be needed to determine the appropriate supply of foreign aid from a security viewpoint has not been carried out. The analysis would be difficult enough even if it were simply a question of comparing the costs of defending a certain territory from various alternative bases. But the decision to give or withhold aid will also have dynamic consequences on military, political, and economic developments, consequences that can virtually never be predicted with confidence. Therefore, the dynamic aspects of the security argument for supplying foreign aid are necessarily a question of judgment in which formal methods of cost analysis play but a minor role. The static aspects are amenable to analysis, however, and are a legitimate subject for further research.

Unfortunately, in the absence of convincing cost analysis there is a great

[2] See Charles Wolf, Jr., "Some Aspects of the 'Value' of Less Developed Countries to the United States," *World Politics*, Vol. 15, July 1963, pp. 623–635.

[3] Committee To Strengthen the Security of the Free World, *The Scope and Distribution of United States Military and Economic Assistance Programs*, Department of State, Washington, D.C., March 20, 1963, p. 5.

I assume that the "dollar for dollar" statement refers to marginal benefits; if it refers to average benefits, then increases in foreign aid at the expense of domestic defense spending need not follow necessarily. However, it hardly seems likely that the Clay Committee was able to determine the shape of the foreign-aid cost-benefit functions empirically.

temptation to indulge in extreme statements concerning the virtues or defects of aid. Perhaps the greatest impetus that official defenders of aid could give to their programs would be to show more modesty in their claims about its past and future accomplishments, while trying to improve the analytical basis for that portion of their program that is subject to quantitative measurement.

Supply of Aid: Nonmilitary Considerations

Foreign aid is offered for a number of reasons other than purely military ones. That is, even if the "Who needs them?" hypothesis were correct, foreign aid could be defended on other grounds, principally—

1. Effects on U.S. society;
2. Economic significance;
3. The existence of prior aid commitments;
4. Humanitarian motives;
5. The desire to set an example of peaceful international cooperation.

The following paragraphs discuss each matter briefly and then go on to some general observations about the relation between foreign aid and the attainment of the implied goals. The discussion offers no simple answers, for there are none. As Schultz puts it, "Whether support for foreign aid is based on humanitarian benevolence, utilitarianism, or long-run self-interest raises issues that are not easy to untangle by simple introspection."[4] Anyone who has tried to analyze these issues must agree; and many would wish to delete the word "simple" from the quotation.

Effects on U.S. Society. It is often argued that the greatest value of our foreign-aid program is not military at all, since in the long run the United States presumably could assure its military security from its Western Hemisphere bases. Rather, so goes the argument, it is vital that we help maintain free societies elsewhere, because the steady growth of a hostile world would foment a garrison-state mentality in the United States, the effect of which would be to erode our freedom and curtail our democratic privileges of diversity and dissent.

It is impossible to test this hypothesis, although there is no lack of historical examples of states surrounded by enemies. Many of them, such as the Soviet Union and ancient Sparta, have been authoritarian and

---

[4] T. W. Schultz, "Value of U.S. Farm Surpluses to Underdeveloped Countries," *Journal of Farm Economics*, Vol. 42, December 1960, p. 1020.

militaristic. It is also true that in U.S. history, periods of antiforeign prejudice and anti-Communist "campaigns" have been associated with attacks on domestic civil liberties. Whether these considerations should be dominant in justifying the supply of foreign aid is clearly a matter of individual belief. I am inclined to consider it a most important factor in the long run.

Economic Motivations. There is no doubt that the United States has important economic interests in underdeveloped countries. Our exports to them in 1961 amounted to $6.6 billion, and our imports to $5.7 billion. In the same year our capital investment in these countries was valued at $12.2 billion.

Foreign aid is not a necessary condition for continuing this trade and investment. It is at least as important to the underdeveloped countries as it is to the United States; whether or not these countries are politically hostile to the United States, they will still have to sell where they can. Of course, one might argue that for certain strategic materials, trade with underdeveloped countries is of great importance; in practice, however, there are normally alternative sources of supply for almost any raw material, although perhaps at a higher cost.[5] In a dynamic setting, it might be argued that foreign aid is sometimes a necessary condition for growth in underdeveloped countries—that the aid will, in fact, stimulate an increase in trade that will more than pay for the present cost of aid. If there were widespread unemployment in the donor country, this argument could be reinforced by pointing out that the real cost of the aid is small. This point will be discussed in more detail below.

Honoring Prior Commitments. Policies are not made in a historical vacuum. Even if it were decided that much aid is not justified on solid military or economic grounds, a donor country would obviously endanger its reputation for trustworthiness and veracity by abruptly cutting it off. A great power can ill afford to withdraw lightly from its international commitments. For the United States, an important consideration would be the political impact of such a withdrawal on our allies. Other members of the North Atlantic Treaty Organization (NATO) might view it not only as a withdrawal from our commitments to less developed countries but also, by inference, as a reduction of all U.S. commitments abroad.

Humanitarian Motives. Foreign-aid appropriations are usually justified

[5] See Wolf.

on military and economic grounds, but there is also a widespread interest in relieving poverty, disease, and ignorance. Welfare programs in the United States are based on such considerations, and public support for foreign aid undoubtedly reflects such motives. Essentially, the argument is simply that the wealthy have some responsibility for the welfare of the poor. We accept such arguments in domestic affairs; and, as in the case of local Community Chest programs, even translate them on occasion into a voluntary effort to redistribute income. In the case of international economic aid, as in domestic affairs, the argument is also supported by an implication that economic aid in the proper amount and composition will ultimately enable less developed countries to stand on their own feet.

A related point is that any move to establish an atmosphere of peaceful international cooperation through such programs as foreign aid is useful in reducing international hostilities and channeling energies toward constructive goals.

Supply of Aid: Ends and Means

For most of these objectives—except questions of military advantage and, to a degree, the gains from trade—there are no valid measures of costs versus benefits. This is immediately clear in the case of humanitarian goals, but it is also true of the other motives discussed above.

Even if it is agreed that the United States has a valid interest in underdeveloped countries' welfare, it does not necessarily follow that economic aid will promote mutual interests. In some cases, to be sure, the reciprocity is clear. For the United States to obtain a foreign military base, for example, the foreign country's asking price may include economic aid; if so, foreign aid may be the least costly way of buying a military advantage. Such machinery occasionally breaks down, of course. The United States has given substantial economic aid to Cambodia and Burma, but presumably is no longer allowed to maintain military, communications, or intelligence facilities there.[6] By the same token, the United States gave Cuba substantial amounts of aid through artificially high sugar prices, and has harvested nettles in return.

In discussing all these motives, except the humanitarian, it is sometimes stated that foreign aid is a necessary but not sufficient condition for

---

[6] This does not necessarily imply that the aid was wasted; it may have been justified—or for that matter, unjustified—on other grounds.

building and safeguarding U.S. interests in underdeveloped countries. This formulation has its appeal, but it is incorrect as a generalization. In some cases foreign aid is a necessary condition for assuring our interests. India may be a case in point. In other cases, of which Ghana is typical, it might be argued that aid is neither a necessary nor a sufficient condition. In many underdeveloped countries U.S. aid is not important enough to assure success for any of the goals discussed above.

One might even argue that our grants of aid sometimes promote forces inimical to U.S. interests. In Cuba, for example, the high prices we paid for sugar may have affected Cuban income distribution in ways that helped incite the revolution there.

This review of the motives for offering foreign aid leaves us in an unsatisfying position, intellectually. It resolves itself, with regard to security, into our resorting to an eclectic series of decisions based on criteria that are either inherently unmeasurable (for example, is the United States better or worse off in the long run by supporting the fragile regimes of Southeast Asia?), or, if measurable, have usually not been measured (for example, how much would it cost to augment the strength of United States military forces by the same amount as we now obtain through our aid to Iran?).

When we turn to some of the other goals, we find that the relationship between ends and foreign aid as a means is still tenuous. It is difficult, for example, to prove that foreign aid effectively fosters a healthy society in the United States by developing free societies in the underdeveloped world. Perhaps it does, but the results are not measurable in the long run. In short, it is probably futile to search for simple and clear-cut ways to measure the costs of foreign aid against the broad benefits to the donor.

Unsatisfactory as these observations may seem to those in quest of infallible touchstones, they are probably preferable to some of the absolutes that have come back to haunt their proponents in the past, such as the square mile view; or the belief that aid was justified on the manifestly absurd grounds that it would forestall *any* Communist take-overs; or the belief that the donor would gain substantial political leverage.

To the extent that economic aid is directed to helping underdeveloped countries increase their rates of economic growth, there is no simple correlation with U.S. national interest.

Ultimately, it seems to me that the case for such a policy rests on the justification that economic growth promotes the development of free societies—or at least independent ones; and that Western values are more likely to prosper in such an atmosphere. Naturally, some of the independent states so fostered may be hostile to the United States; as noted above, there is no necessary correlation between economic growth and pro-Western sentiments. There seems to be a reasonable presumption, however, that societies in which output is increasing rapidly are less likely to be welded through revolution into a totalitarian, anti-Western bloc. Economic growth probably eases social tensions in the long run, although, as the history of Europe in the Industrial Revolution indicates, it may often catalyze social unrest in the short run.

Supply of Aid and Burden Sharing

Among the variety of factors—military, economic, social, humanitarian —discussed above, each person and each nation will have a different balance of interest. Nonetheless, it seems clear that, with the partial exception of economic motives, whatever benefits are derived from foreign aid presumably accrue to all industrialized countries. This is the fact that gives rise to burden-sharing questions.

In a sense the word "burden" is inappropriate, because the aid is given in exchange for expected benefits. Our hopes may be vain, of course; aid may fail to promote Western security, just as an item purchased in a store may fail to give satisfaction. But in the absence of deliberate fraud, in neither aid nor trade can the purchaser be said to bear a burden. He expects a return for his money.

The issue of a burden arises only in respect to cost sharing. All Western countries presumably gain broad security benefits from foreign aid; how should the costs be distributed? In other words, it is a question of public finance, which, like most questions of equity in public finance, is not subject to a single unequivocal answer. These issues are discussed in more detail below.

Normally, burden-sharing considerations do not apply to the humanitarian and commercial benefits from aid. If these benefits impel one country to furnish aid, no benefit necessarily accrues to others. At most, indirect commercial benefits may be diffused through a possible increase in world trade. Undoubtedly these motives are present in all countries' aid; but the logic of the burden-sharing argument in foreign aid, as in everything else, must stem not from these motives but from shared benefits. Of course, one industrialized country cannot very well insist that a second country increase its share of aid contributions to make citizens of the second country richer or happier. When developed countries do ask each other to provide more aid, the ultimate justification is that some countries' benefits have exceeded their costs by more than is equitable. In practice this line of thought reduces to a consideration of security benefits, broadly defined to include domestic political effects on Western societies.

Burden-sharing discussions at the Organization for Economic Cooperation and Development (OECD) and the General Agreement on Tariffs and Trade (GATT), as well as those in economics literature, frequently refer to expansion of private investment and trade with underdeveloped countries as if they were aspects of the problem. As Mason has pointed out, however, reductions of trade barriers do not impose a burden;[7] nor is there any logical reason for all developed countries, in concert, to reduce trade barriers or increase investment in underdeveloped countries. Private investment is clearly motivated by the expectation of benefits, regardless of others' behavior. National gains from specialization and trade are presumably obtainable when any industrial country removes obstacles to trade with underdeveloped countries, although exceptional cases can always be formulated. In practice, however, as the free-trade-protectionist argument indicates, most countries are reluctant to reduce barriers because of the short-term costs, particularly if other countries are unwilling to do the same.

Arguments for sharing the "burden" of more liberal trade and investment policy must essentially be based on two points: (1) Industrial countries are unlikely to move in this direction except in concert. (2) Even if a few do move this way while others do not, there may be less benefit for Western security than if all did. The fact that trade and investment provide their own rewards does not exclude collateral security benefits. Underdeveloped countries' gains from trade and investment are important for economic growth—usually more important than aid—and therefore, by the argument discussed above, presumably bear some relation to the security of the West. For that reason, on practical grounds, it may appear legitimate to regard trade and investment as aspects of the burden-sharing problem.

Nevertheless, on balance, it seems to me that moves to liberalize commercial policies should not be directly included in any burden-sharing

---

[7] E. S. Mason, "The Equitable Sharing of Military and Economic Aid Burdens," *Proceedings of the Academy of Political Science*, Vol. 27, May 1963, pp. 67–68.

calculus. I can think of no sensible way to measure the contributions of each country, fundamentally because no costs are involved. If the United States lowers its tariffs and imports more goods from Brazil, both countries are likely to be better off.

This amounts to saying that commercial policy toward underdeveloped countries should be divorced from the burden-sharing issue. In practice, it is true, industrial countries do not look at the matter this way; a liberal trade policy is always discussed as if it involves granting favors. This attitude is correct only in the restricted sense that underdeveloped countries may derive greater relative benefits because they are poorer; but this position is hard to defend. It is somewhat farfetched to assert that one trading party incurs a "cost" if his gains are less than another's. If this were normally a sticking point, there would be no trade at all.

A more important practical reason for excluding trade from burden-sharing discussions is that the attempt to make the word "aid" embrace everything rich countries do for poor ones inevitably leads to dodging the aid issue. Too many aspects of international economic relations are not susceptible to meaningful and compatible measures. It is much more fruitful to draw a dividing line between things that are and are not measurable by a common scale, and consider them apart. The wisdom of doing so is reflected in the division of labor between the GATT and the Development Assistance Committee (DAC) of OECD. It is all to the good if developed countries move toward more liberal commercial policies in the GATT or in other forums. In the long run such movement may be more significant than changes in the flow of aid. No harm will be done if these countries wish to conceive of their liberalized policies as a form of aid, so long as they do not actually weigh them in the same scales with official aid contributions.

Economic and Bargaining Problems in Cost Sharing[8]

Although this study is primarily concerned with economic aid, the burden-sharing question has arisen in a variety of contexts, including the

[8] This section owes a good deal to T. C. Schelling, "International Cost-Sharing Arrangements," *Essays in International Finance*, No. 24, Department of Economics, Princeton University, Princeton, N. J., 1955; and L. Gordon, "Economic Aspects of Coalition Diplomacy: The NATO Experience," *International Organization*, Vol. 10., October 1956, pp. 529–543. Other important references include Irving B. Kravis and M. W. S. Davenport, "The Political Arithmetic of International Burden Sharing," *Journal of Political Economy*, Vol. 71, August 1963, pp. 309–330; and Mason.

administrative budgets of international organizations, the financing of international lending organizations, and the sharing of costs in military alliances. Accordingly, this section (and Chapter 4, which reviews burden-sharing experience) refers to all types of international cost-sharing arrangements, particularly to NATO.

Some Perspective on Burden Sharing

The following paragraphs discuss factors that affect burden-sharing criteria and their influence on cost-sharing formulas.[9]

Formulas have no particular intrinsic merit. They are normally arrived at by a bargaining process that may or may not reflect considerations of economic efficiency and equity.

If it is agreed that burden-sharing criteria and formulas based on them are simply one method of attaining a goal, the question follows: Under what conditions are such criteria likely to be accepted? In an international alliance there is no method of imposing taxes on sovereign member states. Burden-sharing schemes, "objective" or not, must be accepted by each member, whether the sums are large or small.

In some international organizations—the United Nations, the OECD, the International Monetary Fund—members have agreed on a common formula for contributions. In others, such as NATO and international economic aid programs, they have not. The reasons for this disparity seem clear enough. Agreement on burden-sharing criteria involves at least two steps: (1) a political decision to support the organization; and (2) a politico-economic decision on the advantages of financing the alliance according to burden-sharing formulas.

In the case of organizations like the UN, once the first decision was made, the second followed as the path of least resistance. There was no satisfactory alternative. Besides, the sums involved were relatively small and had little political importance. It hardly seems worthwhile for twenty or more nations to enter into collective bargaining over financing a small increase in, let us say, the UN headquarters budget. When new UN activities have been introduced, however, such as raising the UN Special Fund or funds for policing the Congo, new political considerations have emerged.

[9] Formulas are defined here as cost-sharing arrangements based partly or wholly on such "rational" criteria as ability to pay or benefits received.

In the case of NATO and international economic aid, by contrast, the decision to enter into cost-sharing agreements did not follow automatically once the political decision was made. The amounts of money involved are very large and many members may think they stand to gain from not accepting formulas. Furthermore, countries may be reluctant to accept burden-sharing formulas even if they seem advantageous in the short run, for fear of committing themselves to a precedent they may later regret. For example, several nations were reluctant to agree to a cost-sharing formula for NATO headquarters for fear of establishing a precedent that would lead to more substantial expenditures. It might be argued that one important reason NATO members were able to agree on shares of the $175 million annual NATO infrastructure budget was that the percentage contributions agreed on seemed clearly inappropriate for any broader burden-sharing criteria.[10]

It should be noted that even the UN type of formula, which is based primarily on ability to pay, will itself be the product of bargaining. This is inevitable, even when countries have agreed in principle to accept rational burden-sharing criteria. The reason is simple enough. Because members of an alliance do not have identical interests, each stands to gain from a certain amount of judicious bargaining. When the amounts become large, some countries are increasingly tempted to forsake any explicit allegiance to rational burden-sharing criteria, because of their real or fancied disadvantages under formal criteria. And when one or more important members refuse to accept such criteria, it becomes more difficult to apply them to the other members.

In general, members of an alliance will be most willing to accept a common budget: (1) when the job to be done cannot be carried out by individual national action, or could be so carried out only at a cost that seems prohibitive compared with the benefits (UN headquarters and NATO infrastructure are cases in point); (2) when members see more political advantages in a jointly financed than in an individual action; and (3) when the sums involved are insignificant in relation to national budgets or incomes.

This section concentrates primarily on NATO and DAC (the forum for economic aid donors), where common funding plays only a minor role. Are burden-sharing criteria applicable or even worth discussing in such

---

[10] See Chap. 4 for a discussion of NATO experience.

cases? Basically the answer is yes, if members agree to use them as a guide in determining their separate expenditures for alliance purposes.

Furthermore, arguments for burden sharing are in themselves part of a country's strategy in negotiating a more favorable situation for itself and for the alliance. Finally, although factors not susceptible to a logical solution inevitably hamper the development of logical cost-sharing criteria, there are nonetheless important advantages in reaching agreement on certain aspects of cost sharing, whether or not there is a common budget. As Schelling has said (p. 25):

> If we drop the idea of a formula, and think rather of the develop-
> ment of "criteria," or even more loosely of "relevant considerations,"
> for the negotiation of country shares, many of the theoretical problems
> discussed earlier become, if not "soluble," at least resolvable. While a
> formula has to be simple and precise, "considerations" can be
> numerous and less well-defined; and principles can gradually be
> forged to which exceptions can be made for the cases to which the
> principles are least applicable. The existence of a vague consensus
> may never yield a quantitative formula but still be adequate to permit
> eventual agreement. The posing of unanswerable questions, the
> weighting of conflicting considerations, and the debating of principles
> too numerous and too vague to be included in a formula are not
> necessarily ineffectual just because the final outcome is a negotiated
> compromise.

The discussion of this section is fairly long, but the conclusions can be stated briefly enough. Essentially we emerge with four principal points, two of them negative:

1. Public finance considerations of equity offer us very little guidance in formulating contributions systems.
2. Balance-of-payments considerations should ordinarily be allowed to influence only the form of contributions, not their amounts.
3. It is possible to introduce a definition of foreign aid based on discounted present values that reduces all forms of aid to a logical common denominator.
4. There is a good argument for basing international contributions on real-income rather than money-income equivalents.

The discussion of burden sharing to follow consists of several subsections. The first examines the principal kinds of criteria that have been advanced as guidelines for burden sharing: adequacy of effort, economy of effort, and equity. These categories have been borrowed from Gordon's interesting article on NATO burden sharing.

The later subsections outline various aspects of burden sharing under the following categories: (1) definitions of aid and common defense; (2) valuation of contributions; and (3) contributions systems as balancing devices.

What Kinds of Criteria?

Burden-sharing criteria of themselves will not persuade a country to increase its relative contributions unless it is disposed to do so anyway. A country's willingness to contribute more will depend on its interest in the matter, the pressure it is subjected to, and similar bargaining considerations. Generally speaking, the less money involved, the easier it is to win acceptance for a formula based on ability-to-pay standards. Attempts to impose formulas for military expenditures are therefore least likely to succeed, because the amounts are the largest and the domestic political implications the greatest.

Formulas are likely to be applied, however, when national financing is clearly impossible (such as for NATO headquarters or infrastructure expense), and may therefore be extended some day to such categories as NATO-controlled weapon systems.

For the rest, formulas are used principally as a bargaining device in discussing defense spending—a convenient way for a country to "prove" that inequities prevail in a given situation. The following rather abstract analysis should be read with this fact in mind. We are essentially discussing the rationale for bargaining; the limited relevance of this chapter rests on its value as rationale and as a demonstration of the meager use of formal criteria for determining cost-sharing arrangements.

There are no *a priori* upper or lower limits to alliance defense expenditures or economic aid contributions; as has been frequently stressed, the decision of how much to spend on these objectives is essentially political, a matter of judgment.

Adequacy of Effort. In the case of NATO, an "adequate effort" can presumably be defined as one that enables a country to meet its agreed NATO force goals as expressed in the approved Military Committee documents; however, it might also apply to forces not committed to NATO, such as the Strategic Air Command (SAC) and the French nuclear striking force, because they would probably be used on NATO jobs in the event of war.

For economic aid, the United States has suggested at the DAC meetings that the members contribute a total of 1 per cent of combined GNP. This criterion reflects a 1960 resolution of the UN General Assembly, but there is no particular economic justification for it. It is simply a symbolic amount that would require increases in contributions from the developed countries, but not unrealistically large increases.

The discussion of adequacy of economic aid has long been associated with the idea of "absorptive capacity"—the underdeveloped countries' ability to use the aid effectively. It has been assumed that there is a diminishing marginal productivity of aid within each underdeveloped country; and it has even been implied that underdeveloped countries could not at present effectively use sums exceeding the 1 per cent proposed.[11]

Generally speaking, the same claim has not been applied to defense expenditures. For example, even though it is agreed that expenditures on additional nuclear first-strike capacity may be redundant after a certain point, and even though the same argument presumably would apply to any single category of defense expenditures, a special factor to be considered in defense tends to make the concept of a definite upper limit inapplicable: This factor is the likely response of hostile powers. If the NATO powers increase their defense expenditures by a given amount, the Soviet Bloc may react by increasing its expenditures; if so, the levels of expenditure formerly considered adequate in terms of "marginal productivity" considerations may then become inadequate.[12]

Economy of Effort. Economy of effort, in this context, implies an attempt to assure international specialization in producing goods and in supplying labor and special skills, including military forces. It also implies, in the military sphere, the idea of creating balanced collective forces, that is, an aggregate force that would meet NATO's requirements, on the basis of some national specialization. Another such element is the attempt to standardize military equipment.

At best, NATO has only partially achieved these objectives. To the extent that force expansion has followed the lines recommended by its

[11] Rosenstein-Rodan. See Chap. 2 of this study for a detailed summary and critique. The apparently obvious inference that the marginal productivity of aid declines as aid levels increase is probably incorrect within the ranges so far observed. Diminishing marginal productivity of investment is a valid presumption in economic statics, but in growth situations, investment opportunities feed on themselves.

[12] Theoretically, a similar process would take place if the Soviet Bloc and the West began competing more actively than now in offering economic aid.

Military Committee, NATO has achieved a certain national specialization conducive to the goal of balancing collective forces. It is almost impossible, however, to estimate how the actual force cost diverged from the optimum that might have been achieved if this goal had been scrupulously respected.

The benefits of international specialization in NATO production of goods and manpower supply were partially realized through methods that were not entirely deliberate. The United States has been in fact the principal supplier of heavy military equipment for the alliance. A degree of international specialization arose from U.S. offshore procurement of certain goods, but there was very little conscious effort to specialize in the production of particular goods for exchange within the alliances. The least cost principle in manpower supply was respected to a degree. Thus, Greece and Turkey supplied larger armed forces in relation to their defense budgets than did the wealthier European countries.

This recital presents only one side of the economy-of-effort principle; the other side would be a positive correlation between GNP and equipment expenditures as a percentage of total defense spending. Again, this gauge was respected to a degree, with a relatively large percentage of U.S. and Canadian defense spending.

Because the forms of economic aid are so various and the total contributions so small compared to military expenditures, the criterion of economy has not often been discussed. In the bestowal of economic aid, the United States has not been the chief supplier of the goods lent or given, nor are the arguments for such an imposed specialization as strong. Many elements that are also latent in the field of military supply become particularly evident in the case of economic aid. Each country tends to think of the long-run market for its products. Furnishing aid to underdeveloped countries partly becomes a method of encouraging long-term trade relations with them. Of course, to the extent that aid is untied, underdeveloped countries may strive to buy their products in the cheapest market, thereby benefiting from the existing specialization in the international economy. This is one of the strongest arguments for untied aid.

Equity of Effort. In practice, most of the discussion of economic criteria centers on equity, for a number of reasons. First, international bargaining about the total effort, and hence about adequacy, has tended to take place as part of the bargaining about relative shares. It is easy enough to agree on some total figure for contributions; the difficulty lies in hammering out each nation's quota. Second, many of the issues involved in economy of effort are not so obviously related to national budgets as are the direct payments required under a contributions schedule. In NATO these differences are clearly evidenced by the relative willingness of countries to accept NATO force goals. The trouble comes in meeting the goals.

Equity can be considered at the level of real resources and in money terms. In either case the problems are formidable, and, at the international level, inherently insoluble. Despite its divergence from an ideal, each country's domestic taxing and expenditure process results in some sort of parceling-out of contributions of goods and services, and a financing of those contributions through taxation and borrowing. The result presumably reflects a political consensus about equity. In defense programs, for example, recruitment and the draft provide men; the lowest cost producers are supposed to provide the goods; and domestic taxation presumably reflects the social consensus of who should pay. International equity is far more complex. There is no universal agreement, and no mechanism for introducing it, on such matters as the appropriate percentage of the labor force that should be serving in the armed forces; the correct measure of different countries' capacities to produce military equipment efficiently; and their ability to meet a share of the total cost. Furthermore, there has never been agreement on a method for estimating the value of benefits each country receives from military alliances; therefore it has been impossible to propose any system that could equitably reflect those benefits.[13]

Equity and the Theory of Taxation. Most discussion of equity has focused on the system of money contributions, and therefore on principles of taxation.

Although tax systems are essentially a question of judgment, the two

---

[13] It can be demonstrated that the economics of alliance will diverge from a Pareto optimum unless rather unlikely conditions prevail. However, the proof itself rests on the assumption, apparently reasonable, but on reflection dubious, that each country in isolation would spend on defense to the point that marginal cost equals marginal benefit from defense. In fact, the relations between what a nation might do in isolation and in alliance have been profoundly affected by nuclear strategy, so that marginal benefits may often be less than marginal costs at any level of spending. For example, it would be irrational for most European nations in isolation to spend anything on defense against possible attack from the USSR. Only the existence of the alliance validates their defense expenditures. For an interesting use of welfare economics technique and statistical methods to demonstrate the inefficiencies of an alliance, see Mancur Olson, Jr., and R. Zeckhauser, *An Economic Theory of Alliances*, The RAND Corporation, Santa Monica, Calif., P–2992, October 1964.

principles most commonly referred to are ability to pay and benefit received. The first is normally cited as the basis for progressive taxation; the second as the basis for user fees, and can also be applied to justify proportional or progressive direct and indirect taxes. Thus, it is often stated that if people who are equally well off economically receive an equal benefit, they should pay equal taxes.

In international "taxation," there has been some application of benefit criteria. Contributions to the Universal Postal Union (UPU) are based on volume of postal traffic, area, and population. GATT administrative expenses are based on members' foreign-trade proportions. The UN minimum assessment of $19,000 is based on the proposition that the smallest countries receive disproportionate benefits, because cost of delegates' travel reimbursement and cost of headquarters services normally exceed the minimum contribution.[14]

Sumberg[15] has suggested that international taxation be based on a levy on international travel or on the profits of international business. If we assume, for example, that air and sea belong to all people and that those who use them for pleasure or profit receive a benefit, this proposal also would be an example of the benefit principle.

In general, ever since the League of Nations abandoned the UPU system in 1921–1924 and turned to an ability-to-pay method based on relative national tax receipts and relative national population, the primary emphasis has been on ability-to-pay criteria.[16]

Within the framework of the ability-to-pay principle, almost all expert studies and political discussions have assumed that defense and aid contributions should be progressive, like a domestic income tax; that is, it has been assumed that one should be able to take a measure of each country's output, such as total or per capita GNP, and compare the value of each country's common defense contribution to the output. The countries with the higher incomes would be asked to pay progressively larger shares of the common defense expenditure.

The difficulties have proved insurmountable, largely for political reasons but partly because of the problems of defining aid and evaluating contri-

[14] Kravis and Davenport, p. 314; Schelling, p. 2. See Chap. 4 of this study.
[15] T. A. Sumberg, "Financing International Institutions," *Social Research*, September 1946, pp. 276–306.
[16] See J. D. Singer, "The Finances of the League of Nations," *International Organization*, Vol. 13, 1959, pp. 255–273, for a discussion of the League's efforts to arrive at a financing scheme.

butions.[17] Even assuming that an international body could arrive at common definitions that were not question-begging, this would be only the beginning of the process.

Underlying these barriers to agreement, there remains the basic question: What degree of progressiveness? This is, on the international scene, another manifestation of the question of income distribution. Economic analysis, never having been able to answer this question satisfactorily, has delivered it over to politics.

Briefly, what can tax theory tell us about equity in international contributions systems?

First, a flat-rate tax without exemption is appealing for the same reason as any simple tax: ease of understanding and administration. Another point in its favor, particularly for relatively small expenditures, is that international contributions are too small a proportion of total taxes to have important domestic effects on equity or incentive. The simplest method is therefore the best. This argument does not apply to large expenditures, however, such as those for defense, and it conflicts to a degree with widely accepted notions about the equity of progressive taxation.

Second, proportional contributions with a lump-sum exemption are also relatively simple to administer; they have been used for the Organization for European Economic Cooperation (OEEC) and, in a modified form, for the UN system. Normally, they are applied on a per capita basis; that is, national per capita income is estimated and the contributions are levied on a per capita basis after exempting a specified sum. The progressiveness is not necessarily redistributive within countries, although it probably is among countries.

This system can be made more or less progressive among countries by changing the amount of the exemption. An interesting variant is the UN system, which introduces a variable lump-sum exemption depending on the per capita national income of the country. There is a floor of 0.04 per cent and a ceiling of 30 per cent on the contributions of any one member. Within this range, there is a variable lump-sum exemption depending on the per capita national income of the country: The higher the per capita national income the smaller the lump-sum exemption. The maximum amount that can be deducted from the per capita tax base is 50 per cent

[17] See "Definitions of Aid and Common Defense Expenditures," p. 72, and "The Valuation of Economic Aid Contributions," p. 124.

of per capita income. This percentage declines with increasing national income, and countries with over $1000 per capita annual income receive no exemption. The formula for determining each country's contributions base can be expressed as

$$X_i = Y_i - Y_i\left(0.5 - 0.5\frac{\bar{Y}_i}{1000}\right) \text{ if } \bar{Y}_i < \$1000$$

$$= Y_i \text{ if } \bar{Y}_i \geq \$1000,$$

where X_i = the ith country's contribution base, Y_i = national income of country i, and $\bar{Y}_i$ = per capita national income of country i. Kravis and Davenport express this relation in terms of each country's relative share, as

$$\frac{Y_i\left[-0.5\left(\dfrac{1000 - \bar{Y}_i}{1000}\right)\right]}{\sum Y_i\left\{\left[1 - 0.5\left(\dfrac{1000 - \bar{Y}_i}{1000}\right)\right]\right\}}.$$

The numerator of this formula is equivalent to the preceding formula.

The UN formula assumes that under the benefit principle every country will contribute something; the maximum exemption is 50 per cent of per capita income.

At the same time, it is more progressive than most formulas for simple lump-sum exemptions, in that the exemption declines as income rises.[18] A limitation has been put on the progressiveness of the system, however. The United States has succeeded in restricting its maximum contribution to 30 per cent of the total UN budget. If other countries had not reacted to this event, it could have meant that some of the British Commonwealth and Northern European countries would pay a higher per capita rate than that of the United States; because they consider it inequitable to do so, an adjustment has been made that links reductions in the U.S. percentage contribution with reductions in their own. No country's per capita assessment can exceed that of the United States.

The progressiveness of a per capita tax system will depend on the amount of the lump-sum exemption. Table 3–12 (p. 82) illustrates how a

[18] However, if lump-sum exemptions are large enough, they will be more progressive than the UN formula. Furthermore, for foreign-aid burden-sharing purposes, the UN formula gives about the same result as a proportional tax, because most aid donors have per capita national income of above $1000.

$300 per capita lump-sum exemption would distribute the burden, as compared to a flat-rate tax on total income; it also shows the effect of a diminishing lump-sum exemption, as used by the UN.

Table 3–11 (p. 81), taken from Rosenstein-Rodan's article, illustrates the distribution of a progressive burden-sharing system based on U.S. income tax rates and exemptions for a family of four.

It should be noted that the international cost-sharing systems actually in force are weighted differently from those that would follow from direct application of the systems shown in Tables 3–11 and 3–12. Tables 4–1 and 4–3 show the UN, NATO headquarters, and OECD contributions. The differences are great, partly because Tables 3–11 and 3–12 include only a few countries, while the other organizations are larger; the primary reason, however, is that the United States pays a smaller proportion of contributions than its proportion of world income, as calculated at exchange-rate equivalents. (In the case of military expenditures, however, the U.S. burden is more than equal to its share of alliance income. See Table 3–5, p. 77.) Naturally, when we compare actual contributions percentages to real-income levels rather than to money income, the U.S. share comes closer to the theoretical computations found in the tables in this chapter.

Equity and International Taxation. Progressive taxes correspond to most countries' own ideas of equity as demonstrated by their internal income tax systems, with ability to pay foremost. Their great disadvantage, and the reason they have been little used internationally, is that it is very difficult to obtain agreement on what rates of progression to use, in the absence of any objective standards.

Each country has a different income tax system with different marginal rates. Furthermore, there is a difference between the rates in force and the actual incidence of the tax system. In general, tax incidence in any country is unknown, and the incidence presumably differs in all countries. Of course, one can imagine taking some kind of an average of tax progressions based, for simplicity's sake, on income tax alone; but doing so would be difficult in practice and furthermore would correspond to no particular standard. Rosenstein-Rodan has suggested using the U.S. income tax system with standard exemptions and deductions as applied to a family of four. He proposes this system because U.S. taxes have a relatively high progression, and are therefore consistent with ability-to-pay criteria, as among countries.

The final issue of tax theory treated here is the impact of international contributions systems on domestic taxes.[19] We should realize from the outset that we are dealing with an odd sort of equity in international tax systems: equity among countries, rather than among individuals, which is after all the issue that public finance normally deals with. It seems worthwhile to ask how international cost sharing relates to the traditional idea of fairness—after all, the contributions are ultimately paid by people and firms, not countries. It turns out that international and interpersonal equity are distantly related at best.

One tax principle is that like treatment should be given to people similarly situated. Of course, "similarly situated" has implications both for benefits and for costs. It is by no means clear that member countries or their citizens share equally in the benefits of an alliance. Consequently, it has sometimes been proposed that one should attempt to estimate the benefits each country gains from association in an alliance. The reader can imagine the difficulty of such a task by merely speculating on how he would go about computing the value of SAC to France; and even if such estimates were possible, they might still be unhelpful as guides to equity in contributions.

It is sometimes maintained that, at least within countries, we can say that persons receiving the same benefits and earning the same incomes should pay equal taxes. Again, there is a difficulty in defining equality of benefit. Does a New Yorker receive the same benefits from SAC as a resident of Aroostook County, Maine? If not, what are the differences in value?

Whatever international assessment scheme is used, it implies no specific tax incidence domestically. For example, a system that is progressive among countries may be financed by regressive or proportional taxation within countries. In fact, there is some indication that countries that have emphasized progressiveness in international contributions may have relatively mild progression in their domestic income tax systems.[20]

One simple appeal of a flat-rate international system is that it leads by analogy to flat-rate income tax additions applied to people within each

[19] This has been discussed by M. W. Hoag, "Economic Problems of Alliance," *Journal of Political Economy*, Vol. 65, December 1957, pp. 522–534; and by Charles J. Hitch and Roland N. McKean, *The Economics of Defense in the Nuclear Age*, Harvard University Press, Cambridge, Mass., 1960, pp. 295–296.

[20] L. Needleman, "The Burden of Taxation: An International Comparison," *National Institute Economic Review*, No. 14, September 1961, pp. 55–61.

country. Such a system would mean that persons of the same income in different countries, as well as of the same incomes in the same country, would pay the same price for protection, in the case of military expenditures. If internal tax systems are progressive and the increments are applied to a progressive tax system, there is every likelihood that people in the different countries will pay different amounts at the same income level.[21]

Kravis and Davenport have suggested that international taxation should be based on the worldwide distribution of real income among individuals, with each country paying a proportion of the total tax equal to the proportion that its citizens would pay under any given worldwide proportional or progressive personal tax system. Clearly, it is not necessary to apply a worldwide income distribution for proportional taxes: All we need for this purpose is each country's national income. For progressive taxation, however, their proposal has the advantage of "taxing" equal real personal incomes by the same amount—although it excludes income other than personal income.

Kravis and Davenport's method, which starts with binary comparisons between appropriate U.S. and foreign income distributions, utilizes the lognormal form of national income distributions to fit national populations into income classes. They then arrive at national and world income distributions for the year 1960, with standard deviations of the distributions all based on the U.S. distribution of consumer units by family income level for 1960. The means of the lognormal distributions are, for each country, the geometric means of real per capita incomes. Table 5–15 displays their results for a ten-country world, with various income tax systems applied to the hypothetical "world" income distribution.

Although this method has the great virtue of applying international progressive taxes to individuals, thereby aiming at equal taxation of individuals in similar circumstances, it still is subject to a number of defects:

1. As a technical matter, we lack adequate information on income distributions in most countries; the ingenious method of Kravis and Davenport, as they point out, would be inadequate for a formal burden-sharing effort. In addition to data problems, the method assumes that the relation between the standard deviations of similar pairs of U.S. and foreign income distributions for various years is the same as that between the U.S. distribution for 1960 and the unknown foreign ones in that year.

2. Although it may be defensible to base an assessment system on

---

[21] Hoag, p. 531.

individual income to introduce the traditional public finance concept of individual cost and benefit into international taxation, it is extremely doubtful whether national governments will actually tax their citizens in accordance with the international tax rates used to derive each country's contribution. They will probably continue to use their existing tax systems, and the incidence on individuals will bear no relation to that implied by the international taxing system.

3. Furthermore, what is the appropriate international tax system? Kravis and Davenport have suggested a range of possibilities, from proportional taxation to the mildly progressive German income tax and the more progressive British and American income tax. One could also think of an average of all contributing countries' tax systems, but the construction of such a system runs into such problems as (a) our ignorance of the real incidence of income taxes by country; and (b) the presumably wide differences between income tax incidence and total tax incidence, which is generally unknown anyway.

Whatever the logical appeal of a simple international system directly related to an equally simple domestic tax burden, it is most unlikely that national legislatures will apply such formal tests of fairness in deciding how to finance increased international contributions. In practice, we are forced to admit that there is a certain inconsistency in much of the emphasis on progressive taxation in the international sphere, because we do not know how it will be related to domestic taxes. Domestic taxes will continue to be based on some blend of social consensus about equity plus certain political compromises and certain administrative considerations such as ease of collection. These factors vary greatly among countries.[22] It is unlikely that there could be any effective link between international and national considerations of equity; nor, perhaps, should there be such a link.

Real versus Money Income in International Taxation. So far, in the discussion of equity, I have referred to income without defining it. Presumably, the standard is national product, but there are well-known difficulties in comparing the GNP of different countries by means of exchange rates.[23] Exchange rates do not reflect the true comparative

---

[22] Needleman.

[23] In this analysis, ability-to-pay computations are based on GNP. The UN formula uses national income. In theory, national income is a better tax base than GNP, but the latter is more widely used and more readily available for underdeveloped countries. In international contributions systems, choice of GNP as a base in preference to national income favors countries like the United States that have a relatively high ratio of national income to GNP.

purchasing power of currencies because (1) exchange rates tend to be somewhat inflexible for institutional reasons; and (2) many goods and services are not internationally traded, and those that are face such barriers as tariffs and transportation costs. Two OEEC studies comparing Western Europe and the United States have carefully documented the disparity between national income estimates as converted by exchange rates and estimates based on the relative purchasing powers of the currencies.[24]

In general, the exchange-rate comparisons tend to overstate the relative real income of high-income countries, because the price levels in many service industries in high-income countries are higher than differences in labor productivity would warrant. Furthermore, it is probable that the evaluation of nonmarket goods and services is particularly unsatisfactory in national product accounts, and these items play an important role in low-income countries. This is most evident in exchange-rate comparisons between very wealthy countries, such as the United States, and very poor countries, such as India. Such comparisons typically show low-income countries with annual per capita incomes of $50, compared with a U.S. level of about $2500. In terms of U.S. prices, of course, not even a bare subsistence would be possible on a $50 per capita income. In other words, at U.S. prices, low-income countries have a much higher relative purchasing power than the exchange-rate figures imply. The Appendix to this chapter contains the OEEC comparisons for 1950 and 1955, and extrapolations to 1960. For comparison, the income equivalents at official exchange rates are also shown (see Table 3–18, p. 87). It should be noted that the OEEC comparisons are price-quantity index numbers, and therefore yield two comparisons between each country and the United States, one based on U.S. prices, the other on the European country's prices. As might be expected, European countries' incomes come closer to U.S. levels when U.S. prices are used as weights.

It is generally agreed in the literature[25] that real income is the sounder basis for measuring international ability to pay. Neale has pointed out that

---

[24] M. Gilbert and Irving B. Kravis, *An International Comparison of National Products and the Purchasing Power of Currencies*, OEEC, Paris, 1954; and M. Gilbert and Associates, *Comparative National Products and Price Levels*, OEEC, Paris, 1957; see also the Appendix to this chapter.

[25] Schelling; Rosenstein-Rodan; and Kravis and Davenport. The most obvious example of the defects of exchange rates as a measure of relative contributions arises from the great differences among countries in military pay levels. In France soldiers' pay is low compared to average productivity; in effect there is a tax on the soldier. It is obviously inappropriate to value French and U.S. relative contributions by using their respective military pay scales.

the discrepancy between exchange-rate equivalents of real income and real income means that a flat rate is in fact progressive.[26] He is essentially raising a point about index numbers. The basic question is whether the gap between U.S. and Norwegian output is smaller when both are valued at U.S. prices (Difference A), or at Norwegian prices (Difference B), than when both are valued at own prices and exchange-rate equivalents (Difference C). If Differences A and B are both smaller than C, the flat-rate tax is progressive by either price system. In that case, a flat-rate tax imposed in dollars on both Norway and the United States will be progressive.

There seems little doubt, on theoretical grounds, that real-income equivalents would provide a fairer estimate of ability to pay; however, the OEEC studies of real-income equivalents are for the year 1955 and cover only eight Western European countries and the United States. A serious effort to establish purchasing-power equivalents for international contributions would require recomputing the 1955 figures and extending them to additional countries. Such a recomputation should have a high priority if burden-sharing studies are to be pushed any further. As an interim device to aid this study, Kravis, author of the original OEEC report, has extrapolated the 1955 data to 1960 (see Appendix to this chapter). This measure is a rough estimate, however; it is based on 1950 weights and is aggregative, being computed from only three components (consumption, investment, and government).

It should be noted that if each country wants to value its own contributions at its own prices, taxes based on real income are ambiguous. In that case, there is no common weighting system for contributions; they have to be related either to each country's GNP or to a bill of goods. Thus, under a progressive tax, if one country's contribution is designated as the standard, other countries can pay larger or smaller proportions of their own GNP, as determined by relative real incomes.[27] The defect of this method is that each country's relative sacrifice is appropriate by the progressive tax system, but the value of the relative and total contributions to the taxing agency is inappropriate. Thus, Italy may contribute goods that are high-cost in Italy relative to world prices; and, therefore, although

[26] Alan D. Neale, *The Flow of Resources from Rich to Poor*, Occasional Papers in International Affairs, No. 2, Center for International Affairs, Harvard University, Cambridge, Mass., November 1961.

[27] In this particular circumstance, under a proportional tax (each country paying 1 per cent of GNP), there is, of course, no point to making real-income computations. And it is clearly *not* true that under such a system the real incidence of taxation is progressive. This view is occasionally expressed, however, as in Pierre Uri, *Partnership for Progress*, Harper and Row, New York, 1963, p. 47. It is true only if contributions are in a common unit of account. Compare Kravis and Davenport.

its contribution meets the progressive tax criterion, its value to the taxing agency is less than its cost to Italy. This sort of ambiguity between donor's cost and value to recipient is recurrent in the valuation of aid. It is discussed in Chapter 5.

The Contributions System as a Balancing Device. It has often been suggested that contributors should feel free to use international contribution systems to ease their own domestic economic problems, if they can do so without seriously reducing the systems' effectiveness. Measures taken under such proposals have normally assumed three forms: (1) attempts to moderate balance-of-payments deficits; (2) attempts to reduce domestic unemployment; and (3) attempts to dispose of surplus production.[28]

The opposite viewpoint is also taken—that countries should settle their domestic economic problems in their own houses, so to speak, and not rely on international cost-sharing arrangements to alleviate their difficulties. Proponents of this view sometimes attach primary importance to the end purposes for which burden-sharing systems are established, and contend that progress toward those ends may be deflected if systems are manipulated into serving very different purposes.

Rather than adopt a stand based on inflexible principles, it seems preferable to examine such questions in light of their probable specific effects. If it is likely that aid-tying and analogous measures will severely harm the operation of the military alliance or economic aid effort, the disadvantages of such balancing devices may outweigh the advantages. If not, there seems to be no *a priori* reason for rejecting them. This seems particularly clear when the cost of untied contributions would be so great as to create serious economic difficulties for any member country.

Balance of Payments. If one accepts the proposition that there is no automatic reason for rejecting balancing devices, it follows that balance-of-payments difficulties should not be allowed to affect the amount of member countries' contributions for defense and aid. The only effect should be on the form of the aid—that is, whether it is to be tied or untied.[29]

There are three qualifications to this general statement. First, if a country's exports have a large import component, even in the tied goods

[28] For example, see Neale.

[29] As noted above, however, tied aid will generally mean that the value of aid to the recipient is less than its cost to the donor. The total cost of contributions will be greater than necessary for a given benefit.

it provides for the program, there may be moderately serious consequences for the balance of payments. Even though the aid is tied, the drain on foreign exchange will continue. Typically, this drain will be small— extremely small compared to the drain from untied aid. For some countries that import a large proportion of their industrial raw materials and semifinished products, however, this drain presents a certain hazard in time of real payments stress. The Netherlands and the United Kingdom may be cases in point.

A second qualification applies to countries that simultaneously enjoy full employment and face balance-of-payments pressure. An increase in tied contributions without corresponding reductions in domestic buying power will create inflationary domestic pressures that may worsen a country's balance-of-payments situation.

There is a third category: situations in which tied contributions are inappropriate for the purposes of the burden-sharing system. For example, the UN has allowed only a small proportion of contributions to be provided in local currency instead of dollars. The United Nations' argument has been that it can accept only as much inconvertible currency as it plans to spend during the contributions year. The nature of the organization's activities will not allow contributions in kind.

Another case might be found in military alliances. If strategic requirements call for Country A to station some of its troops in allied Country B, there will inevitably be some expenditure of foreign exchange by and on behalf of the troops; the amounts will depend on the stringency of the requirements for procurement in the home country, and on the negotiability of military pay. The contribution cannot be entirely tied, and some drain on foreign exchange is inevitable. Country A can compensate for it by requesting reimbursement from the government of B, either directly or through purchases of Country A's goods. The United States and Germany entered into such an arrangement in 1961, to compensate the United States for its troop costs in Germany.

When an alliance institutionalizes a system of tied contributions, certain adverse effects may follow if the sums are large. If a country knows that it can tie its contribution in case it runs into balance-of-payments difficulties, and also knows that other countries will purchase from it to relieve its situation, it will probably feel less pressure to take domestic remedial measures. Clearly, a country is most likely to regard military programs in this light, because military outlays bulk large in the national budget. If arrangements for tied contributions encourage countries to follow policies that continue a balance-of-payments disequilibrium, the consequence could be that not enough B countries would be left to buy A-Country goods (unless, of course, all the major trading nations were included in the alliance). Even if the result were not that drastic, inequity would still remain: The system allows certain countries to have their cake and eat it too. One remedy could be to make domestic restrictive measures mandatory after a certain period of time.

Reducing Domestic Unemployment. It has been suggested that countries with persistently high unemployment should provide larger armed forces to military alliances than they otherwise would, and receive reimbursement on an opportunity-cost basis from countries that could thus reduce their force quotas. The argument for such a policy is that the real cost of providing such forces is much lower than the money cost, and that the contributions of the countries whose forces are thereby reduced would alleviate the budgetary problem of the donor country as well as possible balance-of-payments problems. This rationale again reflects the original NATO burden-sharing preoccupation, although economy of effort is translated here into economic rather than military terms.

Several more or less persuasive arguments can be advanced against such an approach. First, it is sometimes stated that international differences in unemployment levels are cyclical, and that no contributions system, whether for defense or economic aid, should be tied to cyclical fluctuations. As can be seen from Table 3-4 (p. 77), however, international differences in the level of unemployment have persisted since 1954. Unemployment has been high in Canada, the United States, Belgium, Denmark, and Italy, and low in France, the Netherlands, Norway, the United Kingdom, and Germany. Greece and Turkey, not listed in Table 3-4, have also had high unemployment.

A more forceful argument against the use of unemployment indexes as a determinant of military force levels is that it is politically unpalatable, both because it results in substantially higher budgets, and because it is an admission of the government's inability to cope with domestic unemployment.

A third argument is theoretically more fundamental, though practically less decisive. There is no particular reason why countries should assign their unemployed manpower to military duties when they can be usefully employed in domestic public works or other work. The practical argument against this point is that countries with persistently high unemployment often seem equally persistent in avoiding fiscal measures that will effectively reduce unemployment. Increases in military budgets sometimes appear more acceptable, politically, than increases in public works expenditure.

The logic of the case for using alliance expenditures to reduce domestic unemployment leads to using all unemployed resources, including capital, as a criterion. In this light, the argument becomes applicable to both defense expenditures and economic aid. Emphasis on unemployment alone conduces to exclusive reliance on such recourses as transmuting the unemployed into troops (or, on a negligible scale, into Peace Corpsmen)—in short, "exporting" unemployment.

Some countries, however, have both persistent unemployment and persistent excess industrial capacity (for example, the United States, Canada, and Belgium). These countries are in a position to export their unemployment in the form of men or goods. Whenever another country buys military equipment from the United States to help the U.S. balance of payments, there is also an employment and income effect. Resources with an opportunity cost of zero are being put to work for the purposes of the alliance. There is a complete divergence between money and real cost in such a case. The same would, of course, be true if the United States itself financed the purchase by domestic borrowing. Political considerations normally favor the export of unemployment in the form of goods rather than troops.

The argument also applies to economic aid. Clearly, the United States, Canada, and Belgium could currently increase their aid shipments at very little real cost, and could do so even if they were relatively inefficient producers of the goods being exported.

Even with this broader definition of unemployment, it may be infeasible, as pointed out above, to require a larger share from countries with surplus resources. In that case, one could still allow indirectly for unemployed resources in the contributions system by another method: evaluating the unemployed labor in each country, above a minimum unemployment level, at its opportunity cost, the average domestic wage. (See Table 3–6, p. 78.) The result would be a rough indication of what full-employment GNP might be. The reader can see from Table 3–6 how such a method would affect proportional shares and shares based on a $300 lump-sum exemption. The advantage of such a system is that it offers a method of partially utilizing unemployed resources without triggering some of the political and budgetary repercussions. Tables 3–6, 3–8, 3–11, 3–13, and 3–15 include several other computations of burden-sharing formulas on a full employment basis.

Surplus Production. Surplus production is a special aspect of the problem of unemployed resources. If, under existing institutional arrangements, a country has more of a product or resource than it can use domestically, one alternative is to make contributions in kind to international organizations. The above example of troops, or of goods produced with excess capacity, are really forms of contributions in kind. Another form is surplus agricultural products. Rosenstein-Rodan has proposed discounting the value of Public Law 480 agricultural commodities by one-third. Logically, the appropriate discount should be based on elasticities of demand for the products. Chapter 5 shows some computations of PL 480 values, based on demand elasticity estimates for 1961 and 1962. A discount seems the simplest procedure to apply, but it would be difficult to decide on the appropriate rate. Another way to reach a similar result is to set a ceiling on contributions in kind, but it should be realized that a strict ceiling might reduce the total flow of resources devoted to alliance purposes.

Definitions of Aid and Common Defense Expenditures

The previous section discussed the kinds of criteria that cost-sharing systems might use, and concluded that real national income theoretically offers a better guide to ability to pay than does national income valued at exchange rates; and that there is something to be said for progressive taxation, even though its significance in equity is ambiguous unless taxes are actually assessed on individuals rather than nations, and according to a common international tax system rather than to national ones. There is no likelihood at present of international acceptance of these conditions; nonetheless, acceptance of a modified progressive system (progressive among nations) for the United Nations may be the precursor of direct international taxation of individuals, either in the form suggested by Sumberg or in that proposed by Kravis and Davenport. This is clearly a case in which economic considerations of equity are negligible compared to political issues.

In this brief section, it seems worthwhile to define what the principal forms of burden sharing include. Because economic aid is the principal topic of this study, we will reserve a detailed discussion of its definition and valuation for Chapter 5. Basically, the definition proposed in this study is founded on a discounted present-value method for official aid. The same method could also be applied to private capital flows, but the effect would presumably be to value the investment at zero.

This section will refer primarily to the definition of common defense expenditures, and the difficulties involved. As we will see, there are a number of analogues in foreign aid.

The 1951 NATO burden-sharing exercise naturally raised the question of what items should be included and excluded in evaluating national contributions to common defense. There were a number of difficulties in arriving at a definition. First, should one include all of a country's defense expenditures as a contribution to the common defense? Doing so would tend to overstate the contributions of countries with colonial empires or with military interests outside of Europe. If, however, one attempts to separate defense expenditures that contribute to NATO common defense from those involving non-NATO objectives, a thicket of statistical and conceptual difficulties arises to bar the way.[30] The colonial powers claimed in 1951 that most of their overseas forces in fact represented a common defense contribution because they were defending the interests of the Western Alliance. Second, a considerable part of the overseas forces could be considered second-echelon troops in an emergency. Third, prorating the overhead costs of forces with a NATO mission and of non-NATO forces presented a number of complexities.

Of course, one can nonetheless try to evaluate each country's contribution to the common defense effort by estimating the costs incurred in providing its share of NATO forces. Any such effort is to a degree artificial. It must either ignore overhead costs or else prorate them arbitrarily. Furthermore, it should involve some discounting system for first- and second-echelon troops, and there is at best a dubious basis for such a system. Finally, there are extremely difficult data problems in separating and correctly stating capital and operating costs.

If one decides, in the interests of simplicity, to define a country's total defense expenditure as the measure of its contributions to common

---

[30] Many of the conceptual problems of defining and evaluating common defense expenditures are discussed in Hitch and McKean, pp. 281–301.

defense, a host of questions still arises, such as (1) Should the costs of veterans' benefits, or of meteorological systems that fulfill both a military and civilian function, be included in national defense totals? The solution adopted by NATO involved specific decisions quite close to those used in OEEC national income accounts. (2) Should military personnel costs be evaluated at the military pay the personnel actually were accorded or, for example, at their opportunity cost in civilian employment as defined by the average national wage level? This is part of the larger question of whether burden sharing should be considered on a real- or a money-income basis.

NATO opted for a definition based on total national defense expenditure, after the first burden-sharing exercise failed to produce agreement on a pooling of national resources and finance. Despite the defects of this method, it has two important advantages: (1) It has been accepted by the member countries. (2) The alternative—to define common defense contributions as each country's effort in meeting NATO force goals—involves measurements that are extremely difficult and sometimes impossible to make.

Nevertheless, it must be remembered that the present NATO definition in no way accords with presently accepted standards of equity. It recognizes, as defense expenditures, outlays that have nothing to do with common defense. Furthermore, to the extent that the wealthier countries have more overseas commitments than the noncolonial powers, it may distort ability-to-pay considerations for common defense. This phenomenon has clearly been operative for France, and to a lesser degree for the UK. The net effect may be to make Germany appear more out of line than it actually is. Finally, in taking money expenditures as an indicator of contributions, it assumes that the price system, as applied to military goods and services in each country, is a good measure of the resource cost of the military establishment.

Burden-sharing Computations

The remainder of this chapter presents computations of burden-sharing formulas for DAC and NATO, based on various real-income and exchange-rate equivalents.[31] The computations reflect some of the ability-to-

---

[31] The DAC data from this chapter should be compared with the results of Chapter 5, where the computations have been worked out on a present-value basis.

pay criteria discussed above, using 1960 income calculations. A few significant points emerge from the data:

1. Real and money incomes are growing faster in Europe than in the United States. Table 3–1 lists the growth rates since 1950, total and per capita, at U.S. weights. Table 3–2 shows the changes in the ratio of European to U.S. real GNP, per capita, at U.S. weights. Table 3–3 compares 1960 real GNP to exchange-rate equivalents; it also gives national GNP as a mean between GNP at U.S. weights and at national weights (this is the figure used to represent real GNP in subsequent tables).

TABLE 3–1: GROWTH OF REAL INCOME, U.S. AND WESTERN EUROPE, 1950–1960
(In $ million; U.S. weights)

Country	Per Capita GNP			Total GNP		
	1950	1955	1960	1950	1955	1960
Belgium	1,051	1,348	1,771	9,079	11,991	16,254
Denmark	1,121	1,290	1,910	4,787	5,725	8,778
France	968	1,285	1,799	40,401	55,613	82,268
Germany	782	1,333	1,882	37,415	66,885	101,168
Italy	545	810	1,218	25,609	39,672	60,293
Netherlands	950	1,215	1,799	9,608	13,062	20,789
Norway	1,076	1,400	1,826	3,509	4,799	6,575
U.K.	1,133	1,470	1,826	57,061	75,293	96,337
U.S.	1,830	2,310	2,768	277,579	381,773	504,400

SOURCES: Gilbert and Associates, *Comparative National Products;* and the Appendix to this chapter. U.S. price weights.

TABLE 3–2: REAL GNP COMPARISONS (RATIOS):
NATO COUNTRIES, 1960

	Ratio to U.S. per Capita GNP		
Country	U.S. Price Weights	National Price Weights	Exchange-rate Equivalent
Belgium	64	52	48
Denmark	69	54	47
France	65	48	46
Germany	68	49	46
Italy	44	26	23
Netherlands	65	47	37
Norway	66	48	44
U.K.	66	52	51

SOURCE: Extrapolated from Gilbert and Associates, *Comparative National Products.* See Appendix below.

NOTE: These comparisons are based on binary comparisons between the United States and eight West European countries; therefore they do not yield valid rankings among the latter.

TABLE 3–3: REAL GNP COMPARISONS: NATO COUNTRIES, 1960
(In $ equivalents)

| Country | 1960 GNP (in $ million) | | | |
	U.S. Price Weights (1)	National Price Weights (2)	Mean of Cols. 1 and 2 (3)	Exchange-rate Equivalent (4)
Belgium	16,263	13,207	14,735	12,160
Denmark	8,778	6,871	7,825	5,964
Canada			35,830[a]	35,830
France	82,362	60,775	71,569	58,159
Germany	101,169	74,398	86,881	71,245
Italy	60,293	35,641	47,967	31,821
Netherlands	20,789	15,034	17,912	11,764
Norway	6,579	4,786	5,683	4,424
Portugal			3,365[b]	2,243
Turkey			7,736[b]	5,157
U.K.	96,337	75,878	86,108	70,683
U.S.	504,400	504,400	504,400	504,400
Greece			4,790[b]	3,193

SOURCE: Extrapolated from Gilbert and Associates, *Comparative National Products*. See Appendix below.

NOTE: These comparisons are based on binary comparisons between the United States and eight West European countries; therefore they do not yield valid rankings among the latter.
[a] Real income assumed equal to nominal income.
[b] Real income assumed to be 50 per cent above nominal income.

2. The United States is paying more than its share of combined NATO defense expenditures, according to all but the most progressive exchange-rate formulas, and to any real-income formula. Even if we estimate the full-employment equivalent of GNP (unemployment data from Table 3–4), the United States' present expenditure is greater than its theoretical share. Tables 3–5 and 3–6 list various formulas estimated on an exchange-rate basis and according to actual GNP and full-employment equivalents. Table 3–5 also gives 1960 defense expenditures by country. Tables 3–7 and 3–8 give burden-sharing computations on a real GNP basis, including a full-employment estimate. However, NATO burden-sharing computations are inherently unsatisfactory in the absence of a logical definition of what constitutes a NATO expenditure.

TABLE 3–4: UNEMPLOYMENT RATES IN NATO COUNTRIES, 1954–1960
(Percentage of nonagricultural employed plus unemployed)

Country	1954	1955	1956	1957	1958	1959	1960
U.K.	1.5	1.2	1.3	1.6	2.2	2.3	1.8
France	2.1	1.8	1.3	0.9	1.0	1.5	1.4
Germany	7.0	5.1	4.0	3.4	3.5	2.4	1.2
Italy	10.0	9.8	9.9	9.0	9.0	8.7	7.9
Belgium	10.9	8.4	7.0	5.5	8.5	9.5	7.5
Denmark	8.0	9.7	11.1	10.2	9.6	6.1	4.3
Netherlands	1.9	1.3	0.9	1.2	2.3	1.8	1.2
Norway	1.3	1.2	1.4	1.4	2.3	2.2	1.7
Canada	4.6	4.4	3.4	4.6	7.1	6.0	7.0
U.S.	5.6	4.4	4.2	4.3	6.8	5.5	5.6

SOURCES: International Labor Organization, *Yearbook of Labour Statistics*, and UN, *Monthly Bull. Stat.*, as reported by Hoeber, Dale, and Lea, Stanford Research Institute.

TABLE 3–5: DEFENSE EXPENDITURES AND GNP OF NATO
COUNTRIES, 1960; AND PROPOSED FORMULAS
(Exchange-rate basis)

Country	1960 Defense Expenditure ($ million)	Per Cent of GNP 1960	Per Cent of NATO Total			
			1960	If based on GNP as Per Cent of NATO Total	Rosenstein-Rodan Formula[a]	$300 per Capita Exemption
Belgium	383	3.2	0.6	1.49	1.1	1.39
Denmark	161	2.7	0.3	0.73	0.4	0.67
France	3,835	6.6	6.1	7.13	4.4	6.50
Germany	3,029	4.3	4.8	9.45	4.5	8.06
Italy	1,136	3.6	1.8	3.90	0.1	2.50
Netherlands	477	4.1	0.8	1.44	0.6	1.22
Norway	148	3.3	0.2	0.54	0.3	0.49
Portugal	105	4.5	0.2	0.27	—	—
U.K.	4,848	6.8	7.7	8.65	6.4	8.02
U.S.	46,545	9.2	73.2	61.80	77.8	65.82
Greece	170	5.3	0.3	0.39	—	0.10
Turkey	239	4.6	0.4	0.63	—	—
Canada	1,654	4.6	3.6	4.39	4.4	4.44

SOURCES: Computed by author from sources of NATO and the Department of Defense, Office of International Security Affairs; and Rosenstein-Rodan.

NOTE: The United Nations formula applied to NATO gives approximately the same results as a proportionate tax, because the formula allows no exemption to countries with more than $1000 per capita GNP.

[a] U.S. income tax rates for family of four applied to exchange-rate equivalent of per capita GNP, based on estimated 1961 GNP.

TABLE 3–6: NATO SHARES UNDER FULL-EMPLOYMENT GNP
(Exchange-rate basis)

Country	GNP 1960 ($ million)	Rate of Unem-ploy-ment	Full-employment Equivalent GNP ($ million)	Per Cent of NATO Total under Full-employment GNP	Full-employment Equivalent GNP minus $300 per Capita ($ million)	Per Cent of NATO Total
Belgium	12,160	7.5	13,437	1.55	10,684	1.47
Canada	35,850	7.0	39,435	4.55	34,025	4.67
Denmark	5,964	4.3	6,100	0.74	4,721	0.69
France	58,159	1.4	58,159	6.72	44,440	6.09
Germany	71,245	1.2	71,245	8.23	55,118	7.56
Greece	3,193	8.0	3,320	0.38	812	0.11
Italy	31,821	7.9	33,698	3.89	18,847	2.59
Netherlands	11,764	1.2	11,764	1.36	8,297	1.14
Norway	4,424	1.7	4,424	0.51	3,344	0.46
Portugal	2,243	8.0	22,333	0.27	—	—
Turkey	5,157[a]	8.0	5,363	0.62	—	—
U.K.	70,683	1.8	70,683	8.17	54,864	7.53
U.S.	504,400	5.6	547,778	63.01	493,101	67.70
Total	817,063		864,739		728,252	

SOURCES: OECD, Gen. Stat.; and Table 3–4 above. For method, see Table 3–8.
[a] 1959 figure.

TABLE 3–7: NATO CONTRIBUTIONS FORMULAS: BASIS,
1960 REAL-INCOME EQUIVALENTS
(Percentages of NATO total)

Country	As Proportion of Real NATO GNP	$300 per Capita Exemption	UN Formula Modified[a]	U.S. Income Tax Rate: Family of 4
Belgium	1.64	1.59	1.57	1.44
Canada	4.00	4.02	4.22	4.17
Denmark	0.87	0.85	0.84	0.75
France	8.00	7.65	7.52	6.79
Germany	9.71	9.36	9.31	8.71
Greece	0.54	0.30	0.37	—
Italy	5.36	4.38	4.20	2.76
Netherlands	2.00	1.91	1.88	1.69
Norway	0.64	0.61	0.59	0.55
Portugal	0.38	0.10	0.24	—
Turkey	0.86	0.20	0.53	—
U.K.	9.62	9.30	9.23	8.55
U.S.	56.37	59.73	59.51	64.60

SOURCES: OEEC, Gen. Stat.; IMF, Intern. Financ. Stat.

NOTE: Real income estimated at mean of GNP at U.S. price weights and GNP at national price weights.
[a] Estimated by (1) dividing per capita GNP by $2000; (2) multiplying quotient by 50 per cent; and (3) subtracting product from 50 per cent. The resulting percentage figure is multi-

TABLE 3–8: NATO SHARES UNDER FULL-EMPLOYMENT GNP
(Real-income basis)

Country	Real GNP 1960 ($ million)	Unemployment Rate 1960	Full-employment Equivalent GNP ($ million)	Per Cent of NATO Total	Full-employment GNP minus $300 per Capita ($ million)	Per Cent of NATO Total
Belgium	14,735	7.5	16,282	1.72	13,529	1.68
Canada	35,830	7.0	39,413	4.16	34,001	4.22
Denmark	7,825	4.3	8,004	0.85	6,625	0.82
France	71,569	1.4	71,569	7.56	57,850	7.19
Germany	86,881	1.2	86,881	9.17	70,754	8.80
Greece	4,790	8.0	4,982	0.52	2,474	0.31
Italy	47,967	7.9	50,797	5.36	35,946	4.47
Netherlands	17,912	1.2	17,912	1.89	14,445	1.79
Norway	5,683	1.7	5,683	0.60	4,603	0.57
Portugal	3,365	8.0	3,499	0.36	763	0.09
Turkey	7,736	8.0	8,045	0.85	—	—
U.K.	86,108	1.8	86,108	9.09	70,289	8.74
U.S.	504,400	5.6	547,784	57.84	493,107	61.29
Total	894,801		946,959		804,386	

SOURCE: Hoeber, Dale, and Lea.

NOTE: Full-employment GNP computed on basis of proportional increase in GNP for all unemployment above 2 per cent. Figures for Canada, United States, and Belgium increased by 5 per cent to reflect excess industrial capacity. Figures for Greece, Turkey, and Portugal increased by 4 per cent total. Real income is mean of real income at U.S. weights and at national weights.

3. In economic aid, as that aid is usually computed (official grants and loans, all at nominal value), the United States is in a less favorable position by ability-to-pay criteria. Under mildly progressive formulas, the United States' relative share should be larger. As pointed out in Chapter 5 below, the present definition is somewhat biased against U.S. aid, because the

---

plied by GNP, and the product subtracted from GNP. The UN method uses national income instead of GNP, puts a 33 per cent ceiling on contributions, and uses a $1000 per capita exemption base (less progressive than modified formula). The formula may be represented as:

$$\frac{Y_i\left[1 - 0.5\left(\frac{2000 - \overline{Y_i}}{2000}\right)\right]}{\sum\left\{Y_i\left[1 - 0.5\left(\frac{2000 - \overline{Y_i}}{2000}\right)\right]\right\}}$$

where Y_i is the GNP of Country i, and $\overline{Y_i}$ is its GNP per capita.

latter has a high percentage of grants and of loans repayable in local currency, or at low interest rates. Tables 3–9 and 3–10 show the composition of DAC aid for 1960. Table 3–11 reproduces Rosenstein-Rodan's U.S. progressive income tax formula for Western countries. Tables 3–12 and 3–13 show the percentage shares under various exchange-rate formulas. Tables 3–14 and 3–15 give burden-sharing formulas under various real-income equivalents. In international organizations the United States uniformly pays less than its fair share under the burden-sharing criteria discussed here (see Chapter 4).

4. The lack of data on real income and on loan terms and conditions affects these computations. For real income I used extrapolations of the OECD data prepared by Irving Kravis (Tables 3–18 and 3–19). His computations are very useful, but as he has pointed out, they are based on 1950 data and are becoming increasingly unreliable. It was also impossible to divide NATO members' defense expenditures into NATO and non-NATO classifications.

TABLE 3–9: DAC MEMBERS' OFFICIAL CONTRIBUTIONS TO UNDER-
DEVELOPED COUNTRIES AND INTERNATIONAL AGENCIES, 1960
(In $ million equivalent)

Country	Grants	Loans Gross Total	Loans Short Term (less than 10 years)	Loans Consolidation Credits	Multilateral Contributions	Gross Official Contributions
Belgium	86	—	—	—	19	105
Canada	48	—	—	—	27	75
France	708	114	14	11	60	893
Germany	8	151	66	73	101	333
Italy	9	19	19	18	89	135
Japan	2	80	61	—	42	124
Netherlands	26	5	—	—	22	53
Norway	1	—	—	—	20	21
Portugal	2	32	—	—	6	40
U.K.	165	184	27	8	92	449
U.S.	1481	854	128	3	235	3009[a]

SOURCE: OECD, *Flow of Financial Resources to Countries in Course of Economic Development in 1960.*

[a] Includes $436 million under PL 480 transfers, unexpended.

TABLE 3–10: DISTRIBUTION OF ECONOMIC AID CONTRIBUTIONS,
DAC COUNTRIES, 1960
(Net official loans and grants)

Country	Per Cent GNP Contributed	Equivalent ($ million)	Actual Per Cent of DAC Total
Belgium	0.82	101	2.07
Canada	0.21	75	1.54
France	1.50	843	17.30
Germany	0.51	343	7.04
Italy	0.41	127	2.61
Japan	0.40	156	3.20
Netherlands	0.41	41	0.84
Portugal	1.52	34	0.70
U.K.	0.56	390	8.00
U.S.	0.55	2764	56.70
Total		4874	

SOURCE: OECD, *Flow of Financial Resources to Countries in Course of Economic Development in 1960.*

TABLE 3–11: DISTRIBUTION OF DEFENSE
OR AID CONTRIBUTIONS; BASIS U.S.
PERSONAL INCOME TAX SCHEDULE

Country	Nominal GNP Contribution (%)	Real GNP Contribution (%)
Belgium	1.1	1.4
Canada	4.3	3.7
Denmark	0.4	0.6
Finland	0.2	0.4
France	4.2	5.3
West Germany	4.3	7.7
Italy	—	1.6
Netherlands	0.6	1.4
Norway	0.3	0.5
Oceania	1.2	1.9
Sweden	1.2	1.6
Switzerland	0.8	1.0
U.K.	6.1	8.4
U.S.	75.2	64.4

SOURCE: Rosenstein-Rodan.

NOTE: Computation also assumes GNP per family as a measure of income, and a family as consisting of four members.

TABLE 3–12: DISTRIBUTION OF DAC SHARES BY BURDEN-SHARING FORMULAS, 1960
(Exchange-rate basis)

Country	GNP ($ million)	Per Cent of Total GNP	Per Cent of GNP less $300 per Capita	Modified UN Formula[a]
Belgium	12,160	1.45	1.39	1.31
Canada	38,850	4.28	4.49	4.64
France	58,159	6.95	6.60	6.18
Germany	71,245	8.51	7.86	7.60
Italy	31,821	3.80	2.54	2.73
Japan	38,669	4.62	1.57	3.03
Netherlands	11,764	1.41	1.24	1.15
Portugal	2,243	0.26	—	0.15
U.K.	70,683	8.37	8.21	7.67
U.S.	504,400	60.35	67.10	65.53

SOURCE: OEEC, *Gen. Stat.*
[a] See Table 3–7 for UN formula.

TABLE 3–13: DISTRIBUTION OF TAXES ON BASIS OF FULL-EMPLOYMENT
GNP: DAC COUNTRIES, 1960
(Exchange-rate basis)

Country	1960 GNP Equivalent ($ million)	1960 Unemploy- ment Rate (%)	Adjusted 1960 GNP Equivalent ($ million)[a]	Per Cent of Total under Adjusted GNP Formula	Per Cent of Total under Adjusted per Capita Formula[b]
Belgium	12,160	7.5	13,360[c]	1.50	1.48
Canada	35,850	7.0	39,227[c]	4.42	4.71
France	58,159	1.4	58,159	6.57	4.80
Germany	71,245	1.2	71,245	8.06	7.36
Italy	31,821	7.9	33,698	3.79	2.63
Japan	38,669	1.3	38,669	4.36	1.46
Netherlands	11,764	1.2	11,764	1.12	1.12
Portugal	2,243	([d])	2,243	0.25	—
U.K.	70,683	1.8	70,683	8.00	7.65
U.S.	504,400	5.6	548,686[c]	61.94	68.77

SOURCES: Tables 3–4 and 3–8. For method, see Table 3–8.
[a] GNP increased by percentage unemployed in excess of 2.0 per cent.
[b] $300 lump-sum per capita exemption.
[c] Full-employment GNP increased by additional 5 per cent, reflecting excess industrial capacity.
[d] Unknown.

5. Chapter 5 includes burden-sharing calculations for economic aid based on a present-value definition of aid. For reasons discussed there, this is a better measure of aid flow than are the figures of Table 3–9. Chapter 5 also includes the Kravis-Davenport method, which bases burden sharing on actual income distribution within each country.

TABLE 3–14: DAC CONTRIBUTIONS, 1960
(Real-income basis)

Country	Real GNP ($ million)	Per Cent of DAC Total	Modified UN Formula (% of DAC total)	Real GNP less $300 per Capita (% of DAC total)	U.S. Income Tax Rates (% of DAC total)
Belgium	14,735	1.59	1.55	1.46	1.45
Canada	35,830	3.86	4.15	3.73	4.22
France	71,569	7.75	7.42	7.09	6.88
Germany	86,881	9.40	9.13	8.66	8.82
Italy	47,967	5.17	4.14	4.05	2.79
Japan	61,870	6.07	4.78	4.13	0.06
Netherlands	17,912	1.93	1.86	1.76	1.71
Portugal	3,365	0.35	0.20	0.08	—
U.K.	86,108	9.31	9.10	8.61	8.65
U.S.	504,400	54.59	58.69	60.40	65.40

SOURCE: Appendix, Chap. 3.

TABLE 3–15: DAC CONTRIBUTIONS UNDER FULL-EMPLOYMENT GNP, 1960
(Real-income basis)

Country	1960 Unemployment Rate	Full-employment GNP ($ million)	Per Cent of Full-employment Total	Full-employment GNP less $300 per Capita (% of DAC total)
Belgium	7.5	16,282	1.66	1.64
Canada	7.0	39,413	4.01	4.12
France	1.4	71,569	7.29	7.02
Germany	1.2	86,881	8.85	8.58
Italy	7.9	50,797	5.17	4.36
Japan	1.3	61,870	6.30	4.09
Netherlands	1.2	17,912	1.82	1.75
Portugal	8.0	3,499	0.36	0.09
U.K.	1.8	86,108	8.77	8.53
U.S.	5.6	547,784	55.78	59.80
Total		982,115		

SOURCES: Appendix, Chap. 3, and OEEC, *Gen. Stat.* For method, see Table 3–8.

6. Tables 3–16 and 3–17, which compare actual U.S. contributions in 1960 to defense and aid with the shares that would be payable under various burden-sharing formulas based on real and nominal income, support the observations of Paragraphs 2 and 3 above. By almost any progressive standard, the United States is spending more than its "appropriate" share for military purposes. This finding undoubtedly reflects in part the high relative cost of military manpower in the United States.

TABLE 3-16: U.S. SHARE OF NATO MEMBERS' DEFENSE BUDGETS, 1960

Item	Per Cent of NATO Total
Actual share	74.2
Shares computed at exchange-rate equivalents:	
Share of total NATO GNP	61.8
UN contributions formula	62.0
$300 per capita exemption	66.3
U.S. income tax rates	77.6
Share of total NATO full-employment GNP	63.3
Share of full-employment GNP with $300 per capita exemption	67.7
Shares computed at real-income equivalents:	
Share of total NATO GNP	56.4
Modified UN contributions formula[a]	59.5
$300 per capita exemption	59.5
U.S. income tax rates	64.6
Share of total NATO full-employment GNP	57.9
Share of full-employment GNP with $300 per capita exemption	61.4

[a] Degree of progressiveness doubled.

TABLE 3-17: U.S. SHARE OF DAC MEMBERS' OFFICIAL CONTRIBUTIONS, 1960

Item	Per Cent of DAC Total
Actual share	56.7
Shares computed at exchange-rate equivalents:	
Share of total DAC GNP	60.3
UN contributions formula	61.8
UN contributions formula, modified	65.5[a]
$300 per capita exemption	67.4
U.S. income tax rates	75.2[b]
Share of total DAC full-employment GNP	61.8
Share of full-employment GNP with $300 per capita exemption	68.8
Shares computed at real-income equivalents:	
Share of total DAC GNP	54.4
UN contributions formula, modified	58.9[a]
$300 per capita exemption	60.4
U.S. income tax rates	65.4
Share of total DAC full-employment GNP	55.8
Share of full-employment GNP with $300 per capita exemption	59.9

[a] Degree of progressiveness doubled.
[b] Rosenstein-Rodan.

The present U.S. contribution for economic aid is not excessive by any standard. The U.S. Government has argued that this "undercontribution" should be balanced by consideration of its relatively high defense expenditures (see Chapter 5). In light of the computations of Chapter 5, U.S. relative aid contributions are understated by the methods used in Table 3–17.

Conclusions

Burden-sharing issues arise in any international activity when the distribution of costs is not considered equitable in view of the distribution of welfare or benefits among participants. The "burden" applies only to the sharing of costs, because aggregate benefits presumably are worth the total costs; otherwise the activity would not be undertaken. In economic aid, however, the relation between cost and benefit in terms of the donor's national interest is often tenuous, because the benefits can be ascertained only over the long run, and economic aid is often a small factor among many variables that determine underdeveloped countries' economic growth and political change.

The cost-sharing issue has arisen in several contexts: contributions to international organizations, expenditures by members of military alliances, contributions to economic growth of underdeveloped countries.

The long discussion of this chapter has brought out one fundamental point about cost sharing: There is no theoretically valid objective criterion for determining alliance contributions. It is not possible to measure the benefits each party receives from membership in NATO; even if it were, there would be no necessary relationship between benefits and ability to pay. Concerning ability to pay, theoretical arguments have undermined the logical rationale for progressive taxation. As a practical matter, however, ability-to-pay criteria, because they are acknowledged as the basis of domestic taxation systems, offer the most acceptable rudder.

A few other points emerge as offering practical interest for burden-sharing policy: (1) Real income (purchasing-power equivalent) offers a better guide to ability to pay than do exchange-rate equivalents of national income. (2) Balance-of-payments problems ordinarily should not affect the amount of national contributions, but only their form (that is, whether

tied or untied).[32] (3) There is some argument for taking account of unemployed resources in developed countries in formulating a burden-
sharing system. (4) Since defense and foreign-aid expenditures are not
perfect substitutes in international contributions, it is illogical to equate,
on a dollar-for-dollar basis, a deficiency in military contributions with a
surplus in economic aid. Similarly, a dollar spent by someone else for
defense is ordinarily not worth as much to the United States as a dollar it
spends for itself (assuming that the dollar is calculated at its purchasing-
power equivalent in each country). (5) Because exchange rates fail to reflect
purchasing power adequately, any flat-rate tax imposed on national
income in a common unit of account will in fact be progressive in incidence
as among countries. (6) Discounted present value provides a logical basis
and common denominator for measuring foreign-aid contributions (see
Chapter 5). (7) In practice, burden-sharing formulas are likely to be
accepted only when the sums are relatively small and when the formulas
offer no binding precedents for the future.[33]

Equity and economy of effort call for some international specialization
in providing various resources for the alliance. The present NATO system
partially answers this need, but the nature of an alliance makes it unlikely
that great progress can be made in specialization. In economic aid untied
contributions and a more comprehensive mobilization of European technical assistance resources should presumably work in this direction.

In short, general considerations offer only the most fragmentary guidelines. If we want to improve the present distribution of burdens, we will
have to adopt an approach that takes account of long- and short-run
alliance goals and embodies a realistic view of the limits on what can be
done without unduly compromising those goals.

---

[32] Defense expenditures that involve troop costs abroad are a partial exception, unless
one maintains the extreme principle that deficit nations should withdraw troops and
offer equipment instead.
[33] See Schelling, p. 9.

APPENDIX, Chapter 3

EXTRAPOLATIONS OF REAL-PRODUCT AND PURCHASING-POWER COMPARISONS

Extrapolations to 1960: Eight European
Countries and the United States[1]

Tables 3–18 and 3–19 contain the results of extrapolations of the OEEC real-income and purchasing-power comparisons to 1955 and 1960.

TABLE 3–18: PER CAPITA GNP'S OF EIGHT EUROPEAN
COUNTRIES, 1950, 1955, AND 1960
(United States = 100)

Country	OEEC 1950 (1)	OEEC 1955 (2)	1955 (Kravis) Global — Three Components (3)	1955 (Kravis) Global — Factor Cost (4)	1955 (Kravis) Global — Market Price (5)	1960 (Kravis) Global — Three Components (6)	1960 (Kravis) Global — Factor Cost (7)	1960 (Kravis) Global — Market Price (8)
			A. U.S. Price Weights					
Belgium	57	58	60	58	58	64	62	62
Denmark	61	56	58	58	58	69	68	68
France	53	56	57	57	56	65	64	64
Germany	43	58	56	55	55	68	67	68
Italy	30	35	35	35	34	44	43	43
Netherlands	52	53	58	56	57	65	64	63
Norway	59	61	60	59	59	66	65	64
U.K.	62	64	63	62	61	66	65	65
			B. National Price Weights					
Belgium	48	49	49	48	48	52	51	51
Denmark	48	44	45	45	45	54	53	53
France	39	42	42	42	41	48	47	47
Germany	30	42	39	38	38	49	46	47
Italy	18	20	21	21	20	26	26	25
Netherlands	37	39	42	40	40	47	45	45
Norway	44	46	44	44	44	48	48	48
U.K.	48	50	49	48	47	52	50	50

[1] The material under this heading is entirely the work of Irving B. Kravis of the Wharton School of Finance and Commerce, University of Pennsylvania.

Table 3–19: Purchasing-power Equivalents for GNP's of Eight
European Countries, 1950, 1955, and 1960
(Units of domestic currency per U.S. dollar)

Country	Currency Unit	OEEC 1950 (1)	OEEC 1955 (2)	1955 (Kravis) Three Components (3)	1955 (Kravis) Global Market Price (4)	1960 (Kravis) Three Components (5)	1960 (Kravis) Global Market Price (6)
			A. U.S. Quantity Weights				
Belgium	franc	45.00	44.90	44.50	44.80	44.20	44.30
Denmark	kroner	5.58	5.94	5.99	6.00	6.06	6.06
France	franc	312.00	394.00	370.00	377.00	477.00	454.00
Germany	mark	3.70	3.51	3.82	3.89	3.86	3.97
Italy	lira	577.00	605.00	595.00	601.00	574.00	576.00
Netherlands	florin	2.76	2.93	2.93	2.96	2.96	2.98
Norway	kroner	5.78	6.58	6.73	6.80	6.71	6.78
U.K.	pound	0.294	0.319	0.329	0.335	0.338	0.316
			B. National Quantity Weights				
Belgium	franc	37.00	37.60	36.30	36.90	35.90	36.52
Denmark	kroner	4.32	4.57	4.64	4.64	4.70	4.69
France	franc	223.00	287.00	267.00	270.00	323.00	325.00
Germany	mark	2.54	2.54	2.69	2.67	2.73	2.73
Italy	lira	330.00	337.00	342.00	344.00	330.00	329.00
Netherlands	florin	1.96	2.17	2.11	2.10	2.13	2.13
Norway	kroner	4.11	4.78	4.74	4.83	4.64	4.82
U.K.	pound	0.219	0.243[a]	0.245	0.250	0.255	0.237

[a] Reported in apparent error as 0.272 in Gilbert and Associates, *Comparative National Products*, p. 30; see pp. 31 and 40 of the same work.

Table 3–18 lists real GNP per capita for each of eight European countries, expressed as percentages of that of the United States. The upper bank of figures gives the quantity ratios of European to U.S. GNP per capita, calculated from U.S. price weights. The lower bank shows the quantity ratios in terms of the price weights of the European country. Note that national rather than average European price weights were used in the second set of calculations.

Column 1 lists the OEEC estimates for 1950, as revised in the study by Gilbert and Associates.[2] Column 2 gives the OEEC extrapolations of the

[2] *Comparative National Products.*

1950 figures to 1955. (These ratios have been calculated from the data in the third and fifth columns of Table 22 of the Gilbert and Associates study.)

Columns 3, 4, and 5 tabulate the results of three methods that Kravis used in extrapolating the 1950 OEEC estimates to 1955. The first and preferred method, labeled "Three Components," is based on separate extrapolations of consumption, investment, and government purchases. The other two methods are global, in that total GNP per capita was extrapolated, first on a factor-cost basis (Col. 4) and second on a market-price basis (Col. 5). In principle, the factor-cost basis is preferable because it is the concept employed in the original Gilbert-Kravis estimates of the quantity ratios; however, it is impossible to distinguish between factor cost and market prices in the indexes used for extrapolation; the same indexes were simply used to extrapolate the GNP estimates at factor cost and the GNP estimates at market prices.

The extrapolations to 1955 were made to provide a check on the somewhat summary methods used here against the more detailed extrapolations made by the OEEC from 1950 to 1955. A comparison of Cols. 2 and 3 indicates a close correspondence between the results obtained by the three-component method and the more detailed OEEC extrapolation. Even closer agreement might have been obtained if the national account figures available in 1956 had been used, when the OEEC extrapolations were made, rather than subsequently revised series.

Columns 6, 7, and 8, relating to 1960, are, of course, the end product of this work; it is worth mentioning again that the three-components method probably yields the best approximations to the actual relationships. It is interesting to note that the dispersion of the quantity ratios to the United States is much smaller in 1960 than it was in 1950; the European countries with the lowest per capita incomes have had the most rapid expansion over the decade.

The extrapolations were based on national accounts data for the individual countries reported in the OEEC, *General Statistics,* for July 1961 and September 1961. The current-price and constant-price estimates were used to obtain quantity and price changes between 1950 and 1955, and between 1950 and 1960 for each of the three components of GNP, and for total GNP both at factor cost and market prices. The quantity changes were adjusted for population increase to reduce them to a per capita basis.

The price changes and the per capita quantity changes were then used to extrapolate four basic aggregates:

1. U.S. product at U.S. prices;
2. U.S. product at the foreign country's prices;
3. The foreign country's product at U.S. prices; and
4. The foreign country's product at the foreign country's prices.

The quantity changes for the United States were used to adjust upward aggregates containing U.S. quantities (that is, the first two aggregates listed above), and quantity changes for the foreign country were used to adjust upward aggregates containing foreign quantities (that is, the last two aggregates listed above). The four aggregates thus adjusted for quantity changes were next adjusted for price changes by applying the price indexes for the United States to the adjusted aggregates containing U.S. prices (first and third in above list), and the foreign price indexes to the adjusted aggregates containing foreign prices (second and fourth). The result of these two sets of adjustments was a set of four aggregates corrected to 1955 or to 1960, according to the case, from which quantity ratios for 1955 or 1960 could be computed directly.

Essentially the same procedure was used to derive the purchasing-power equivalents of Table 3–19; however, the changes in the adjusted aggregates referred to in the preceding paragraph were used here to extrapolate the purchasing-power equivalents for 1950 shown in the Gilbert and Associates volume (p. 30). Table 3–19, like Table 3–18, has two banks of figures, the first showing the purchasing-power equivalents calculated with U.S. quantity weights, and the second with the quantity weights of each country. Because the factor-cost basis is less relevant for purchasing-power comparisons, only the three-components estimate and the global estimate at market prices are given.

Real-product and Purchasing-power Extrapolations to 1961

Using the method described above by Kravis, I have made similar estimates on factor-cost and market-price bases for the year 1961, shown as Table 3–20. No factor-cost data were available for Norway, Belgium, and France. No market-price data were available for Belgium. These results were used for the computations of Table 5–14. The other real-income computations, in both Chapters 3 and 5, are based on Kravis's 1960 estimates.

TABLE 3–20: PER CAPITA GNP AND PURCHASING-POWER
EQUIVALENTS OF GNP: SEVEN EUROPEAN COUNTRIES, 1961

	Per Capita GNP[a]				Purchasing-power Equivalents[b]	
	U.S. Price Weights		National Price Weights			
Country	Factor Cost	Market Price	Factor Cost	Market Price	U.S. Quantity Weights	National Quantity Weights
Denmark	70	71	55	56	6.37	4.87
France	—	66	—	48	468.50	334.60
Germany	70	73	49	52	4.14	2.84
Italy	48	47	28	28	582.80	331.70
Netherlands	64	64	44	44	2.89	2.05
Norway	—	68	—	51	7.04	4.99
U.K.	66	67	51	52	0.346	0.261

[a] U.S. = 100.
[b] Units of currency per U.S. dollar.

CHAPTER

4

The Record
of Cost-sharing
Arrangements

Theoretical discussions of cost sharing in terms of the adequacy, economy, and equity of effort (such as the one in Chapter 3) are likely to remain, in the end, largely scholastic exercises. In the actual course of affairs, a give-and-take bargaining process determines the cost shares for international activities, just as it determines domestic taxation in most countries. Around the conference table, jointly accepted views of efficiency and equity may or may not play an important role; but in general, the more money involved, the less altruism.

This chapter reviews the experience of the Universal Postal Union (UPU), the League of Nations, the United Nations, the International Monetary Fund (IMF), the International Bank for Reconstruction and Development (IBRD) and its associated organizations, the North Atlantic Treaty Organization (NATO), and the Development Assistance Committee (DAC) of Organization for Economic Cooperation and Development (OECD). Each organization faced a different problem, and the negotiating processes yielded widely inconsistent results—an indication, among other things, that willingness to pay is at least as important a consideration as ability to pay.

The Universal Postal Union

As pointed out in Chapter 3, the UPU is one of the organizations that base contributions systems largely on the benefit principle.[1] The UPU

---

[1] Among them are the Hydrographic Bureau (which bases its system on shipping tonnages), the General Agreement on Tariffs and Trade, and the Bureau of Customs Traffic (the latter two basing their systems on value of foreign trade).

TABLE 4–1: CONTRIBUTIONS SCHEDULES FOR INTERNATIONAL ORGANIZATIONS

Country	Universal Postal Union (1931)	League of Nations (1935)	United Nations (1961)	OECD (1962)
Argentina	0.55	2.9	1.11	—
Australia	2.77	2.7	1.79	—
Belgium	1.66	1.8	1.30	2.90
Brazil	1.66	2.9	1.02	—
Canada	2.77	3.5	3.11	4.91
China	2.77	4.6	5.01	—
Czechoslovakia	1.66	2.9	0.87	—
Denmark	1.11	1.2	0.60	1.33
France	2.77	7.9	6.40	12.88
Germany	2.77	7.9	—	14.35
Greece	1.66	0.7	0.23	0.70
India	2.77	5.5	2.46	—
Ireland	0.55	1.0	0.16	0.40
Italy	2.77	6.0	2.25	6.95
Japan	2.77	6.0	2.19	—
Netherlands	1.66	2.3	1.01	2.57
Norway	1.11	0.9	0.49	1.02
Poland	1.66	3.2	1.37	—
Portugal	1.11	0.6	0.20	0.51
Spain	3.21	4.0	0.93	2.62
Sweden	1.66	1.8	1.39	2.82
Switzerland	1.66	1.7	—	1.26
Turkey	1.11	1.0	0.59	2.05
U.K.	2.77	10.5	7.78	16.29
U.S.	2.77	—	32.51	25.00
U.S.S.R.	2.77	7.9	13.62	—
Other members	48.50	8.6	11.61	1.44
Total	100.00	100.0	100.00	100.00

SOURCES: Data for UPU from Sumberg, pp. 292–293; for League of Nations, from Denys P. Myers, *Handbook of the League of Nations*, pp. 78–79; for the UN, from J. D. Singer, *Financing International Organization: The United Nations Budget Process;* for OECD, from Department of State.

regulates the conditions of international postal movements, including both terminal and transit traffic. Presumably the larger and wealthier countries, which have the most international postal traffic, benefit most from UPU activities. Since 1878 the Union has divided its members into seven classes, based on population, area, and volume of postal traffic.[2] If a country

[2] See Sumberg, p. 286; and Schelling.

considers itself "bigger" than the formula implies, however, it has some leeway to change its class voluntarily; and because the UPU budget is small ($707,000 in 1962), it costs very little to buy an extra bit of prestige in this way.

The highest share of the budget any one member can pay is 4.18 per cent. There are 17 members in this class, including the United States, the larger countries of Western Europe, the major British Commonwealth countries, China, India, and Russia. The other 97 members (as of 1961) were spread over the other six classes, with the lowest class paying one-twenty-fifth as much as the larger members.

The UPU formula was originally based on the Telegraphic Union formula (based on population, extent of lines, and number of telegraphic offices). Both were developed during a period when measurement of national income was unknown. In the period since World War II, when most cost-sharing discussions have introduced national income as a criterion, the UPU has remained loyal to its own formula—presumably on the principle of *de minimis*. As is clear from Table 4–1, the system's claims to equity must be based on benefit principles. In terms of ability to pay, it is highly regressive; but because most countries' payments come to less than 1 cent per capita annually, the social injustice is presumably bearable. Incidentally, the regressiveness may have increased over the past forty years for a number of countries; in 1919 the largest contributors paid 6.33 per cent each. With the growth of membership and postal volume, there are more contributors in Class I, but they pay relatively less.

The League of Nations

The League started out by deciding to base its contributions on the UPU system, but it proved to be entirely unsuitable. The exact point at which regressive taxation becomes unbearable to the taxpayers has always been a matter of dispute (as the genesis of national revolutions indicates); but in the sphere of international taxation in 1922, it can be defined as the point at which the total tax rose from 125,000 Swiss francs to 6,000,000.[3] India, Canada, and Australia were not anxious to match British, French, and Italian contributions, even though their attachment to the League was perhaps no less strong than to the UPU.

[3] Schelling, p. 5.

The League then turned to a system that retained the class structure of the UPU, but was presumably less regressive in incidence, both because the contributions range was larger and because the formula included some reference to national income. Thus in 1935 the contributions of the highest class (which included the UK) were 104 times greater than those of the smallest class (see Table 4–1). The formula for determining class was an index number, the product of each country's relative government revenues (presumably closely correlated to GNP) and relative population (with UK population taken as the ceiling to prevent overtaxing India and China). This method was formally adopted in 1924. In subsequent years the Allocations Committee of the League, which was responsible for apportionment recommendations, turned increasingly toward national income as a measure of relative shares.[4] Consequently, the original spread (of 95 to 1) between largest and smallest contributors increased over the years to 104 to 1, although it remained much less than that of the United Nations (825 to 1). Undoubtedly, it was still largely regressive in impact. For example, the GNP of the UK was clearly far more than three times that of Poland and more than 80 per cent greater than that of India. Singer is probably incorrect in stating that after 1924 the League tended to adopt a formula based on national income less minimum per capita subsistence income, because countries like India and China would have contributed virtually nothing under such a system. He refers to the importance of logrolling, which in fact probably explains much of the change that took place after the 1924 formula was adopted.[5]

Whatever the actual incidence of the system, its intent was clearly to shift from a benefit principle (which the League explicitly rejected) to one based on capacity to pay. In that way, it set a precedent for postwar cost-sharing arrangements. In practice, adhering only remotely to the principle, it also set a precedent for postwar financing systems.

The United Nations

The League's early financial difficulties stemmed in part from the fact that the UPU schedule was originally written into the covenant. The United Nations Charter avoided this mistake by stating simply, "The

---

[4] J. D. Singer, "Finances of the League of Nations," pp. 266–267.
[5] *Ibid.*, p. 267.

expenses of the Organization shall be borne by the Members as apportioned by the General Assembly."

The Organization set up a Committee on Contributions and directed it to base its assessments on ability to pay. The report of the committee was submitted to the General Assembly in 1946.[6] The report proposed a contributions percentage for each member. The method of arriving at the recommendations was not specified, but it was based on progressive taxation in the sense of higher percentages of national income paid by members with higher per capita national incomes. Thus, among countries of equal national income, those with higher populations would pay less, but would have paid more under the League formula.

Other factors considered included (1) dislocations caused by war; (2) foreign-exchange problems; and (3) the decision not to allow any one country (the United States, in this case) to pay more than 50 per cent of the costs.

The 1946 proposals included a figure of 49.89 per cent for the United States. The United States succeeded in bargaining this down to 39.89 per cent, while aiming at the goal of one-third (reached in 1954 and replaced by a new "goal" of 30 per cent). The United States was able to gain support for this position by agreeing that no other country should pay a higher per capita contribution than the United States, which would have been the case for such nations as Canada, Sweden, and New Zealand.[7] At the same time, minimum contributions (currently at 0.04 per cent of the budget) were agreed to, reminiscent of the benefit principle (see "Economic and Bargaining Problems in Cost Sharing," p. 51).

The current situation then is as follows: (1) The United States pays about 32 per cent. (2) Other countries with high per capita income pay no more per capita than does the United States. (3) Low-income countries receive a deduction from their assessment base of a maximum of 50 per cent of GNP (see Table 4–1).[8] As a result, per capita incidence is equal among the higher per capita income countries, and to that extent the system does not meet the progressiveness criterion set by the Committee on Contributions. Because of the advantage thus gained by high-income

[6] *Report of the Committee on Contributions*, General Assembly Document A/80, New York, October 11, 1946.

[7] This provision was changed in 1954 to one having similar effects. These countries' percentage share was frozen until their per capita shares declined to the U.S. per capita share.

[8] See Chap. 3, pp. 60 ff.

countries, medium- and low-income countries pay more than they would in a system in which countries with equal per capita incomes paid equal proportions of national product. However, the deductions accorded to the low-income countries reintroduce a progressive element in the lowest brackets. Thus, in effect, most of the regressiveness introduced by the ceilings is probably thrown onto the middle-income countries (for example, those with per capita incomes in the range of $300 to $900, at official exchange rates).

The UN system makes no direct reference to real income, although the relative underpayment by the high-income countries works in the same direction as would an assessment based on real incomes. Naturally, if we reconsider the progressiveness of the system in terms of real incomes, the high-income countries would pay relatively less than they would under a UN system without ceilings; and the deductions for low-income countries under such a system would be smaller.

The UN Committee on Contributions had to deal with an issue that has frequently been raised in cost-sharing discussions over the past two decades: the foreign-exchange problem. A number of countries wanted to pay in their own currencies, valued at official exchange rates, to save their supply of gold and dollars. The Secretary-General has announced annually since 1948 (on the basis of geographic distribution of budgetary expenditures) the amounts of nondollar currencies that will be accepted, and allocates them among members. In 1959, 32.45 per cent of all contributions were in other currencies, mostly pounds sterling and Swiss francs.[9] To the extent that some countries pay in nonconvertible currencies, the real value of their contribution is reduced; it is a tied payment and should be valued at less than official exchange rates (see "The Valuation of Economic Aid Contributions," p. 124). To the extent that the expenditures are for relatively cheap goods that are not internationally traded, the real benefit of the contribution is greater than the nominal value, although real costs are not disproportionately large.

If ability to pay is the criterion, the UN system is a substantial advance over the prewar arrangements. From the long-term viewpoint, it is a step closer to the application of progressive taxation to international organizations. India, for example, paid 5.77 per cent of the League budget, but pays only 2.44 per cent of the UN budget. Mexico, with higher per capita in-

---

[9] J. D. Singer, *Financing International Organization*, p. 138.

come, pays 0.71 per cent of the UN budget, compared to 1.28 per cent under the League. In other words, among low-income countries contributing both to the UN and the League, changes in contributions reflect not only the larger membership of the UN, but also differences in per capita income.

Bargaining is still very important to the large contributors, however. The sums are not large enough to make them reject a formula approach, but enough money is at stake to make the percentages worth negotiating over, particularly because of fears that present shares will set a precedent for future assessments.

Because of the defects of formulas, and—more important—because of the desire to give the UN a measure of financial independence, it has been suggested that the organization impose taxes itself. Proposals include taxes on international travel and on international trade, patents, and postage. It has also been proposed that the UN go into business as an international bank, seller of atomic energy, and the like. The organization does earn small sums from the sale of postage, publications, and tour services;[10] but direct taxation or large-scale business enterprise seems a long way off.

The International Monetary Fund, The International Bank for Reconstruction and Development, and The International Development Association

The Bretton Woods agreements of 1944 provided for establishment of the IBRD and the IMF, the first postwar institutions to set up a cost-sharing system; both differed from the UN system in that contributions went toward an initial capital stock, rather than being annual payments for operating and capital requirements. Furthermore, except for admission of new members and proportional quota increases by all members in 1959 (the Fund quotas were increased 50 per cent and Bank subscriptions 110 per cent), no additional payments were anticipated. None have yet proven necessary, because interest on loans finances operating expenses.

Under the IMF charter, quotas are related to drawing rights. Each member subscribes 25 per cent of its quota in gold, and 75 per cent in national currency (or in noninterest-bearing notes payable in national

[10] *Ibid.*, p. 144.

currency). In general, no country may borrow more than 125 per cent of its quota from the Fund.

At Bretton Woods members were faced with conflicting incentives: the desire to minimize quota payments (particularly in gold), and the desire to have large quotas, both to be able to borrow large sums in case of payments difficulties, and also as a sign of national prestige associated with voting power.[11] Bargaining became a vital element, and the formula actually adopted was essentially a basis for discussion. The formula therefore produces results that differ considerably from actual quotas (Table 4–2, p. 101, shows 1962 IMF quotas). The formula was the sum of the following elements:

1. 2 per cent of national income for 1940;
2. 5 per cent of holdings of gold and dollars as of July 1, 1943;
3. 10 per cent of average annual imports, 1934–1938; and
4. 10 per cent of maximum variation in annual exports, 1934–1938.

This sum is multiplied by

5. 1 plus the ratio of average annual exports (1934–1938) to national income.

The principal nonformula considerations in arriving at quotas were agreement (1) that the U.S. quota would be about twice the UK quota; (2) that other large countries should have an "appropriate" quota in relation to these two; and (3) that the total resources of the Fund should be about $10 billion, including allowance for new members. Thus, computations based on the formula (for which basic data are often not available anyway, very few underdeveloped countries having national income data for the prewar period) would vary substantially from actual quotas.

Several aspects of the formula are worth discussing. First, a system based on these quotas gives relatively heavy weight to national income. In a welfare or capacity-to-pay sense, this is appropriate; but the IMF is designed to make the international payments system work, and, as Schelling has pointed out, the extent and variability of trade then become relevant. According to the benefit principle, however, it might be argued that foreign trade and its fluctuations should be given greater weight. As we remember from Chapter 1, the effect of this would be to give larger quotas to small countries (which generally have high trade

[11] Oscar L. Altman, "Quotas in the International Monetary Fund," *International Monetary Fund Staff Papers*, Vol. 5, August 1956, pp. 140–142.

ratios) and to commodity exporting countries (which generally have more fluctuation in export earnings) than under the present formula.[12] Given the present system of drawing rights related to quotas, the argument for such a change essentially would rest on the fact that countries to which trade is important are more likely to run into payments difficulties than are countries less dependent on trade; or that those who gain a good deal from trade should be willing to put up money to make the system work effectively. The first of these justifications is often clearly invalid (for example, trade is important to Iraq, which has no payments problems, and no great matter to the United States, which considers that it has severe ones). The second justification is unverifiable in detail, but is consistent with the benefit principle.

Another change that might be argued for in any revision of the Bretton Woods formulas would be the elimination of Step 5 in the above formula. Multiplying the sum of 1 through 4 by 5 makes the relation between quotas and national income (or any other variable) nonlinear, so that strange results emerge for low-income countries, keeping other variables constant. They pay much higher quotas than do countries with high incomes.[13] The smaller the income weight in the formula, the more marked the nonlinearities resulting from applying the Bretton Woods formula.

Although there is some argument for setting up Fund quotas on a basis that reflects factors other than ability to pay, it is not clear why gold and dollar reserves should be an element. In the first place, the value of a country's reserves as of any date is subject to changes that are not necessarily related to income or trade levels. To the extent that they reflect variation in exports, Step 4 in the formula already accounts for that factor. Second, if reserves are to enter the formula at all, it would be more consistent to make quotas negatively correlated to reserves or to the reserves-trade or reserves-export variation ratios.

Finally, it should be remembered that the Bretton Woods quotas were arrived at after a long British-American debate on the Fund's purposes and methods of operation. For that reason, the principal factor determining quotas was each major power's desire to obtain the maximum voting strength (votes are virtually proportional to quotas). Formulas and their

---

[12] But not necessarily larger in all cases than they are under the present quotas, because of their divergence from formulas.

[13] This might be appropriate, if trade is the contribution base, but there is no particular reason for a nonlinear formula.

vagaries must be considered in light of this conflict and the effort to resolve it.[14]

As can be seen in Table 4–2, IMF quotas and the subscriptions of IBRD and associated agencies are generally close to each other for major countries, although the U.S.-U.K. ratio is higher in the IBRD and in the new organizations[15] than in the Fund.

TABLE 4–2: SUBSCRIPTION TO IMF, IBRD, IFC, AND IDA

Country	Percentage Subscription, 1962			
	IMF	IBRD	IFC	IDA
Argentina	1.83	1.80	1.69	1.94
Australia	2.61	2.57	2.26	2.08[a]
Belgium	2.20	2.17	2.54	—
Brazil	1.83	1.80	1.18	1.94
Canada	3.59	3.62	3.67	3.91[a]
China	3.59	3.62	—	3.13
Denmark	0.85	0.84	0.77	0.90[a]
France	5.14	5.07	5.92	5.47[a]
Germany	5.14	5.07	3.72	5.47[a]
Greece	0.39	0.24	0.28	0.26
India	3.92	3.86	4.51	4.17
Ireland	0.29	0.29	0.34	0.31
Italy	1.76	1.74	2.03	1.87[a]
Japan	3.27	3.21	2.82	3.47[a]
Netherlands	2.69	2.65	3.10	2.86[a]
Norway	0.65	0.64	0.56	0.69[a]
Portugal	0.39	0.39	—	—
Spain	0.98	0.97	1.13	1.04
Sweden	0.98	0.97	1.13	1.04[a]
Turkey	0.56	0.55	0.48	0.60
U.K.	12.74	12.54	14.66	13.54[a]
U.S.	26.95	30.63	35.81	33.06[a]
Other countries	17.65	14.76	11.40	12.25
Total value of subscriptions ($ million)	15,306	20,730	98	969

SOURCES: IBRD, *The World Bank, IFC, and IDA Policies and Operations;* IMF, *Intern. Financ. Stat.*

[a] Subscription 100 per cent payable in convertible currency; other countries pay 10 per cent convertible currency.

[14] The Bretton Woods negotiations are described in J. W. Beyen, *Money in a Maelstrom*, The Macmillan Company, New York, 1949, Chap. 10; R. N. Gardner, *Sterling-Dollar Diplomacy*, Clarendon Press, Oxford, 1956, Chap. 7; and R. F. Harrod, *The Life of John Maynard Keynes*, The Macmillan Company, New Yorik, 1951, Chap. 13. The official record is found in *Proceedings and Documents of the United Nations Monetary and Financial Conference, Bretton Woods*, 2 vols., U.S. Department of State, Washington, D.C., 1948.

[15] International Finance Corporation and International Development Association.

Partly, this difference reflects differences between the IMF and IBRD subscription formulas. The IBRD formula was alleged to consist of 4 per cent of each country's national income in 1940 and 6 per cent of its average annual foreign trade, 1934–1938, with a 20 per cent quota leeway allowed for negotiation.[16] As in the case of IMF, not too much reliance should be placed on the formulas. The objective was to set up a capital fund of $10 billion (increased in 1952 to $21.5 billion) in which the U.S. contribution would be somewhat more than twice as large as the British contribution. Furthermore, only 2 per cent of the $10 billion (less than 1 per cent of the increased sum) was payable in gold and dollars; 18 per cent of the original sum was payable in national currency to be spent only with the member's consent. The rest was simply backing for Bank bonds or other obligations.

If the Bank in its postreconstruction phase is viewed essentially as a device for transferring private funds to underdeveloped countries, then much of the subscription mechanism is beside the point, except as it relates to voting power. Votes are roughly proportional to subscriptions, with smaller subscribers receiving slightly heavier weights; thus the United States, with 30.63 per cent of the subscription, has 27.89 per cent of the voting power; Honduras, with 0.03 per cent of the subscription, has 0.14 per cent of the voting power.[17] For that reason, the apparent absurdity of including foreign trade in the formula (which corresponds neither to ability to pay nor benefits received) can be overlooked. The point was to emerge with a politically acceptable distribution of votes.

Most of the Bank's outstanding loans ($4.3 billion plus $1.1 billion sold to private investors, as of December 1961) have been financed by borrowing in capital markets. If a genuine burden-sharing issue arises at all, it is obviously, "who finances the loans?" Because investors need no more than customary urging to buy Bank bonds and loans ($2.5 billion in bonds and $1.1 billion in loans sold were outstanding at the end of 1961), the issue is not genuine. The bonds pay market rates of interest. The fact that more than two-thirds of the bonds are dollar bonds is irrelevant—as it would be if 100 per cent were dollar bonds.

In short, the Bank as now operated is very much like any other bank. It borrows money cheap and lends it dear. Burden sharing is a minor con-

[16] Sumberg, pp. 289–290.

[17] Each member has 250 votes, plus one vote for each $100,000 of capital subscription. For a summary of Bank operations and sources of funds, see IBRD, *The World Bank, IFC, and IDA Policies and Operations*, Washington, D.C., April 1962.

sideration.[18] The same observation applies to the International Finance Corporation (IFC), which finances private investment in underdeveloped countries by lending and equity investment.

The International Development Association (IDA), established in 1960 to make long-term (50-year) loans at low rates of interest (currently $3/4$ of 1 per cent), is a very different matter. By present-value criteria, these loans are virtually grants (see "The Valuation of Economic Aid Contributions," p. 124); the capital must be replenished periodically if IDA is to remain a going concern. In this case the Bretton Woods formula is clearly inappropriate. As a result, the membership is divided into two groups. Group I, consisting of North America and Western Europe, pays its contributions (76 per cent of total) in convertible currencies. All other countries pay 10 per cent of their contributions in convertible currency, and the rest in national currency, released only with their consent. These stipulations raise the relative real contributions of developed countries above Bretton Woods levels. The United States, for example, pays about 42 per cent of Group I contributions, and the United Kingdom pays about 17 per cent

From the viewpoint of cost sharing, and according to ability-to-pay principles, the United States pays less to IDA than it would under any of the formulas described in Chapter 3, "Definitions of Aid and Common Defense Expenditures," and less than it does for bilateral aid, however that aid is valued (see Chapter 5). Therefore, the logic of U.S. efforts should be to encourage a greater flow of funds through IDA, assuming it approves of the Association's methods and wants to maintain the flow of capital to underdeveloped countries while paying less than its "fair share." In a sense it is potentially the most effective way of encouraging a more satisfactory distribution of costs from the U.S. viewpoint; and possibly a more effective way of spending money than under bilateral programs, where day-to-day political pressures may unduly dominate long-run political and economic goals. This might well be true even if U.S. relative shares were raised, as long as a substantial flow of funds was assured.

Three salient observations emerge from this review of the burden-sharing aspects of the Bretton Woods organizations:

1. Although each organization had a different purpose, the formula system used as a basis for negotiations produced similar results in each case. An appropriate formula for the IMF would have weighted foreign

---

[18] That is, in effect real costs are zero.

trade and fluctuations more heavily than national income. An appropriate IBRD or IDA formula would have been based entirely on national income. However, the subscription system in IBRD was largely irrelevant to the major source of funds, so that the primary significance of quotas was in the voting system.

2. The fact that different formulas produced the same results demonstrates that they were essentially bases for bargaining, not rules for determining contributions.

3. The IDA is in effect a system for parceling out grants on a large scale. Its subscription system should therefore presumably be based on national income if the theoretical postwar standard for international organizations is to be accepted. There has been some *de facto* tendency in that direction. It is less regressive compared to GNP or per capita income than the Bretton Woods organizations or the United Nations (because of the local-currency provision of the subscription system), but is still regressive.

Cost Sharing in NATO

Cost sharing in NATO is quite different from contributions systems in international organizations. NATO is an alliance of states, each of which budgets and spends its own defense appropriations, selecting the amount and distribution of expenditures as it sees fit, that is, on the basis of its domestic and international political calculus. Formal cost-sharing systems are used but little (see below).

As the tables in Chapter 3 make clear, the United States has paid a larger proportion of total NATO defense budgets than it would have under all but the most progressive of tax formulas. The reasons are simple. The United States—which has high manpower costs and high costs for some kinds of equipment, perhaps because of the frequent and often necessary practice of using cost-plus procurement contracts—looks primarily to itself for defense against Soviet Bloc aggression. Other NATO countries look primarily to the United States. If economy and equity considerations were applied, both total NATO defense expenditures and the U.S. share would be less than now. Europe would provide more manpower, goods, and money than it now does.

As a practical matter, a full-employment Europe can hardly be expected to raise taxes and spend money for increased military forces when it knows that the United States will do it anyway. Some countries (for example, France) may spend large sums to fight colonial wars or to maintain a European power status or, as with Germany, to maintain a "good soldier" posture. But there is no fundamental and compelling inducement for Europe to pay its "fair share" in NATO; at least there has been none up till now.[19]

Even so, NATO burden-sharing efforts were not entirely fruitless. Although a specific formula for cooperation was never found, some of the results a formula might have achieved were achieved by other means: (1) Total contributions for defense increased fairly rapidly after 1950 in response to the Korean War. (2) Financing the increased effort was considered and carried out on a different basis from that used for manning and equipping the member-country forces; that is, the military estimate of national force goals, as adopted by the NATO Lisbon Conference in the spring of 1952, did not imply that each member should fully finance the approved contributions. In practice, two countries, the United States and Canada, supplied extra financial resources and equipment to those countries economically unable or politically unwilling to pay for the entire cost of the expanded defense program.[20]

The rapid growth of NATO forces during the early 1950's was not a result of NATO's only formal burden-sharing exercise. This effort, conducted initially in 1951 by NATO's Finance and Economics Board, and then in late 1951 and early 1952 under the aegis of the Temporary Council Committee of the NATO Council of Ministers, failed in its goal of maximizing each country's defense expenditure in terms of various ability-to-pay criteria. The success of the Temporary Council Committee was essentially political. It established force goals under which the member countries were willing to make some effort to meet, and it helped promote national and U.S. financing of increased costs.

For a variety of reasons, the burden-sharing exercise was not repeated. It was impossible to agree on defining NATO defense expenditures, or appropriate contributions criteria. Fundamentally, each country wanted to maintain its freedom of action in dealing with sums that were typically

[19] Sentiments of "responsibility" and carrying one's share may play some role, particularly for the smaller countries. It is difficult to distinguish between this and the desire to keep on the right side of the United States and other allies.

[20] For the discussion of the 1951 NATO burden-sharing exercise, see Gordon.

more than 5 per cent of GNP annually. In a sense, the Temporary Council Committee had achieved one of its main objectives: sharp increases in the defense efforts of the member countries. After 1952 the adequacy of national defense efforts was examined by NATO annual reviews. It is significant that during the course of these reviews, formal recommendations for increased national defense budgets were never made.

From 1951 to 1956 U.S. military aid to NATO was of major importance, averaging about $2 billion a year. Beginning in 1957, however, with the continuing growth of the European economy, the reduction in U.S. national defense expenditures, and the apparent decline in the political urgency of NATO expansion, this assistance leveled off at $600 to $700 million a year. Furthermore, with the worsening U.S. balance-of-payments situation, U.S. assistance increasingly became tied assistance, whereas in earlier years a substantial part of our military assistance expenditures had been in the form of overseas procurement. Tied assistance has not done away with the problem entirely; it does not affect U.S. troop expenditures overseas, particularly for NATO forces. In recent years, therefore, the United States has attempted to get financial "compensation" by urging European countries, notably Germany, to procure military supplies in the United States. Germany has done so in the past three years (1961–1963), with procurement in the United States at least equal to our troop expenditures in Germany—a sort of balance-of-payments compensation for the U.S. presence in Germany.

In two domains NATO did reach agreement on a burden-sharing formula. From the beginning in 1951, the members worked out a payment schedule for NATO headquarters expense. The annual headquarters budget, currently equivalent to about $7.5 million, is shown in Table 4–3. The United States provides 24.2 per cent of the total, with the United Kingdom, France, and Germany paying 19.5, 17.1, and 16.1 per cent, respectively. This is somewhat reminiscent of the OECD formula, in which the United States set a 25 per cent limit to its contributions and other countries paid the balance on a progressive scale.

The other example of a burden-sharing formula used by NATO is the infrastructure program. Table 4–4 shows the contributions of member countries in recent years. It should be noted that the U.S. contribution has followed the trend established in the military aid program. During the early years of the infrastructure program, when construction of airfields, pipe lines, docks, and other transportation and communication facilities

TABLE 4–3: NATO HEADQUARTERS BUDGET, 1962

Country	Percentage	Amount ($)
Belgium	2.86	211,068
Canada	5.08	428,040
Denmark	1.65	121,770
France	17.10	1,261,980
Germany	16.10	1,188,180
Greece	0.39	28,272
Iceland	0.05	3,690
Italy	5.96	439,848
Luxembourg	0.09	6,642
Netherlands	2.85	210,330
Norway	1.15	84,870
Portugal	0.65	47,970
Turkey	1.65	121,770
U.K.	19.50	1,439,610
U.S.	24.20	1,785,960
Total	100.00	7,380,000

seemed urgent, the United States contributed a large percentage of the total. This effort encouraged a larger European contribution than might otherwise have been possible. Since 1951 the U.S. contribution has declined from 48.1 to 30.85 per cent of the total. In renegotiating the infrastructure agreement in 1964, the United States bargained for a reduction of its share to substantially lower levels. As in the case of OECD, the UN, and NATO headquarters, setting the U.S. contribution at one-third or less of the total tends to mean that the poor countries pay a higher amount per capita than the United States. Nevertheless, certain objective considerations led to agreement on this formula for infrastructure investment. First, almost all the construction work is in Europe, and there is some evidence that it benefits European economies more than it does the U.S. economy. Second, the awards for construction are usually let to European contractors, with a consequent income effect favoring the European countries.

A few points from the NATO experience seem worth noting. First, though no burden-sharing scheme was formally adopted, the U.S. military assistance program was in effect a political-economic judgment of the relative abilities of Europe and the United States to provide resources and finance them, respectively.

TABLE 4-4: SHARES OF NATO INFRASTRUCTURE COSTS

Country	Per Cent Share 1961–64	Cost ($ million)
Belgium	4.24	29.68
Canada	5.15	36.05
Denmark	2.87	20.09
France	12.00	84.00
Germany	20.00	140.00
Greece	0.67	4.69
Italy	5.97	41.79
Luxembourg	0.17	1.19
Netherlands	3.83	26.81
Norway	2.37	16.59
Portugal	0.28	1.96
Turkey	1.10	7.70
U.K.	10.50	73.50
U.S.	30.85	215.95
Total	100.00	700.00

Second, it proved impossible to gain agreement on any formal review of national defense budgets and their adequacy; the process had to operate indirectly through the annual NATO review system.

Third, during the time European countries faced balance-of-payments problems and the United States remained in a surplus position, U.S. military aid was not tied to U.S. procurement. When the position was reversed, the United States began tying its aid and asked other countries to spend part of their national defense budgets for U.S. equipment.

Fourth, the post-1956 decline in U.S. aid corresponded to a general slackening in national defense expenditures among NATO members. It is difficult to relate this falling-off directly to the decline in military assistance; it seems to reflect primarily a political judgment on the part of the members that the threat from the USSR was less immediate. It is therefore difficult to accept fully the claim that U.S. military assistance exercises a sort of multiplier effect on the budgets of other NATO members. It may be more accurate to say that the two are correlated with members' general estimates of the urgency of increased military expenditures.[21]

Fifth, although burden-sharing formulas have been arrived at in two limited spheres of NATO activity—headquarters expense and infrastructure financing—these are unlikely to set a pattern for a more ambitious formula system.

[21] A similar tendency was noticeable after the 1961 Berlin crisis.

Cost Sharing for Economic Aid

Relative aid costs are discussed in detail in Chapter 5. This section simply reviews the history of Western efforts at burden sharing in providing economic aid to underdeveloped countries.

Starting in the late 1950's, the United States began to encourage other countries to provide more economic aid. Initially, the United States exerted pressure on Europe primarily by encouraging increased contributions to multilateral programs, notably UN Technical Assistance. Since 1959 there has been a shift in the tempo and emphasis of U.S. efforts. The Draper study on foreign military assistance emphasized this viewpoint in its report to the President:

> Other free world industrialized countries . . . have the combined capacity to furnish development aid roughly comparable to that provided by the United States. There are already clear indications that the European countries are providing increasing assistance to the underdeveloped world. The United States should encourage further steps in this direction.[22]

In 1960 the Development Assistance Group was established, representing nine donor countries of Western Europe; its primary real purpose from the U.S. viewpoint was less to "coordinate" than to raise the total flow of aid and Europe's share of it. With the establishment of OECD, the Development Assistance Group became the Development Assistance Committee (DAC) of OECD. In the London and Tokyo meetings of DAC in March and July 1961, the United States attempted to introduce a burden-sharing scheme based on two principles: (1) DAC members (which were then the United States, Canada, France, Germany, Italy, Japan, the Netherlands, Belgium, Portugal, and the United Kingdom) should agree to contribute 1 per cent of their combined annual gross national product as aid to underdeveloped countries. (2) Contributions to that total should be made on the basis of a "progressive income tax" self-levied by the member governments. No common aid fund was proposed; but each country was supposed to refer its own aid effort to these criteria.

[22] *Report of the President's Committee To Study the Military Assistance Program*, Government Printing Office, Washington, D.C., 1959, pp. 67, 86.

At the July 1961 meetings the other countries rejected the U.S. proposal, both in respect to total amount and composition. As with NATO, the reason seemed to be primarily political: Countries were not willing to accept constraints on the national budget process that would follow from accepting an international contributions scheme of that magnitude. Furthermore, many countries were not sufficiently impressed by the urgency of the matter to sharply increase their current level of aid expenditures. In effect, the U.S. proposal was aimed at getting other countries to contribute more money to economic development; other countries were unwilling to commit themselves to any formula that would ensure greater contributions.

The members agreed on an annual review procedure, on the NATO model, which would not make specific recommendations on the size of national foreign-aid budgets. It was an even less coercive review than the NATO system. The NATO reviews included an analysis of national defense programs in terms of agreed NATO force levels. The annual DAC reviews referred to no agreed level of aid, but only to the much more general criterion of adequacy of effort.

Despite the failure of DAC efforts to provide an agreed formula for aid, it had the merit from the U.S. viewpoint of creating a forum where aid could be discussed and where pressure for increased expenditures could be maintained. By the same token, Europe was able to use DAC data to point out that U.S. aid was not disproportionate relative to GNP (see Table 5–10), and that much of it was composed of surplus farm goods, conveniently dumped. The United States still chose to feel put upon and to urge relatively larger European contributions, as in the Clay Committee's report to the President in April 1963:

> We are convinced that the burden of sustaining foreign assistance to the less-developed countries is falling unfairly upon the U.S. and that the industrialized countries can and should do more than they are now doing. The present inequity is even more apparent when one adds defense expenditures to economic assistance to determine the national shares in the total expense of protecting and advancing the free world's well-being.[23]

In fact, considering economic aid only, U.S. contributions were not disproportionate, at least not by ability to pay as usually defined. They

[23] Committee To Strengthen the Security of the Free World, *The Scope and Distribution of United States Military and Economic Assistance Programs,* p. 14.

were undoubtedly disproportionate compared to U.S. shares in international organizations, and somewhat greater than they might be under mildly progressive real-income formulas. On the second point, the excessive U.S. contribution to defense plus aid, the Clay Committee was on stronger ground. As the 1961 Tokyo meetings of DAC showed, however, such an approach is useless in the absence of (1) an agreed rate of substitution between aid and defense expenditures; (2) an agreed "fair shares" system of taxation; (3) a valid method of comparing real defense costs among countries (see "Cost Sharing in NATO," p. 104); and (4) any realistic possibility that the United States would cut its defense budget on burden-sharing grounds.

Conclusions

It is clear from the experience of recent decades that international tax systems cannot be imposed on a formula basis in the manner of domestic taxation, so long as interests are divergent and there is no central authority to impose a solution. When sums are small, as in the UPU, it is easy enough to reach agreement on a formula, and countries may even want to increase their shares as a matter of prestige.

When sums are large (or seem likely to set a precedent), formulas become no more than a basis for negotiation. Furthermore, when sums are large, the benefit principle tends to be replaced by ability-to-pay considerations. At the same time, countries with the greatest ability to pay have the most leverage. In every formal cost-sharing system (excluding DAC and military budgets), the United States pays less relative "tax" than its proportion of total income, whether valued at exchange rates or in real-income terms. Under progressive tax standards applied either to individuals or nations, of course, this discrepancy is widened. In other words, there is a correlation between income level and bargaining ability. The very rich get away with paying smaller shares than they should and the poor usually receive exemptions (UN system) or most of the benefits (IBRD). Thus, the middle-income countries (Europe) tend to be overtaxed in the UN agencies, the IBRD, and the OECD, by both ability-to-pay and benefit criteria. The case is not so clear for NATO infrastructure, where pipelines, communications systems, and the like may benefit Europe more than the United States.

In fields where there is no common effort, burden-sharing exercises have primarily consisted of attempts by the United States to remove some of the burden from its back and to shift it, in particular, to countries that are either conspicuously remiss (Canada, Germany) or conspicuously beholden to the United States (Germany, United Kingdom). It is impossible to say how effective or justifiable this effort has been. There is certainly a widespread impression in the military sphere that it is justified; and there is evidence to support the view.[24] The effort to spread the military mantle to cover economic aid shares has clearly been unsuccessful. On its own merits, the case for a lesser U.S. share in economic aid is not very strong, at least by the present official definition of aid. Under the definition to be discussed in Chapter 5, the situation changes slightly, because every country but France, Belgium, and the United States is underpaying by any equity criterion. However, if there is one point that emerges from the cost-sharing record, it is that changes in definition will not automatically change the contributions system. There are no Marquis of Queensbury rules that still hold fast when money and national interest are at stake.

Finally, there is clear evidence that with the increasing importance of international activities, there has been notable progress toward basing discussions of shares on ability-to-pay considerations. The differences among the UPU schedule, the League system, and the UN system offer striking evidence of the relation between discussion and action, even though discrepancies between the existing system and the uncertain "ideal" of progressive international taxation are still wide. Ironically, however, it is in the areas where efforts at cost-sharing formulas have failed (DAC, NATO) that the United States, at least, comes closest to paying its appropriate share according to this ideal. Because the sums in defense and aid are orders of magnitude larger, small discrepancies in relative shares have far larger practical effect; so the United States is less inconsistent than a reading of the percentages might make it appear. If, in terms of ability to pay, the United States is overpaying by as little as 1 per cent in NATO military expenditures, that more than compensates for its underpayments to all 70 international organizations of which the United States is a member.

---

[24] E. S. Mason, *Foreign Aid and Foreign Policy*, Harper and Row, New York, 1964, Chaps. 2, 3.

CHAPTER

5

The Costs of
Economic Aid

This chapter begins by defining economic aid and discussing possible
alternative definitions. It then goes on to describe how to value aid that is
offered in different forms and under varying conditions. A later section
presents computations of Western aid values, under the revised definition
suggested here, for the years 1961 and 1962. These values are compared to
nominal values as reported to the Organization for Economic Cooperation
and Development (OECD), and to theoretical shares under various burden-
sharing systems.

This chapter applies only to economic aid officially offered by Western
governments. It does not discuss aid by private and international organizations, although the same criteria would apply. Economic aid in the form
of trade, investment, and commodity policies is discussed in Chapters 6
and 7.

Defining Economic Aid

The Official Definition of Aid

In 1961 the principal donors of aid to underdeveloped countries agreed
to hold annual reviews of each other's aid efforts on the basis of an agreed
definition; these reviews are conducted by the Development Assistance
Committee (DAC) of OECD.

The present DAC system for analyzing members' aid flows defines total official aid as the sum of six elements: (1) contributions to international organizations for development purposes; (2) bilateral grants; (3) bilateral loans repayable in lenders' currency; (4) bilateral loans repayable in borrowers' currency; (5) consolidation credits; (6) transfer of resources through sales for recipients' currency (this consists almost exclusively of U.S. contributions of surplus agricultural commodities under Public Law 480).

This classification indicates both an awareness that various types of aid have different impacts on donor and recipient and an inability to devise a system that could deal systematically with these differences. For example, DAC realizes that a loan repayable in soft currency is different in effect from one repayable in hard currency; separate categories are therefore established. These and other subtotals are then added together, however, to form a single aid total. Table 5–1 shows U.S. aid commitments for 1961 as computed by this method.

TABLE 5–1: U.S. ECONOMIC AID COMMITMENTS IN 1961:
OECD DEFINITION
(In $ million)

Item	Amount	
Bilateral aid:		
Grants	1549[a]	
Loans repayable:		
In dollars	1540[b]	
In borrowers' currency	337	
Contributions in kind	1030[c]	
Total bilateral aid		4456
Multilateral aid		258
Total 1961 commitments		4714

SOURCE: Computed by author from data supplied by the Agency for International Development.

[a] Of which $461 million was in commodities, PL 480, Titles II and III.

[b] Excludes loans of five years or less, by DAC agreement.

[c] $438 million of PL 480 sales proceeds granted to purchaser, $592 million loaned to purchaser, repayable in local currency.

Clearly, whatever its merits, a method that weights equally grants, loans of any term and condition,[1] contributions in kind, etc., fails to establish an economic measure of resource sacrifice, which should presumably be one element of a formal foreign-aid burden-sharing system.

[1] The DAC exclusion of loans of less than five years' duration is discussed below.

A Revised Definition of Aid

The discussion of what constitutes economic aid has been confused by the simultaneous use of two implied definitions. One definition tends to regard as aid anything that benefits the economy of a recipient country—including private investment and loans at interest rates lower than those prevailing in the underdeveloped countries, even if as high as those in the more developed countries. The second definition recognizes only the donor country's sacrifice of real resources. Depending on the purpose of the argument, either definition has some claim to legitimacy.

A related point is the motivation of the aid. In one sense, private investment is surely not aid, because it is done with the expectation of profit and is of no less benefit to the investing country than to the host country. If private investment is discouraged by primary reliance on public-fund transfers, however, the flow of resources to underdeveloped countries may decrease.[2] The case is therefore far from clear-cut. Similarly, reparations payments constitute a sacrifice of real resources, but they are not motivated by the desire to promote economic development.

Let us first take up a definition of aid based on public-fund transfers. What shall be included in the definition of aid—grants, long- and short-term loans, loans repayable in local currency, tied and untied loans, contributions in kind, consolidation credits? The first thing to do is to reduce all types of contributions to a single standard for ranking their relative value. The most appropriate method for doing so is to define aid as the present value of aid disbursements minus the present value of repayments, discounted at an appropriate rate of interest reflecting domestic opportunity cost of public capital.[3] This rate would differ for each donor. Eckstein has estimated it at between 5 and 6 per cent in the United States. A less satisfactory but more uniform discount rate would be the borrowing or lending rate of the International Bank for Reconstruction and Development (IBRD). Loans extended at interest rates above the discount rate would count as negative aid. These issues are discussed below in more detail under the heading "The Valuation of Economic Aid Contributions" (p. 124).

[2] See pp. 49–51 above for discussion of private investment and burden sharing.

[3] For a comprehensive discussion of factors affecting the choice of interest rates, see Otto Eckstein, "A Survey of the Theory of Public Expenditure," in National Bureau of Economic Research, *Public Finances: Needs, Sources, and Utilization*, Princeton University Press, Princeton, N.J., 1961, pp. 439–504.

The sovereign advantages of a present-value definition are (1) it allows us to forgo arbitrary decisions about such matters as whether short-term loans or consolidation credits are aid; and (2) it provides a single compatible weighting for different forms of aid.

This definition combines all forms of aid, and weights their values according to the donor's sacrifice. The shorter the loan term and the higher the interest rate, the greater the ratio of present value of repayment to nominal value, and, consequently, the smaller the aid component. Let us take a specific example: loans at different terms and interest rates. Table 5–2 lists the terms of three dollar-repayable loans actually extended by the United States in 1961; the reader can see the effect of changes in interest rates and repayment terms on present value. The method consists of computing the stream of repayments due on the loan, and summing that stream after dividing by a compounded rate of discount (interest), which represents the alternative rate that money could earn if it had not been loaned as foreign aid. In this example, 7 per cent was used.

TABLE 5–2: DISCOUNTED PRESENT VALUES OF THREE TYPICAL U.S. LOANS
(In $ thousand)

Loan and Agency	Amount of Loan	Interest Rate	Loan Term and Grace Period	Discounted Present Value, 7% Discount	Subsidy Element: Amount and Per Cent of Total Loan
Loan A[a]	$ 3,500	5.70%	7 yr + 2 yr grace	$ 3,102.5	$ 397.5 (11.35%)
Loan B[b]	$ 3,500	4.00%	7 yr + 3½ yr grace	$ 2,888.5	$ 611.5 (17.47%)
Loan C[c]	$65,000	0.75%	30 yr + 10 yr grace	$17,645.0	$47,355.0 (72.85%)

NOTE: Computed on equal semiannual payment basis. Includes discounted present value of interest during grace period.
  [a] Export-Import Bank.
  [b] International Cooperation Administration.
  [c] Agency for International Development.

If a discount rate of 5¾ per cent had been chosen, the present value of Loan A would have been $3,500,000—equal to its face value; however, if long-term invested capital in the United States could earn 7 per cent, the loan represents a total sacrifice of $397,526. This is the subsidy or aid element of the loan. As can be seen from the table, the lower the interest rate and the longer the repayment term, the greater the aid component. Loans made by the Agency for International Development (40 years maturity at $3/4$ of 1 per cent interest, including 10 years' grace) are almost 75 per cent subsidy. In other words, they have much of the character of a grant, which can be considered as a "loan" with 100 per cent subsidy. A later section of this chapter, "Computing the Value of Economic Aid," applies this method to determine and compare the subsidy element of DAC members' aid.

Let us first see how aid can be defined if both public and private capital flows are included. This method amounts to defining aid as benefits received by the underdeveloped countries, rather than as sacrifices self-imposed by the donor governments, because private investment is made with the expectation of profit and involves no sacrifice of resources by the investor. Total net capital flow is defined as the measure of benefits received. The appropriate discount rate in this case should be the domestic opportunity cost of equity investment. There is even something to be said for setting the discount rate at the rate of return of foreign private investment, in order to include all capital flows at some positive value. Tables 5–11 and 5–12 (pp. 136–137) include computations discounting official aid at 10 per cent, a figure taken to reflect domestic private opportunity cost. Naturally, the result is to increase substantially the aid value of official contributions compared to the lower discount rate discussed above.

Whether or not the aid definition includes private capital flows, two aspects of the definition problem are still unresolved. One aspect corresponds roughly to the idea of measuring both parties' gains from trade. We have found a measure of the rich countries' sacrifice, but it does not correspond exactly to the poor countries' benefit—our discounted total capital flow is only an approximation. The "true" measure of the poor countries' gains is the difference between what they pay the rich countries for capital (in the case of grants, the payment is zero), and what they would have to pay in the international market for the same capital flow. If there were differences in the annual capital streams, they could be discounted to present value by a rate based on social time preference. Because this process involves two unknown factors—free-market rates for international lending and the rate of marginal social time preference—I have proposed total discounted capital flows as a possible substitute.

This problem of measuring the difference in two parties' gains from trade would exist whether or not international transactions were involved (except that the recipient's benefit would then be measured by the difference between the recipient's actual borrowing rate and the going rate in his domestic capital market). The second issue arises specifically because of foreign-exchange shortages. If Germany lends to India, India may use the money to increase domestic production; but this increase may not result in increased exports or import substitution—that is, it may not generate capacity to repay in foreign exchange. In the simplest case, if India has no export receipts, it may have to ask the United States, for example, for a grant or long-term loan to finance repayment to Germany.[4] Even if India has export earnings, the sacrifice of foreign exchange may entail a greater opportunity cost than would the sacrifice of domestic resources. Still, it should theoretically be true that the value of the loan to India is greater than the sacrifice in repayment; otherwise, there would be no reason to borrow. Nevertheless, what is true under perfect knowledge and rationality assumptions is not necessarily true in India—or elsewhere— today. Perhaps, then, India's sacrifice in repayment might be greater than anticipated, and its rate of time preference in foreign-exchange expenditures might decrease. In other words, the poor countries would prefer the annual flow of aid disbursements to exceed the flow of repayments. Furthermore, this preference may be justified by the poor countries' circumstances. Therefore, perhaps some extra credit should be given to countries that provide an increasing aid and investment flow. The discussion of choice of interest rates below points out how this problem of foreign-exchange valuations could be handled in theory.

The general approach taken in this study is to consider burden sharing in terms of donors' costs, not recipients' gains. Much of the difficulty in theoretical and practical discussions of burden sharing comes from confusing or combining the two elements. This is the basis for efforts to include private investment or loans at high interest rates as aid. Such inclusion is legitimate enough, as noted above, if we look on recipients' opportunity costs as the criterion; but burden sharing is normally concerned with allocating donors' costs, not analyzing recipients' alternatives. Therefore, although the following discussion refers occasionally to recipients' benefits, the computations are based on a donors' cost definition. The consequent

---

[4] The United States may be particularly unwilling to finance Indian loan repayments to Germany, if the United States has a shortage of foreign exchange and Germany a surplus.

disadvantage is that it typically understates the value of the transfer to the recipient, because rates of return on the capital are presumably higher in underdeveloped countries than in donor countries.[5]

Some Alternative Definitions

It has often been pointed out that donors can be said to give aid only if there is a net outflow of goods and services to underdeveloped countries. In other words, the underdeveloped countries' import surplus is the real measure of aid received.

TABLE 5–3: REAL AND FINANCIAL TRANSFERS IN AID OF
DEVELOPMENT: SELECTED COUNTRIES, 1960
(Percentage of gross national product)

Country	Real Transfer[a]	Financial Transfer[b]		
		Total	Public	Private
Belgium-Luxembourg	0.4	1.4	0.8	0.6
Canada	([c])	0.4	0.2	0.2
France[d]	2.8	2.2	1.4	0.8
Germany	3.0	0.9	0.5	0.4
Italy	0.4	0.9	0.4	0.5
Japan	0.5	0.7	0.4	0.3
Netherlands	1.8	2.2	0.4	1.8
U.K.	([c])	1.2	0.5	0.7
U.S.	0.3	0.7	0.5	0.2

SOURCE: U.S. Congress, Joint Economic Committee, *Outlook for United States Balance of Payments.*

[a] Global balance-of-payments surplus on current account, less transfer payments and investment income when identified and included in the national statistics.

[b] Aid and long-term lending as defined in the OECD questionnaire. Total of financial transfers is much larger than the sum of real transfers, because the cash transfers include large financial flows that are not matched by resource flows (e.g., reinvested earnings), and the payments data unavoidably include certain offsets to the flows of goods and services.

[c] Negative.

[d] Estimated from trade data and the payments figures for the franc area.

Kenen has attempted to measure the real transfer for the year 1960 (see Table 5–3) by defining it as the donor's balance-of-payments surplus on current account less transfer payments and investment income. It has been pointed out that the discrepancy between real and financial transfers shown in his computation has an important disadvantage for burden-

[5] In other words, the recipients' benefit is normally greater than the donors' sacrifice. This need not be the case, if rates of return on capital are higher in aid-giving countries than in aid-receiving ones.

sharing estimates: The discrepancy may mean that one donor is financing the real transfer of another donor.[6]

Mme. E. Betout-Mossé has carried this type of analysis a good deal further.[7] She states that in order to qualify as aid the donor's export surplus must (1) be a continuing one between two countries, not simply a reflection of short-term changes in current accounts; (2) be financed by loans or grants; and (3) be between countries of substantially different economic levels. She points out that in some cases (such as Kuwait and Iraq), the less developed countries may actually be aiding the more developed, if there is an excess of exports over imports.

TABLE 5-4: MME. BETOUT-MOSSE'S METHOD FOR MEASURING FRENCH AID TO A LESS DEVELOPED COUNTRY OF THE FRANC ZONE

Item	Resources	Uses
1. Trade balance	Imports, CIF	Exports, FOB
2. Balance of commercial services	*a.* Premiums paid to external insurance companies	*a.* Indemnities paid by foreign insurance companies
	b. Use of French or foreign airlines	*b.* Use by Frenchmen or foreigners of host country's airlines
	c. Use of foreign telecommunications facilities	*c.* External use of the host country's telecommunication facilities
	d. Tourist and external travel expenditures of host-country citizens	*d.* Tourist and travel expenditures of foreigners in the host country
	e. Expenditures for external licenses, copyrights, etc.	*e.* Receipts for external use of licenses and copyrights of host country
3. Payments balances related to the presence of French agents in the host country furnishing services to the latter	*a.* Salaries of Frenchmen working in host-country enterprises	*a.* Final consumption of local goods and services by French agents
	b. Salaries of Frenchmen working in host-country administrations	*b.* Final consumption of imported goods and services by French agents

[6] U.S. Congress, Joint Economic Committee, *Outlook for United States Balance of Payments,* Hearings before the Subcommittee on International Exchange and Payments, December 12, 13, and 14, 1962, Testimony of Peter Kenen, Government Printing Office, Washington, D.C., 1963, pp. 134–147. For a similar approach, see P. A. Simonet, "L'Aide au 'Tiers monde': Efforts de conception et procédés d'évaluation," *Développement et civilisations,* No. 14, March 1963, pp. 65–78.

[7] E. Betout-Mossé, "Sur quelques problèmes posés par l'aide aux pays sous-développés," *Revue économique,* No. 4, July 1962, pp. 590–628.

TABLE 5–4—*continued*

Item	Resources	Uses
4. Payments balances related to the presence of French agents furnishing services to the benefit of France	*a.* Production of French enterprises valued globally as they leave the enterprise, excluding taxes and commercial margins	*a.* Final consumption of local and imported goods and services by French military and civil administration personnel and French wage earners of French enterprises *b.* Final consumption of local and imported goods and services of French military and civil administrations: 　*i.* Commercial goods and services 　*ii.* Pay of local military 　*iii.* Salary of local employees of French civil administrations 　*iv.* Special services; use of airports, military bases, public buildings *c.* Final consumption of local and imported goods and services of French enterprises: 　*i.* Commercial goods and services 　*ii.* Salaries of local employees
5. Payments balances related to the presence in France of agents of the host country furnishing services to the benefit of France	*a.* Expenditures in France of host-country workers	*a.* Salaries received by host-country workers in France
6. Payments balances related to the presence in France of agents of the host country whose services are furnished for the benefit of host country	*a.* Total net expenditures of administrations, delegations, banks of issue, scientific and research organizations *b.* Support of students *c.* Part of operational expenditures of educational institutions	
7. Balances of "common" services (possibly)	*a.* Military protection *b.* Diplomatic services *c.* Monetary services of the franc zone	

SOURCE: Betout-Mossé.

Her method, as applied to French aid to the franc zone, includes a revision of the standard balance-of-payments approach, shown below as Table 5–4. It not only includes the import surplus on current account, but also counts as aid the salaries of Frenchmen working in the franc zone less their consumption of imported and domestic goods and services (if the Frenchmen did not import, the external resources would be available for the local economy). Also, she includes as a resource ("import") the local production by French firms; and as a use ("export") these enterprises' final consumption and that of their employees.

Using this method for 1959, she compares nominal French aid to Africa with the actual net resource flow. Table 5–5 summarizes her results. The totals are considerably less than those reported to OECD. They would be still lower if the correction for overpricing of tropical goods were matched by an adjustment for overpricing of French goods sold in Africa. As Mme. Betout-Mossé points out, however, such a computation would be extremely difficult because of the diversity of African imports and the differences in quality and taste that would have to be introduced (Danish pâté is cheaper than French, but it is not the same product in many a buyer's eyes).

TABLE 5–5: FRENCH AID TO INDEPENDENT COUNTRIES OF BLACK AFRICA AND MADAGASCAR, 1959

Item	Value of Aid (million new francs)
Global trade deficit of these countries (= net French provision of goods and services)	482
Correction, to allow for high prices paid by France for certain tropical crops, as compared to world prices	287
Net value of services provided by French personnel (technical assistance plus French employees of local governments)	501
Total	1270
Flow of official aid, reported to OECD	2221
Flow of official aid plus private capital, reported to OECD	3000

SOURCE: Betout-Mossé.

This method has the merit of concentrating on the real flow of goods and services as distinguished from financial transfers. Its disadvantages for use in burden-sharing analysis are that (1) it is most appropriate for measuring the long-term aid flow; (2) it is very difficult to compute because of lack of data; (3) like Kenen's method, it may overlook the short-run tendency for one donor country to finance the real transfers of another; and (4) since it is based on the relation between two countries (or the members of a single centrally controlled currency zone), it would require thousands of pairs of computations, even if there were adequate data.

Some discussions of aid have emphasized the relation between trade and aid. Measures to expand the flow of trade clearly aid the economies of underdeveloped countries, unless we believe there are no gains from trade. Precisely because there are gains from trade, I have argued above (Chapter 3) that increases in trade in a sense involve no burden for donor countries (although they may involve burdens for some people in those countries). This is the analogue of the point that if aid is really the cheapest way to attain national goals, there is no aid burden, except in the sense that anything one buys costs something.

If trade is regarded as "burden-free" aid, then there is some argument for including, in any evaluation of aid, measures that restrict or expand its flow or that change the terms of trade. None of the methods discussed above take these factors into account. Both Kenen and Mme. Betout-Mossé would give a country the same aid credit if it had a $100 million export surplus, no matter what the level or trend of the trade volume with underdeveloped countries.

Pierre Uri has therefore suggested that burden-sharing criteria include a component for changes in the donors' volume of trade with underdeveloped countries.[8] By the same token one could include an allowance for increases or decreases in quantity of imports, with or without extra weighting for imports of "new" products not previously imported in quantity. As Mme. Betout-Mossé has pointed out, when donors pay more than world-market prices for their imports, or charge more for their exports, these differences should be included as additions to and subtractions from aid. In a more sophisticated version, allowance would also be made for demand elasticities (for example, if a donor fixes high import prices for goods with elastic demand, he is reducing the flow of aid).

These attempts to include the real transfer, whatever computational problems they pose, perform a useful service by concentrating on the actual flow of goods and services as the ultimate measure of aid.

As explained in Chapter 3, it seems preferable as a practical matter to limit burden-sharing analysis to official contributions, and the remainder of this chapter is based on that approach.

---

[8] *Partnership for Progress*, pp. 48–50.

The Valuation of Economic Aid Contributions

Establishing present value as the basis for aid computations is a useful step in valuing the costs of aid; but there is a host of additional difficulties in valuing economic aid, some easily resolved, others intractable. Let us examine them in turn.

Choice of Interest Rate for Discounting

The appropriate discount rate for computing present value of repayments depends on the purpose of the computations. The marginal domestic long-term return on capital is appropriate if we are interested in the domestic opportunity cost of capital. On the other hand, for the sake of consistency among countries, we might want to discount by the international lending rate, which, in the virtual absence of a private long-term market for lending to underdeveloped countries, is presumably represented by the IBRD lending rate. Or, if we wanted to avoid counting any contributions as negative, we could discount at the highest average rate offered by any donor country. Finally, we might want to approximate the rate that long-term private investors would have to earn in these areas.

Any of these rates has its uses; accordingly, under the heading "Computing the Value of Economic Aid" (p. 131), I have included computations discounted at domestic interest rates, 5¾ per cent, 7 per cent, and 10 per cent, approximately representing each of the four alternatives suggested here.

Donor's sacrifices and recipient's benefits are likely to be different.[9] In the present example, the domestic interest rate is taken as an approximation of the former, the 10 per cent rate of the latter. If there were a large free market in long-term loans to underdeveloped countries, its long-term

[9] See above, p. 118. Since this manuscript was written, two publications have appeared, both providing a more rigorous treatment of these issues, notably the distinction between donor's sacrifices and recipient's benefits. See Wilson Schmidt, "The Economics of Charity: Loans vs. Grants," *Journal of Political Economy*, Vol. 71, August 1964, pp. 387–395; and Richard Cooper, *A Note on Foreign Assistance and the Capital Requirements for Development*, The RAND Corporation, Santa Monica, Calif., RM–4291–AID, January 1965. An interesting recent report by Goran Ohlin, *Reappraisals of Foreign Aid Policies*, published by the OECD Development Center (Paris, December 1964), includes an annex with a mathematical treatment of these questions. Ohlin's study also reviews a number of the matters raised in Chaps. 2, 3, and 5 of this volume. In several respects his monograph carries the analysis of aid policies well beyond the points reached in this study.

rate would represent both the lender's and borrower's alternatives. In the absence of such a market, because of risk and capital rationing, the lender's opportunity cost will usually be less than the rate that the borrower would have to pay on the free market. The 10 per cent figure used here is a rough approximation of the free-market rate—the long-term private lending market to underdeveloped countries is too thin to allow a precise estimate. Theoretically, one could also arrive at this free-market rate by estimating for the borrower his domestic equilibrium rate for long-term loans in foreign exchange. Conceptually, this would involve two steps: an estimate of the price of foreign exchange if sold on a free auction market in the borrowing country, and an estimate of the interest rate that individual borrowers would be willing to pay for the use of foreign exchange, so valued, in investment projects. (This assumes that a fixed quantity of foreign exchange is available in each period.)

Terms of Loans

DAC excludes all loans of five years or less. It is illogical to do so, because a short-term loan regularly renewed is no less aid than is a long-term loan, as commercial banks and their customers are well aware. In practice, most countries offer relatively few short-term loans. The computations in the latter part of this chapter discount them at the same rate as long-term loans, on the assumption that if not lent abroad they could have been invested at home at the normally higher long-term rate.

Contributions in Kind

What value should be put on contributions in kind? One could argue for a number of possible values: the price the product would fetch on the world market; the opportunity cost of factors of production; the value in the domestic market of receiving country, etc. In general, "objective" considerations would lead one to value such surplus contributions at less than the market value in the producing country and possibly below world-market price, if the quantities involved would be large enough to affect the commodity's price when sold on the open market. There has been a good deal of analysis of the elasticity of demand for different agricultural products, and one could estimate the real value of contributions on the basis of elasticity coefficients.[10] It might be claimed that, in terms of an aid

[10] If the elasticities of demand are less than one, the total value of world marketing will decline; however, the valuation of the contribution in kind will still be positive.

definition that uses resource sacrifice as a criterion, the value should be still lower because the domestic surplus production reflects factor immobility in the producer country; there are no effective alternatives open to the factors of production.[11]

In practice most contributions in kind are U.S. farm products sold or granted under the provisions of PL 480. The United States now values its PL 480 contributions at world-market prices in the case of Title I sales (about 75 per cent of 1961 shipments), and at Commodity Credit Corporation (CCC) cost in the case of Title II and III shipments.[12] Title I shipments are sold for local currency; in 1961, 13.7 per cent of the revenues were earmarked for U.S. uses in the country. The rest of the proceeds are either granted or loaned to the host government to be used for economic development. Title II and III shipments are outright grants. Title I proceeds reserved for U.S. use are not included as aid here.[13] Title I grants are counted as grants; Title I "loans" are basically grants because the repayments cannot be used to buy other currencies or to export recipient's products; and the United States already has ample local currency for its own uses in the country. However, in the computations I have counted 20 per cent of these sums as loans and 80 per cent as grants, on the grounds that some of these currencies may eventually become convertible.

At what price should these contributions be valued? I have used two measures: (1) valuation of 1961 PL 480 shipments at 1961 world-market prices;[14] and (2) an estimate of the prices that would have prevailed if PL 480 shipments had been sold on world markets with the qualification that wheat prices would not be allowed to fall low enough to compete with feed grains. This meant that only 53 per cent of 1961 wheat and flour shipments

[11] This is the basis for observations that U.S. aid or Canadian aid should be valued at zero, because labor and capital are unemployed. It also is reflected in Kenen's testimony, which states that there is no sacrifice in aid if there are unemployed resources. This statement is not necessarily true if the alternative to aid is domestic works. It also ignores the fact that capital may depreciate faster if used than if left idle; and that some kinds of capital or labor in short supply act as a constraint on the productive use of scarce resources.

[12] This practice frequently gives absurd results. In 1962 the world price of wheat was about $60 per metric ton, while Title II exports of wheat were valued at about $150 per ton.

[13] They often have a grant element in countries where the reserved portion is far in excess of immediate U.S. neeeds, particularly where there is domestic inflation, not affected by a "maintenance of value" clause in the PL 480 agreement.

[14] The data submitted to DAC are based on local currency transfers, but shipments are probably a more accurate measure of aid value. Delays are frequent in the actual transfer of local currency to the U.S. authorities.

could have been sold at the price implicit in the demand elasticity assumed here (implicit export price of $1.36 per bushel). The rest of the wheat is valued at zero, because our existing stockpiles are large enough to take care of any likely future demand; and even if there were some slight probability of its being used, storage costs in the interim would outstrip its value.

It is true that world commercial demand for food would have been greater in the absence of PL 480; however, I have taken 1961 world prices as a point of departure for computing effects of selling PL 480 commodities in world markets, on the assumption that production adjustments in response to higher prices would soon bring world prices back to current levels.

Despite the obvious inaccuracy introduced by using estimated demand elasticities for U.S. exports as a method of computing values of PL 480 shipments, it probably comes closer to representing the real cost of PL 480 aid than does the world-market price. In 1961 PL 480 shipments made up a substantial percentage of world trade in a number of commodities (see Table 5–6).

TABLE 5–6: PUBLIC LAW 480 SHIPMENTS OF SELECTED COMMODITIES
AS PERCENTAGE OF WORLD TRADE, 1961

Commodity	1961 PL 480 Shipments (thousand metric tons)	1960 or 1961 World Trade (thousand metric tons)	PL 480 as Per Cent of World Trade
Wheat ⎱	8,467 ⎱	42,300[a]	25.9
Flour ⎰	2,475[a] ⎰		
Corn	1,362	11,800	11.5
Soybean and cottonseed oils	175	720	24.3
Dried milk	277	1,037[b]	26.7
Cotton	239	3,600	6.6

SOURCES: FAO, *Trade Yearbook, 1960* and *Monthly Bull. Agr. Econ. Stat.;* and U.S. Congress, House of Representatives, *15th Semiannual Report on Activities Carried on under Public Law 480, 83d Congress*, House Document No. 385, 87th Cong., 2d sess., April 1962.
[a] Wheat equivalent.
[b] Includes condensed and evaporated milk.

Tied Aid

Contributions in kind are a class of the larger category of tied aid. This is the commonest form in which the problem of valuation arises. Should contributions expendable only in one country be valued differently from contributions expendable anywhere in the world? Normally, these issues arise when a country faces balance-of-payments difficulties and wants to halt the drain on foreign exchange. They may also reflect a country's desire to increase national employment and income by assuring that orders be placed domestically.

Tied aid has two important effects from the donor's viewpoint: (1) It allows him to contribute without impairing his foreign-exchange position. (2) It may have favorable effects on domestic employment and income.

From the viewpoint of the recipient, tied aid reduces his freedom of choice among suppliers, possibly causing him to pay a higher price or accept inferior quality. (This need not necessarily be true if the donor country is an efficient producer of the goods being purchased.) In general, tying aid means that the total cost of aid in terms of world resource use is higher than it need be.

In the long run, then, there is good reason for encouraging untied aid to a maximum extent. One way to discourage countries in favorable balance-of-payments condition from tying their aid would be to apply discounts to the valuation of tied aid except when the donor is running balance-of-payments deficits. Normally, it is stated that balance-of-payments difficulties should affect only the form of aid, not its level. This pronouncement is subject to exception in countries that have a large import component in their aid exports. In a formal system, deficit countries would reduce their contributions now, and countries with favorable payments could increase theirs. When the deficit countries regained balance, they could reimburse the countries that paid out extra aid on their behalf.

Another form of tied aid is the tied purchase. This can take a number of forms, such as quantitative or tariff preference for the products of certain countries, which allows them to sell more or receive higher prices than they otherwise would, and purchase agreements under which the purchase price is above the world price. An example of the former is European Economic Community preference for the products of overseas territories; examples of the latter include the high prices France pays for imports of agricultural products from the franc zone, or that the United States pays for quota sugar imports. This is a sort of converse of tied aid. In a burden-sharing system, it should be added to the total value of donor's aid, as Mme. Betout-Mossé has done in the case of France. In practice, because of lack of data, I have not included it. Presumably, the appropriate measure is the difference between world prices and the actual purchase price. The effect of excluding such an arrangement is to reduce the relative contributions of France, and to a lesser extent of the United Kingdom and the United States, because France pays high prices for a number of commodities, while the United States and the United Kingdom normally pay more than the world price for sugar.

Tied contributions are more widespread than tied purchases. The appropriate discount to apply is the difference between the price charged for tied goods and their world-market price. Because of the difficulty of measuring this discount, and because all countries in practice do tie their contributions, I have not made a correction for tying in the section below entitled, "Computing the Value of Economic Aid."

Loans Repayable in Local Currency

Until the end of U.S. fiscal year 1961 (July 1961), a large proportion of U.S. loans to underdeveloped countries, made by the Development Loan Fund, were repayable in local currencies. In valuing these loans, some of the comments made about contributions in kind are applicable. In general, the United States was not allowed to use these funds for conversion to dollars or for imports of borrowers' goods and services. These loans, therefore, primarily have the character of a grant. Again, as in the case of PL 480 loans, there is some prospect that the United States may someday use these currency credits; consequently, most of it is treated as a grant and a small portion as a loan (80 per cent and 20 per cent, respectively), reflecting the relatively distant prospects of its availability for effective U.S. use.

Consolidation Credits

Consolidation credits are loans that enable the borrower to refinance existing international obligations at lower interest rates and longer terms. If the consolidation credit lender is the lender of the original obligation, then the additional sacrifice he has made by extending the consolidation credit is measured by the difference (in discounted present values) between the original and the new credit. If the lender advances the credit so that the borrower can pay off a variety of other creditors and repay the lender on easier terms, then the consolidation credit should be valued by the simple discounted present-value method. Because there is a lack of data on the terms of the refinanced credits, the latter method is used in this study.

Substitution between Aid and Defense

A special and potentially important aspect of the valuation of contributions is the substitution between contributions for defense and economic aid. It is clear that a defense dollar is not a perfect substitute for an aid dollar, despite the similarity of certain aims of defense and foreign-aid programs. If they were perfect substitutes, it would be immaterial whether the country spent its combined defense and aid appropriation on one of these purposes alone. Clearly, there is a diminishing rate of substitution in terms of some kind of national utility system.

Some countries, for domestic political reasons, may find it more acceptable to spend money on defense than on aid, or vice versa. In cases in which there are political barriers to transfer between the two categories, it is surely better in terms of burden-sharing goals to encourage expenditures in at least one category rather than risk having no increase at all through a stubborn insistence on one or the other. Some European countries have shown the greater reluctance toward increasing their economic aid contributions. This may be one argument for promoting a formula approach, which may furnish national governments with stronger arguments for increasing their economic aid contributions, even if self-levied and not paid into an international pool.

Another possible line of approach is to subtract defense expenditures from GNP, when economic aid contributions are being considered under ability-to-pay criteria. The effect would be to increase the "tax exemption" of countries that spend more on defense. The advantage of this method is that it does not consider defense and aid as perfect substitutes. The exact degree of substitution will depend on the progressiveness of the contributions system chosen for economic aid. One could adopt the same method in considering defense contributions; however, economic aid is such a small part of national income that the net effect on the progressiveness of defense contributions would be negligible.

The Basis for Comparing Contributions

Despite the uncertainties of the valuation methods outlined above—such as choice of interest rates for discounting, and the necessarily inexact nature of elasticity estimates in world commodity markets—it is an improvement on present DAC practice, because it aims to measure systematically the donors' sacrifices on a comparable basis for the various countries.

Once this is done, the computations can be used for rating donors' sacrifices, presumably by comparing their contributions with their national incomes or gross national products. It is theoretically preferable to make the comparison on the basis of real incomes rather than money incomes, because exchange rates do not accurately reflect the purchasing power of money in each country. The following section therefore includes comparisons of both real and money GNP to relative aid contributions.

Computing the Value of Economic Aid

This section estimates the cost of foreign aid in 1961 and 1962 for seven Western European countries, the United States, and Canada, on the basis of the criteria discussed above. To review briefly—

1. Nominal aid figures are as reported to DAC, except for United States B and United States C computations (see below).

For discounted computations, the following rules are used:

2. Grants are valued as aid at nominal value, except that in United States B and C commodity grants are discounted to reflect current world-market price or market-clearing price, respectively.

3. Loan interest and amortization streams are discounted, loan by loan, for each repayment year, at four alternative rates of interest:

> a. Each country's domestic long-term interest rate, equal to the mortgage rate, or to the long-term bond rate plus 1 per cent;
> b. 5.75 per cent—an approximation of the IBRD lending rate;
> c. 7.00 per cent—the highest average rate at which any DAC member makes long-term loans;
> d. 10.00 per cent—a rough approximation of the return on private investment in underdeveloped countries.

The total present value of each country's loans is subtracted from the total face value. The difference is the aid value of loans.

4. Loans repayable in borrowers' currency are discounted by the same method, but each loan is counted as 80 per cent granted, 20 per cent loan.

5. Consolidation credits are computed like any other loan.

6. No deductions are made for tied aid other than PL 480.

7. United States A, B, and C are computed as follows—

United States A:

    a. Dollar grants—as reported to DAC.

    b. Dollar loans—totals as reported to DAC.

    c. Transfer of resources for recipients' currency (PL 480, Title I)— as reported to DAC.

    d. Commodity grants (PL 480, Titles II and III)—as reported to DAC.

    e. Local currency repayable loans—as reported to DAC.

Category *c* was divided among loans and grants, as reported to DAC. Eighty per cent of the Title I "loans" were treated as grants and 20 per cent as loans, for reasons explained above. Category *e* loans were treated the same way. Category *d* grants were valued as reported by the U.S. Government, at CCC cost.

United States B: Categories *a*, *b*, and *e* were treated as in United States A. Category *c* includes the then-current world-market value of actual PL 480, Title I commodity shipments less the estimated value of local currency receipts retained for U.S. uses. Category *c* divides 1961 loans and grants: 42.7 per cent loan, 43.6 per cent grant, 13.7 per cent U.S. uses, as specified in 1961 U.S. Title I agreements (weighted average); the 1962 percentages are 64.2, 21.3, and 14.5, respectively. As in United States A, the "loans" are treated as 80 per cent grant, 20 per cent loan. Category *c* pays only the difference between shipping costs on U.S. vessels and those on foreign flag ships. Category *d* includes world-market value of Title II and III commodity shipments.

United States C: Categories *a*, *b*, and *e* were treated as in United States A. Categories *c* and *d* were treated as in United States B, with one difference. The commodities were valued at the estimated prices they might have brought if sold on world markets, as shown in Tables 5–16 and 5–17 (pp. 144–145), except that all wheat that could not have been sold at $1.36 or more per bushel was valued at zero (listed in the tables as "Wheat and flour B").

These special measures were necessary for PL 480 because Food for Peace exports form a large percentage of world trade in many products (see Table 5–6).

On the basis of these ground rules, the following computations were carried out:

1. Summary of official economic aid commitments as reported to DAC, 1961 and 1962 (Tables 5–7 and 5–8);
2. Comparison of these nominal aid totals to national GNP and relative GNP, both valued at official exchange rates (Tables 5–9 and 5–10);
3. Real values of 1961 and 1962 official aid using the discounted value method, compared to GNP (Tables 5–11 and 5–12);
4. Relative shares of discounted aid, 1961 and 1962 (Table 5–13);
5. Comparisons of 1961 and 1962 discounted aid shares with various proportional and progressive tax formulas based on real income (Tables 5–14 and 5–15);
6. Estimation of world-market values and market-clearing values of U.S. exports of PL 480 products (Appendix).

TABLE 5-7: DAC OFFICIAL ECONOMIC AID COMMITMENTS IN
1961 AS REPORTED BY MEMBERS
($ million equivalent)

Country	Bilateral Aid	Bilateral Grants	Bilateral Loans Repayable in: Lender Currency[a]	Bilateral Loans Repayable in: Borrower Currency	Contribution in Kind	Multilateral Aid[b]	Total Bilateral and Multilateral Aid
Canada	96	56	40			15	111
France[c]	913	787	126			73	990
Germany	472	125	347			73	545
Italy	205	29	176			16	217
Japan	338	81	257			9	347
Netherlands	40	34	6			44	84
Portugal	65	3	62			8	70
U.K.	424	150	274			40	464
U.S.	4,485	1,549	1,575	337	1,024[d]	285	4,770
Belgium[c]	71	71				23	94
Denmark	1	1				6	7
Norway	1	1				6	7
Total							7,706

SOURCE: Computed by author from OECD sources.

[a] Includes short-term (1–5 year) commitments as follows: Germany, 71; Italy, 141; Japan, 30; Portugal, 7; United Kingdom, 22; United States, 67.

[b] Excluding purchase of IBRD obligations.

[c] French and Belgian data reported on gross flow of funds basis; commitments data unavailable.

[d] Excluding $461 million in PL 480 grants, Titles II and III, reported under "Bilateral Grants."

TABLE 5–8: DAC OFFICIAL ECONOMIC AID COMMITMENTS IN 1962
AS REPORTED BY MEMBERS
($ million equivalent)

Country	Bilateral Aid	Bilateral Grants	Bilateral Loans Repayable in:		Contribution in Kind	Multilateral Aid[b]	Total Bilateral and Multilateral Aid
			Lender Currency[a]	Borrower Currency			
Canada	58	44	14			14	72
France[c]	918	772	146			116	1,034
Germany	469	151	315		3	29	498
Italy	131	19	112			6	137
Japan	287	104	183			9	296
Netherlands	41	11	30			22	63
Portugal	60	3	57			—	60
U.K.	557	159	398			14	571
U.S.	4,724	1,629	1,700	220	1,175[d]	251	4,975
Belgium	70	66	4			28	98
Denmark	2	1	1			8	10
Norway	4	4				7	11
Total							7,825

SOURCE: Computed by author from OECD sources.

[a] Includes short-term (1–5 year) loan commitments as follows: Denmark, 1.4; Germany, 41; Italy, 71; Japan, 22; United States, 69.

[b] Excluding purchase of IBRD obligations.

[c] French and Belgian data reported on gross flow-of-funds basis; commitments data unavailable.

[d] Excluding $555 million in PL 480 grants, Titles II and III, reported under "Bilateral Grants."

Before turning to a summary of the results, we should note some of the data problems:

1. All data (except for France and Belgium) are expressed on the basis of aid commitments by donors, not in terms of actual flow of funds. The totals are therefore greater than those shown in the OECD annual publication, *Development Assistance Efforts and Policies*. It was necessary to present the data on a commitment basis, however, because exact data on loan terms and conditions were not available on a flow-of-funds basis.

2. Data on the terms and conditions of each loan were obtained from OECD. The data were relatively complete (averaging 85 per cent of all loans) except for Italy and Portugal, which reported terms and conditions for only 57 and 33 per cent of their loans in 1962, and Japan, which reported about 20 per cent in 1961. In all cases except Japan (1961), loans for which no data were available were discounted at the weighted average terms and conditions for that country's loans. In 1961 for Japan, so few specific data were available that the estimate had to be based largely on official Japanese reports to DAC of typical terms and conditions.

TABLE 5-9: DAC AID COMMITMENTS COMPARED TO GNP, 1961 AND 1962
(Official exchange rates)

Country	1961				1962			
	GNP ($ million)	Aid ($ million)	Aid as Per Cent of GNP	Rank, Aid as Per Cent of GNP	GNP ($ million)	Aid ($ million)	Aid as Per Cent of GNP	Rank, Aid as Per Cent of GNP
Canada	34,050	111	0.33	10	37,000	72	0.19	11
France	62,610	990	1.58	2	68,580	1,034	1.51	2
Germany[a]	77,600	545	0.70	6	84,275	498	0.59	6
Italy[a]	35,000	217	0.62	8	38,400	137	0.36	9
Japan	47,700	347	0.72	5	52,700	296	0.56	7
Netherlands	12,260	84	0.69	7	13,100	63	0.48	8
Portugal	2,600	70	2.69	1	2,800	60	2.15	1
U.K.	75,000	464	0.62	8	79,115	571	0.72	5
U.S.	518,700	4,770	0.91	3	553,600	4,975	0.90	3
Belgium	12,670	94	0.74	4	13,400	98	0.73	4
Denmark	6,540	7	0.11	12	7,130	10	0.14	12
Norway	4,824	7	0.15	11	5,186	11	0.21	10
Total	889,554	7,706	(0.83)		955,286	7,825	(0.81)	

SOURCES: Tables 5-7 and 5-8, and data supplied to the author by the Agency for International Development.
[a] Excluding short-term loans, Italy and Germany show the following percentages:

Italy	1961	1962	Germany	1961	1962
Per cent of GNP	0.22	0.17	Per cent of GNP	0.61	0.54
Per cent of DAC aid	1.0	0.9	Per cent of DAC aid	6.3	5.9
Italy drops to rank	10	11	Germany drops to rank	9	8

TABLE 5-10: RELATIVE DAC AID SHARES COMPARED TO RELATIVE GNP,
1961 AND 1962
(Official exchange rates)

Country	1961		1962	
	GNP as Per Cent of DAC GNP	Aid as Per Cent of DAC Aid	GNP as Per Cent of DAC GNP	Aid as Per Cent of DAC Aid
Canada	3.8	1.4	3.9	0.9
France	7.0	12.9	7.2	13.2
Germany	8.7	7.1	8.8	6.4
Italy	3.9	2.8	4.0	1.8
Japan	5.4	4.5	5.5	3.8
Netherlands	1.4	1.1	1.4	0.8
Portugal	0.3	0.9	0.3	0.8
U.K.	8.4	6.0	8.3	7.3
U.S.	58.5	61.9	58.0	63.5
Belgium	1.4	1.2	1.4	1.3
Denmark	0.7	0.1	0.7	0.1
Norway	0.5	0.1	0.5	0.1

SOURCE: Table 5-9.

TABLE 5-11: DAC AID COMMITMENTS AND GNP, 1961; DISCOUNTED VALUE BASIS
(At official exchange rates, $ million equivalent)

Country	Nominal Value[a]	Own Interest Rate[b]	Discounted Value, Loans Discounted at: 5.75%	7.00%	10.00%	Own Interest Rate	Aid as Per Cent of GNP, Discounted at: 5.75%	7.00%	10.00%	Rank, Aid as Per Cent of GNP Discounted at Own Rate
Canada	136.9	71.0 (6.00%)	69.9	73.4	83.0	0.20	0.21	0.22	0.24	9
France	1,079.0	934.7 (6.00%)	931.5	946.4	973.3	1.49	1.49	1.51	1.55	1
Germany	531.5	258.6 (6.75%)	242.0	262.6	303.2	0.33	0.31	0.34	0.39	7
Italy	86.2	49.0 (6.20%)	48.2	50.3	534.5	0.14	0.14	0.14	0.16	11
Japan	317.3	114.3 (8.00%)	89.0	104.7	136.2	0.24	0.19	0.22	0.29	8
Netherlands	83.6	78.6 (5.25%)	78.9	79.5	80.5	0.64	0.64	0.65	0.66	3
Portugal	64.6	14.6 (5.00%)	17.2	21.0	28.4	0.56	0.66	0.81	1.09	5
U.K.	525.0	281.0 (7.30%)	247.0	275.0	326.1	0.38	0.33	0.37	0.44	6
U.S. A	4,714.0	3,125.0 (5.00%)	3,224.0	3,368.0	3,643.0	0.60	0.62	0.65	0.70	4
U.S. B	4,237.0	2,689.0 (5.00%)	2,785.0	2,924.0	3,182.0	0.52	0.54	0.56	0.61	(6)
U.S. C	3,874.0	2,372.0 (5.00%)	2,466.0	2,601.0	2,852.0	0.45	0.48	0.50	0.55	(6)
Belgium	94.0	94.0 (NA)	94.0	94.0	94.0	0.74	0.74	0.74	0.74	2
Denmark	7.0	7.0 (NA)	7.0	7.0	7.0	0.11	0.11	0.11	0.11	12
Norway	7.0	7.0 (NA)	7.0	7.0	7.0	0.15	0.15	0.15	0.15	10
Total with U.S. A	7,646.1	5,034.8	5,055.7	5,288.9	5,736.2	0.57	0.57	0.59	0.65	
Total with U.S. B	7,169.1	4,598.8	4,616.7	4,844.9	5,275.2	0.52	0.52	0.55	0.59	
Total with U.S. C	6,806.1	4,281.8	4,297.7	4,521.9	4,945.2	0.48	0.48	0.51	0.56	

SOURCES: OECD, *The Flow of Financial Resources to Developing Countries in 1961*; and author's computations.

NOTES: 1. United States A: aid totals as reported to DAC; local currency repayable loans and PL 480 loans included as 80 per cent grant, 20 per cent loan. United States B: aid totals include PL 480 shipments at world-market price. United States C: aid totals include actual PL 480 shipments at estimated value if actually sold on open market. 2. Domestic interest rates equal mortgage rate on long-term bond rate plus 1 per cent.

[a] Nominal values differ from Table 5–7, which is based on data not available when these computations were made. Also, most short-term loans were omitted from these computations; their real aid value is usually nearly zero.
[b] Each country's domestic long-term interest rate shown in parentheses.

TABLE 5–15: PERCENTAGE COMPARISON OF DISCOUNTED AID SHARE WITH BURDEN-SHARING FORMULAS, 1960 REAL-INCOME BASIS

| | Proportional Taxation | | Progressive Taxation of Real Income | | | | | | Commitments | |
| | | | Applied to Individuals | | | Applied to Nations | | | | |
Country	Nominal Income (1)	Real Income (2)	U.K. Rates (3)	German Rates (4)	U.S. Rates (5)	U.K. Rates (6)	German Rates (7)	U.S. Rates (8)	1962 Discounted Aid Share (9)	1962 Nominal Aid Share (10)
Canada	4.0	3.7	4.1	4.0	4.0	3.9	5.4	3.8	1.3	0.9
France	6.7	7.7	5.7	6.9	5.7	5.9	9.9	6.5	19.4	13.5
Germany	7.8	9.0	6.9	8.6	7.0	7.6	12.3	8.1	4.9	6.6
Italy	3.8	4.9	1.8	3.7	2.1	1.2	4.4	3.6	0.6	1.8
Japan	4.8	7.0	2.5	5.5	4.7	0.5	5.8	2.4	2.8	3.9
Netherlands	1.4	1.9	1.2	1.6	1.2	1.4	2.5	1.6	0.8	0.8
U.K.	8.7	9.4	7.6	8.9	7.5	7.7	12.3	8.2	4.5	7.5
U.S.	62.8	56.3	70.4	60.8	67.8	71.8	47.5	65.8	65.6	65.0

SOURCES: Kravis and Davenport, p. 323; and Tables 5–10 and 5–12. Portugal, Norway, Belgium, and Denmark excluded.

TABLE 5–13: AID AS PERCENTAGE OF DAC TOTALS, DISCOUNTED
VALUE BASIS, 1961–1962

| | Loans Discounted at: | | | | | | | | | | | |
| | Own Interest Rate | | | 5.75% | | | 7.00% | | | 10.00% | | |
Country	A	B	C	A	B	C	A	B	C	A	B	C
						1961						
Canada	1.4	1.5	1.7	1.4	1.6	1.7	1.4	1.6	1.7	1.3	1.4	1.6
France	18.6	20.5	22.5	18.4	20.0	22.3	17.9	19.6	21.4	17.0	18.3	20.3
Germany	5.1	5.6	6.2	4.8	5.2	5.9	5.0	5.4	6.0	5.3	5.8	6.4
Italy	1.0	1.0	1.2	0.9	1.1	1.2	1.0	1.1	1.1	1.1	1.1	1.2
Japan	2.3	2.4	2.7	1.8	2.0	2.2	2.0	2.2	2.6	2.4	2.6	2.8
Netherlands	1.6	1.7	1.9	1.6	1.8	2.0	1.5	1.7	1.6	1.4	1.6	1.7
Portugal	0.3	0.3	0.4	0.3	0.4	0.4	0.4	0.4	0.6	0.5	0.6	0.6
U.K.	5.6	6.1	6.8	4.9	5.4	6.0	5.2	5.7	6.2	5.7	6.2	6.9
U.S.	62.1	58.7	53.9	63.7	60.2	55.7	63.7	60.2	56.2	63.6	60.4	56.5
Belgium	1.9	2.0	2.2	1.9	2.1	2.2	1.8	2.0	2.2	1.6	1.8	1.9
Denmark	0.1	0.1	0.2	0.1	0.1	0.2	0.1	0.1	0.2	0.1	0.1	0.1
Norway	0.1	0.1	0.2	0.1	0.1	0.2	0.1	0.1	0.2	0.1	0.1	0.1
						1962						
Canada	1.1	1.3	1.3	1.1	1.2	1.3	1.1	1.2	1.3	1.0	1.1	1.2
France	16.8	19.0	20.0	16.8	18.8	19.8	16.2	18.2	19.0	15.4	17.1	17.8
Germany	4.4	4.9	5.2	4.2	4.8	5.0	4.6	5.1	5.4	5.1	5.7	5.9
Italy	0.5	0.6	0.6	0.5	0.6	0.6	0.5	0.6	0.6	0.5	0.6	0.6
Japan	2.4	2.7	2.8	2.1	2.3	2.5	2.2	2.4	2.5	2.3	2.5	2.6
Netherlands	0.7	0.8	0.8	0.7	0.8	0.8	0.7	0.8	0.8	0.7	0.8	0.9
Portugal	0.1	0.1	0.1	0.2	0.2	0.2	0.2	0.2	0.3	0.3	0.4	0.4
U.K.	3.9	4.4	4.6	3.0	3.4	3.6	3.7	4.2	4.4	4.8	5.3	5.6
U.S.	68.0	64.0	62.1	69.3	65.6	63.7	68.8	65.1	63.3	67.9	64.5	62.9
Belgium	1.7	2.0	2.1	1.7	2.0	2.1	1.7	1.9	2.0	1.5	1.6	1.7
Denmark	0.2	0.2	0.2	0.2	0.2	0.2	0.2	0.2	0.2	0.2	0.2	0.2
Norway	0.2	0.2	0.2	0.2	0.2	0.2	0.2	0.2	0.2	0.2	0.2	0.2

SOURCES: Tables 5–11 and 5–12.

NOTE: A, B, C denote totals with United States A, B, and C. Totals may not add to 100 per cent, because of rounding.

Actual computations were programmed and run off on an electronic computer.

3. In computing market-clearing values for PL 480 products (Appendix), analytical estimates of demand elasticities were unavailable for 10 to 15 per cent (by value) of the products. I arbitrarily set the elasticity values for most of these products at −1.0—which is too low—in order to be on the conservative side. This may have resulted in a slight underestimate (of less than 1 per cent) of the real value of U.S. aid.

4. Consolidation credits are treated here like any other loan; for reasons previously described in this chapter, this is an inexact procedure. Consolidation credits form a very small percentage of all loans, however.

5. The 1961 data do not include short-term loans, because no data on terms and conditions were available. Normally, the aid value of these loans is close to zero.

TABLE 5–14: DISCOUNTED AID SHARES, 1961 AND 1962,
COMPARED WITH REAL GNP, 1961

Country	1961 Real GNP ($ million equivalent)[a]	Share of Total Real DAC GNP, 1961 (%)	Share of DAC Aid Discounted 1961 (%)	Share of DAC Aid Discounted 1962 (%)
Canada	36.9	3.85	1.5	1.3
France	78.1	8.14	20.5	19.0
Germany	90.8	9.47	5.6	4.9
Italy	49.8	5.19	1.0	0.6
Japan	72.5	7.56	2.4	2.7
Netherlands	18.3	1.91	1.7	0.8
Portugal	3.5	0.36	0.3	0.1
U.K.	89.3	9.31	6.1	4.4
U.S.	520.1	54.22	58.7	64.0
Total	959.3			

SOURCES: Real income, from Appendix, Chapter 3; at geometric mean of U.S. and national weights. Discounted aid values from Tables 5–11 and 5–12 "Own Interest Rate B."

[a] 1961 real-income data not available for Belgium, Denmark, and Norway. DAC aid shares shown here are therefore slightly larger than shown in Table 5–13.

With these qualifications in mind, we can summarize the results of the computations.

First, for most countries, there is a wide discrepancy between the real cost of aid and aid totals as reported to DAC. Only Canada and France—countries whose aid is preponderantly in the form of grants—show essentially the same aid value whether their aid is valued as reported to DAC or as discounted by their domestic long-term interest rates. Therefore, the rank of each country as an aid donor (in percentage of GNP) rises in relation to other countries: France from second to first by a wide margin, and Canada, a small donor, from twelfth to tenth. Portugal and Germany, who offer loans rather than grants, show a sharp fall in the ratio of aid to GNP by the criteria of Table 5–12, compared to totals reported in Table 5–8.

Second, the real value of total Western aid discounted by any of the interest rates used here is much smaller than official reporting systems indicate.

Total reported aid in 1962 was $7.8 billion; real cost varied, depending on the discount rate, from $5.4 to $6.1 billion as valued by totals including United States A; $4.8 to $5.5 billion, including United States B (which values U.S. food aid at world-market prices rather than at the higher CCC

TABLE 5-12: DAC Aid Commitments and GNP, 1962; Discounted Value Basis
(At official exchange rates, $ million equivalent)

Country	Nominal Value[a]	Discounted Value, Loans Discounted at:				Aid as Per Cent of GNP, Discounted at:				Rank, Aid as Per Cent of GNP Discounted at Own Rate
		Own Interest Rate[b]	5.75%	7.00%	10.00%	Own Interest Rate	5.75%	7.00%	10.00%	
Canada	73.1	58.8 (6.10%)	58.8	59.8	60.8	0.16	0.16	0.16	0.16	10
France	1,034.6	908.4 (6.00%)	907.4	917.4	937.4	1.32	1.32	1.34	1.37	1
Germany	497.4	231.4 (6.00%)	225.7	251.6	301.2	0.27	0.27	0.30	0.36	4
Italy	137.1	27.7 (6.25%)	25.7	29.7	31.7	0.07	0.07	0.08	0.08	12
Japan	295.6	128.7 (8.30%)	110.7	119.7	139.7	0.24	0.21	0.23	0.27	7
Netherlands	63.5	35.4 (5.20%)	37.4	39.4	44.4	0.27	0.29	0.30	0.34	4
Portugal	60.2	6.2 (5.00%)	9.2	12.2	19.2	0.22	0.33	0.44	0.69	8
U.K.	570.4	210.8 (7.00%)	166.8	210.8	290.8	0.27	0.21	0.27	0.37	4
U.S. A	4,975.0	3,661.0 (5.00%)	3,759.0	3,897.0	4,139.0	0.66	0.68	0.70	0.75	(3)
U.S. B	4,383.0	3,069.0 (5.00%)	3,167.0	3,305.0	3,547.0	0.55	0.57	0.60	0.64	(3)
U.S. C	4,145.0	2,830.0 (5.00%)	2,928.0	3,064.0	3,306.0	0.51	0.53	0.55	0.60	(3)
Belgium[c]	98.0	94.0 (NA)	94.0	94.0	94.0	0.70	0.70	0.70	0.70	2
Denmark[c]	10.0	9.0 (NA)	9.0	9.0	9.0	0.13	0.13	0.13	0.13	11
Norway	11.0	11.0 (NA)	11.0	11.0	11.0	0.21	0.21	0.21	0.21	9
Total with U.S. A	7,825.9	5,382.4	5,414.7	5,651.6	6,078.2	0.56	0.57	0.59	0.64	
Total with U.S. B	7,233.9	4,790.4	4,822.7	5,059.6	5,486.2	0.50	0.51	0.53	0.57	
Total with U.S. C	6,995.9	4,551.4	4,583.7	4,811.6	5,245.2	0.48	0.48	0.50	0.55	

SOURCE: Computed by author from OECD sources.

NOTES: See Table 5-11.

a Totals may differ slightly from Table 5-8 because of rounding. Short-term loans included.

b Each country's domestic long-term interest rate shown in parentheses.

c No data on loan terms available. Loans (Belgium $4 million, Denmark $1 million) are counted at zero aid value throughout.

costs used in official submissions); or \$4.6 to \$5.2 billion including United States C (which values food aid at market-clearing prices). In terms of percentage of donors' combined GNP, valued in U.S. dollars, the nominal value of the nine countries' combined aid was 0.81 per cent of combined GNP in 1962. This is not far from the target of 1 per cent of GNP for flow of funds to less developed countries, proposed by a UN General Assembly resolution in 1960. When valued by the methods of Table 5–12, however, the aid value falls to a range of 0.48 to 0.64 per cent of combined GNP, depending on the discount rate used and the method of valuing U.S. food grants.

Third, the U.S. aid share in 1962 is about 64 per cent of the total of either combined nominal aid or of combined discounted aid, using United States B totals. This means that the relatively generous terms of U.S. aid offset the overvaluation of food grants. If United States C totals (allowing for lower market prices resulting from free-market sales of U.S. surpluses) are used, the U.S. relative contribution is 62 per cent of combined discounted totals. In 1962 the United States shifted to a new lending policy based on long-term, low-interest loans (30 to 40 years at $3/4$ of 1 per cent interest). This policy resulted in a relatively larger real contribution, as Table 5–13 indicates. Some of the increase in U.S. shares in 1962 compared to 1961 is also accounted for by the relative increase in nominal shares (Table 5–10), but the relative increase in discounted aid is much larger than that in nominal aid. Beginning with commitments made in U.S. fiscal year 1964, the aid legislation has specified a minimum interest rate of $2\frac{1}{2}$ per cent, so that the grant element of U.S. loans is presumably smaller now than it was in 1962.

Fourth, the distribution of contributions seems to be only loosely related to such measures of equity as per capita GNP. Thus, in 1962 the two poorest countries, Italy and Portugal, are far down on the list of contributors by discounted value methods, but the United States and Canada rank third and tenth, respectively, in terms of GNP ratios. Table 5–9, a comparison of aid totals on a nominal basis, ranks Belgium, France, Portugal, and the United Kingdom relatively high as aid donors by per cent of GNP, indicating a possible link between colonial traditions and aid levels. By the criteria of Tables 5–11 and 5–12, however, Portugal and the United Kingdom drop down to the modal level of contributions (about 0.25 per cent of 1962 GNP discounted at own interest rates). Perhaps the appropriate inference is that countries with long colonial traditions feel obliged to make at least a show of offering substantial aid. It should be remembered, however, that the present official system overstates combined aid totals by more than 50 per cent. Among major donors only France, and to a lesser degree the United States, emerge with real aid totals relatively close to the levels reported officially.

Finally, is the United States carrying more than its share of the aid burden? If we use nominal GNP as the basis for valuing contributions, the answer seems to be no. The United States has increased its relative share since 1960 (see Table 3–19), but the contribution is not notably larger than its proportion of DAC members' GNP. As soon as we introduce progressiveness in the tax base, it might be argued that the United States is underpaying relatively.

When we shift from a nominal income tax base to one based on real income (Tables 5–14 and 5–15), there is a stronger argument for claiming that the United States is paying its fair share. But the argument that it is overpaying is in no case overwhelming unless we insist on proportional or regressive tax rates as optimal—an argument the United States supports in international organizations, but is not usually accepted in domestic taxation. The German tax rate shown in Table 5–15 is an example of the latter. It is regressive at low-income levels; thus when German taxes are applied to per capita income (Col. 7), the U.S. contribution is low. When they are applied to individuals according to the actual income distribution, the net effect on real income is mildly progressive.[15]

Conclusions

The conclusions that can be drawn from the data, both for the United States and for other countries, are all fairly obvious.

1. In terms of real cost, the United States is doing significantly less than its DAC submissions indicate. Other major donors, except France, overstate their aid values even more. Some minor donors (Canada, Belgium, Denmark, Norway) overstate aid values relatively little.

2. The methods now used to value PL 480 aid result in important overstatements of U.S. contributions. United States C yields values for agricultural commodities of no more than half the amounts stated to DAC.

[15] For a description of the methods by which Table 5–15 was computed, see pp. 64–65.

3. To the extent that some countries provide their aid in the form of loans (particularly loans at high rates of interest), their actual contributions will be less as a proportion of GNP than they appear to be, and there will be systematic differences among countries in the degree of overstatement. This overstatement is particularly evident in the cases of the United Kingdom, Germany, Italy, and Portugal. Some countries, notably France, Canada, and Belgium, which offer mostly grants, are relatively unaffected by changing from a nominal value to a discounted value basis in aid computations.

4. This suggests that DAC reviews would benefit from considering aid contributions on some such basis as set forth here. It also reinforces the case for providing aid in the form of grants and long-term, low-interest loans.

5. In terms of burden sharing, the contention that the United States is overpaying is not strongly supported, but a number of tentative conclusions do emerge. France is clearly paying far more than its share by any criterion. Denmark, Norway, Italy, Canada, the United Kingdom, and Germany are paying too little by any criterion shown here. Belgium and the United States are paying about the right amount: too little by highly progressive criteria, too much by the proportional standard (Table 5–15).

6. A more thorough effort at valuing real costs would include a discount for tied aid, as discussed above under the heading "The Valuation of Economic Aid Contributions." Because all countries tie their aid, however, it is unlikely that rankings would be greatly affected, although real costs would certainly decline, as the analysis of PL 480 aid demonstrated. Even so, this is an extreme case; in general, it seems safe to assume that overstatement of aid values through tying is considerably less than the PL 480 results imply. The United States values about one-third of its food aid at two to three times the world-market price. Furthermore, it is the only country whose tied aid is a large proportion of world trade in some commodities. For most countries' tied aid, market-clearing prices would not be significantly below world prices, nor would domestic prices typically be such large multiples of world prices as is the case for a large fraction of PL 480 exports.

APPENDIX, Chapter 5

Tables 5–16 and 5–17 show the method that was used to compute market-clearing prices for PL 480 commodities in 1961 and 1962. The world-trade quantities were taken from the Food and Agriculture Organization (FAO), *Monthly Bulletin of Agricultural Economics and Statistics* (or the 1962 FAO *Trade Yearbook*). Where figures appeared to be unusually high or low, a three-year average was taken.

Total PL 480 market-clearing value, setting a minimum export price for wheat of $1.36 per bushel ("Wheat and flour B") is $729 million in 1961

TABLE 5–16: PUBLIC LAW 480 SHIPMENTS, 1961, VALUED AT 1961 WORLD-MARKET PRICES AND AT ESTIMATED MARKET-CLEARING PRICES

Commodity	1961 Shipments (000 metric tons)	Market-clearing Price ($ per metric ton)	Market-clearing Values ($million)	1961 Export Price ($ per metric ton)	Export Value at 1961 Price ($ million)	1960 or 1961 World Trade (000 metric tons)	Assumed Demand Elasticity
Wheat and flour A	10,942	42.86	469.0	60.41	661.0	42,300	−0.7
Wheat and flour B	(10,942)	(50.00)	290.0		(350.4)[a]		
Barley	319.6	45.40	14.5	47.18	15.1	6,200	−1.3
Corn	1,362.3	44.74	60.9	48.61	66.2	11,800	−1.3
Sorghum	117.6	39.36	4.7	41.17	4.8	2,304	−1.3
Rice	395.1	105.03	41.1	109.90	43.4	7,000	−1.0
Fats and oils	175.4	237.30	41.6	294.96[b]	51.7	720[e]	−1.0
Poultry	0.4	761.53	0.3	761.53	0.3	153	([d])
Dried milk	276.8	121.74	33.7	155.52	43.1	1,037	−1.0
Tobacco	12.1	1,652.14	20.0	1,679.00	20.3	760	−1.0
Cotton	239.2	613.09	146.7	624.90	149.5	3,600	−3.3
Tallow	5.4	194.93	1.1	196.30	1.1	856	−1.0
Pulses	14.5	147.20	2.2	149.00	2.2	1,180	−1.0
Shortening	33.5	271.05	9.1	271.05	9.1	NA	([d])
Fruits	3.7	180.00	0.6	180.00	0.6	NA	([d])
Ocean freight (Titles II and III)			62.6		62.6		
Total					1,131.0		
Total with wheat and flour A			908.1				
Total with wheat and flour B			729.1				

SOURCES: U.S. Congress, House of Representatives, *14th and 15th Semiannual Reports on Activities Carried on under Public Law 480, 83rd Congress,* House Document No. 223, 87th Cong., 1st sess; House Document No. 385, 87th Cong., 2d sess. Elasticities estimated by the author, except for wheat (K. W. Meinken, *Demand and Price Structure for Wheat*), feed grains, fats and oils, and cotton (G. E. Brandow, *Interrelations among Demands for Farm Products and Implications for Control of Market Supply*). World trade from FAO, *Monthly Bull. Agr. Econ. Stat.,* and USDA, *Agricultural Marketing Service Reports.*

NOTE: Does not include transactions under barter provisions of PL 480, Title III, valued at $78.6 million, or loans under Title IV, valued at $5 million. Title II data available only on authorization basis; shipment figures may have varied somewhat.

[a] Figures in parentheses do not appear in column total.

[b] Weighted average of soybean oil and cottonseed oil prices.

[e] Soybean oil and cottonseed oil only.

[d] Market-clearing prices assumed unchanged from actual 1961 prices.

TABLE 5–17: PUBLIC LAW 480 SHIPMENTS, 1962, VALUED AT WORLD-MARKET PRICES AND AT ESTIMATED MARKET-CLEARING PRICES

Commodity	Quantity (000 metric tons)		Price ($ per metric ton)		Value ($ million)		
	1962 PL 480 Shipments	1962 World Trade	Market-clearing Price	1962 Export Price	Market-clearing Value	Export Value at 1962 Price	Assumed Demand Elasticity
Wheat and flour A[a]	11,500	46,822[b]	45.05	62.46	518.1	688.3	−0.7
Wheat and flour B[a]			50.00		379.9	(688.3)[c]	(−0.7)
Corn and meal[d]	993	13,766[e]	45.61	48.10	45.3	43.0	−1.3
Barley	397	7,330	52.85	55.02	21.0	21.8	−1.3
Sorghum	70	2,373	44.11	45.10	3.1	3.2	−1.3
Fats and oils[f]	370	579	176.83	290.00	65.4	107.0	−1.0
Lard	51	554	255.92	281.23	13.0	14.3	−1.0
Dried milk	272	653	93.73	132.05	29.5	35.3	−1.0
Evaporated and condensed milk	62	522	391.60	441.16	24.3	27.5	
Dry beans	55.2	1,341	172.00	180.00	9.4	9.9	−1.0
Cotton	219	780	579.22	620.42	126.8	135.8	−3.3
Tobacco	14	868	1,606.24	1,632.19	22.1	22.1	−1.0
Poultry	1.7			640.90	1.1	1.1	
Dried eggs	0.01	NA		3,000.00	0.0	0.0	(g)
Canned fruits	0.2	NA		344.63	0.1	0.1	(g)
Fresh fruits	1.0	NA		111.50	0.2	0.3	(g)
Rice	566	6,138	125.86	136.37	71.2	77.1	−1.0
Miscellaneous dairy products	104	NA	NA	NA	27.8	27.8	(g)
Ocean freight					64.7	64.7	
Total						1,279.2	
Total with wheat and flour A					1,038.6		
Total with wheat and flour B					900.4		

SOURCES: U.S. Congress, House of Representatives, *16th and 17th Semiannual Reports on Activities Carried on under Public Law 480, 83rd Congress,* House Document No. 526, 87th Cong., 2d sess.; and House Document No. 79, 88th Cong., 1st sess. Other sources as in Table 5–16.

NOTE: Does not include transactions under barter provisions of PL 480, Title III, valued at $75.3 million; or transactions under Title IV for which no data on shipments were available (authorizations totaled about $90 million at export market prices, or roughly $70 million at market-clearing prices). Since Title IV shipments are dollar-repayable loans, the operative price is world-market price (= sales price).

[a] Includes flour in wheat equivalent.
[b] And bulgur wheat equivalent of flour.
[c] Figures in parentheses do not appear in column total.
[d] Includes cornmeal in corn equivalent.
[e] And cornmeal equivalent of corn.
[f] Cottonseed, soybean, and linseed oils.
[g] Market-clearing price equals actual export price.

($900 million in 1962). At this price only 53 per cent of 1961 PL 480 wheat shipments could have been sold on the world market at the assumed demand elasticities (66 per cent of 1962 sales). At lower prices, wheat would have competed with feed grains, and demand would have been much more elastic, but I have not computed the values for feed grains because it seems very unlikely that such competition would, in fact, be allowed by the producing countries. The "Wheat and flour A" computations show the price at which *all* PL 480 wheat could have been sold at a demand elasticity of −0.7.

CHAPTER

6

Burden Sharing and Commodity Policy[1]

In this study, we have been primarily concerned so far with "direct" burden sharing—arrangements by which countries contribute to a common budget, or spend directly for defense or foreign-aid budgets.

We have occasionally (as in Chapters 3 and 5) discussed the aid effects of trade, but have concluded that on the whole, and despite their great importance, they should not be included as part of economic aid in burden-sharing discussions, because of difficulties of conception and measurement.

One form of trade, however, clearly constitutes aid and should be included in any discussion of burden sharing. This is what Chapter 3 referred to as "tied purchases"—purchases in which a country deliberately pays more than the open-market price for imports, either directly or through a subsidy system. No matter how it is justified—whether as a method of orderly marketing, or of maintaining equitable terms of trade or parity prices—it involves a transfer of resources in excess of what would be necessary to buy the goods, and is therefore a form of economic aid.

Alternative Commodity Policies

Aid through tied purchases commonly takes the form of commodity agreements, because commodity trade accounts for over 85 per cent of the value of underdeveloped countries' exports (see Table 1–2). Normally, these agreements attempt to maintain high prices by restricting exports.

[1] Much of this chapter previously appeared as *Commodity Policy and Economic Development*, The RAND Corporation, Santa Monica, Calif., RM–3887–ISA, October 1963.

Since demand is price-inelastic, the result of successful restriction is to raise total export revenues. In bilateral arrangements, such as those between France and her former colonies, there may be no explicit quantitative restrictions; such restrictions are simply implied by fixing a price and, if necessary, by instituting an informal allocation system among producers. In multilateral arrangements, it is usually necessary to assign each exporter a quota based on past exports. The system, as expressed in the International Coffee Agreement, for example, is somewhat analogous to the U.S. agricultural price support system in assigning each exporter a marketing quota, with the total of individual quotas aimed at meeting some target price. Some international agreements, such as the Tin Agreement, include buffer stocks, roughly analogous to the Commodity Credit Corporation stocks in the United States.

Another method of using commodity markets as a device to transfer aid operates through subsidy payments. Commodities are sold at their market prices and the seller (or the exporting country, in the case of international commodity agreements) receives a cash subsidy aimed at bringing him to some average income level or to some implied average price level. This is the method used to support wool farmers' incomes in the United States and most commercial farmers' incomes in the United Kingdom.

This study discusses primarily the price-fixing version of commodity agreements. For policy purposes this approach seemed preferable, because adoption of the subsidy approach is extremely unlikely. The United States, the principal financer of such programs, has never been willing to adopt domestic farm subsidies, and would probably be most unwilling to subsidize foreign agricultural output by direct subsidy. Price fixing, on the other hand, has a long history in domestic and international commodity policies. It is often unpopular but often accepted.

Subsidies or deficiency payments, even if accepted, are all too clearly a form of economic aid. In voting aid credits, parliaments would presumably view subsidy payments as virtually a perfect substitute for aid. Price-fixing agreements, once in operation, tend to produce the appearance of being the result of market forces. Thus, if the objective is to increase the total aid flow, price-fixing agreements are likely to be preferable, even though they offer a number of economic disadvantages.

In terms of welfare objectives, however, subsidies may often be preferable. Before we go on to discuss price-fixing methods in more detail, it may be worthwhile to point out the welfare disadvantages of such a system compared to a direct subsidy. The diagram below compares the results of a system of price supports and of subsidy payments.

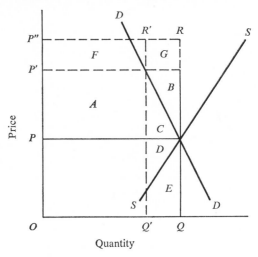

OP is equilibrium price, *OP'* is price-fixing price, *OQ* is equilibrium quantity, and *OQ'* is quantity demanded by the market at price of *OP'*. If the price-fixing program includes a buffer stock purchased by the fund, producers' revenue will be *OP'* × *OQ*.[2] This is larger than equilibrium revenues by the amount *A* + *B* + *C*. It costs the buffer stock *B* + *C* + *D* + *E* to increase revenues this much, and costs the public *A* more to buy the quantity *OQ'* than it would have cost in a free market. To consume *OQ'*, the public is therefore directly or indirectly paying *A* + *B* + *C* + *D* + *E* more than it should pay at equilibrium prices. Under a subsidy system, which bases payments on a target price *OP'*, the public consumes *OQ* at an additional total cost, compared to equilibrium revenues (*OP* × *OQ*), of *A* + *B* + *C* only.

Direct buffer-stock payments in the first case are *B* + *C* + *D* + *E*; in the second case, subsidy payments are *A* + *B* + *C*. The latter amount will always be larger than the former if demand is inelastic. It is therefore sometimes claimed that subsidies are more expensive than price fixing, but the claim is obviously untrue if excess public and private costs combined are included.

---

[2] For a similar analysis, see L. D. Howell, "Benefits versus Costs of Price Supports," *Quarterly Journal of Economics*. Vol. 68, February 1954, pp. 115–130. The diagram is taken from his article.

Of course, the scheme does not have to include a buffer stock (if there is provision for export control). In that case, a price-fixing scheme will not cost the buffer-stock agency anything.[3] But it will still cost the public more than it should by the amount A, while gross revenues increase only by A minus $(D + E)$.[4] Furthermore, because retail markups are often based on a percentage of cost, the public will probably pay a price such as OP'', so that the increase in the public's costs will be considerably greater than the increase in producers' revenues. Under a subsidy system, there will be no pyramiding of markups. The public's cost will equal OP' times OQ. In a welfare sense, price-fixing schemes mean that the public directly or indirectly pays more than the seller receives in increased income, while in a subsidy scheme the two magnitudes are equal. In a subsidy scheme, the buyer pays more than he should for what he wants; in a price-fixing scheme he pays more than he should for less than he wants, particularly if there is a buffer stock. From the sellers' viewpoint, net revenues under the two schemes will be the same if sales are equal and subsidies are set on the basis of price OP'. But buyers will always be worse off in the aggregate under a price-fixing scheme, because they pay the same amount for less goods than they could have under a subsidy.

Despite the theoretical advantages of a subsidy scheme, we will not consider it further here; the rest of this chapter will discuss price-fixing agreements. It should be clear, however, that these agreements are not being proposed as an optimum. They are simply a device for transferring aid from rich to poor countries without going through a formal appropriations process. There may be political motives in both donor and recipient countries that would make such a policy advisable. In that case, as the following discussion emphasizes, workable commodity agreements will be difficult to achieve.

Finally, there are a number of alternative "tax" methods by which price-fixing agreements can operate under an export restriction scheme. They all involve raising market prices, but the actual mechanism can be in the form of export taxes levied in the underdeveloped countries (including marketing board retentions); import taxes in the developed countries, reserved for economic aid; an international commodity council tax spent by agreement of importers and exporters; or, finally, no tax

---

[3] A successful price-fixing policy will require someone to hold stocks, however, as pointed out below under the heading, "Proposals for Commodity Policy."

[4] Net revenues increase by A minus D.

device at all may be built into the system. This chapter discusses primarily the straight price-fixing version; the choice of particular tax schemes is a matter of political convenience.

The Commodity Trade of Developing Countries

A Survey of Recent Trends, by Commodity

We have already pointed out (Chapter 1) that underdeveloped countries' earnings from commodity trade were stagnant from 1954 to 1963. Furthermore, until the end of 1963, there was a clear movement against them in the aggregate terms of trade. The United Nations index for underdeveloped countries' commodity export prices fell from 100 in 1953 to 90 in 1961. During the same period, the export price index for manufactured goods rose from 100 to 109.[5] Analysis of the index components shows that a few commodities affect the index heavily: falling prices for coffee, cocoa, tea, and sugar accounted for more than 90 per cent of the decline in the 32-commodity index. The prices of some products (rubber, jute, tin) rose during the period, partly offsetting the 13-point decline caused by falling prices for coffee, cocoa, sugar, cotton, and rice.

The fact that a handful of commodities exert so preponderant an effect on the index implies that they may be the key ones for any program aimed at raising commodity export earnings. In 1953 coffee, cocoa, sugar, cotton, and rice accounted for 55 per cent of the value of commodity exports in the UN index, excluding petroleum.[6] By 1959 their prices had fallen faster than those of the other components and accounted for only 42 per cent of the value of nonpetroleum exports in the index.

An effective commodity policy requires not only that we concentrate on major products where possible, but also on products that are important to the economies of the countries we want to help. Here we find a number of different trends in operation.

Some countries export tropical products, such as cocoa, coffee, tea, bananas, rubber, and jute, and face no trade competition from developed

---

[5] UN, *Monthly Bull. Stat.*, June 1962.

[6] The 1953 index includes only 32 commodities exported by developing countries. There is a large number of other commodities, exported in relatively small amounts; if they were all included in the totals, the 1953 and 1959 percentages of the five commodities would be about 48 and 34 per cent, respectively.

countries, although substitutes threaten some of their industrial raw materials. In general, these countries depend heavily on crop exports for foreign exchange. A considerable number of countries rely on one or more of these six products for over 75 per cent of their export earnings. These include such Latin American countries as Colombia, Ecuador, and Guatemala; such African countries as the Ivory Coast, Ghana, and Cameroons; and such Asian nations as Ceylon and Malaya. For many other countries, such as Brazil and Ethiopia, trade in these noncompeting tropical products provides half or more of total export earnings. In 1960 these six noncompeting crops accounted for $5 billion in export earnings, or about 30 per cent of the total value of underdeveloped countries' commodity exports, excluding petroleum. The earnings level for these crops was virtually unchanged from the 1953–1954 average. Prices of all the commodities, except rubber and jute, fell during the period, but the tendency was for increases in the volume of trade to compensate partially for declining prices. (See Tables 6–1 and 6–2.)

Sugar and rice are produced both in industrialized and underdeveloped countries, but are exported preponderantly by underdeveloped countries. The export prices of these two crops have also fallen sharply. Export revenues from rice have fallen by 20 per cent since 1953; revenues from sugar have risen somewhat, reflecting the rising trend of world consumption.[7] Most of the production in industrialized countries is subsidized; probably not much of it could be maintained without subsidies and tariffs. It has been estimated that abolition of customs duties on sugar, but not of domestic subsidies, would mean the end of most sugar production in Europe and Japan. Germany, Sweden, and the United States protect their sugar industries primarily by import quotas, and presumably these industries would also suffer greatly in the absence of quota protection. The annual increase in imports into Europe and Japan in the event of abolition of tariffs and charges, under conditions existing in 1959, would have been more than $400 million (see Table 6–7, p. 168). The principal exporters are Cuba, Taiwan, the Philippines, Brazil, and Peru. Smaller countries, such as British Guiana and Jamaica, also rely on the sugar trade.

Rice presents a special case. Underdeveloped countries are not only the principal exporters but also the principal importers. As with sugar, the

[7] In 1963 there was a sharp rise in the world price of sugar, followed by a sharp decline in mid-1964. The discussion of sugar price and policy here assumes that such rises are temporary.

TABLE 6-1: VALUE OF EXPORTS OF SELECTED COMMODITIES, 1953–1961
(In $ million)

Commodity	Area	1953	1954	1955	1956	1957	1958	1959	1960	1961
			A. Agricultural Products							
Sugar	UDW[a]	1,014	913	994	1,034	1,368	1,179	1,034	1,184	1,209
	World[b]	1,264	1,165	1,257	1,283	1,707	1,411	1,249	1,425	1,466
Tobacco	UDW	246	277	267	295	303	323	297	331	NA[c]
	World	729	716	786	771	887	828	796	848	922
Cotton	UDW	1,305	1,330	1,357	1,262	1,028	1,039	1,065	1,002	1,047
	World	1,886	2,167	1,875	2,011	2,252	1,729	1,643	2,151	2,065
Rice	UDW	560	492	470	468	504	458	407	426	446
	World	751	617	562	516	681	567	516	552	571
Oranges and tangerines	UDW	55	75	85	96	133	144	121	137	NA
	World	221	241	258	256	309	317	286	331	344[d]
Soybeans	UDW	5	5	8	7	4	6	6	2	NA
	World	129	140	186	192	226	213	292	343	NA
Groundnuts	UDW	155	184	154	205	185	214	185	173	NA
	World	160	203	162	218	203	222	195	186	NA
Olive oil	UDW	26	69	26	30	49	32	45	23	NA
	World	59	112	66	88	97	65	78	111	NA
Coconut oil	UDW	77	75	72	80	75	69	76	75	NA
	World	97	94	81	93	91	87	93	99	NA
Palm oil	UDW	104	107	108	122	120	117	118	113	NA
	World	108	112	111	125	123	120	121	116	NA
Linseed oil	UDW	37	47	52	39	45	51	54	48	NA
	World	77	86	73	72	74	60	59	60	NA
Linseed	UDW	15	8	5	6	6	5	7	13	NA
	World	31	51	56	85	100	67	79	79	NA
Palm kernel oil	UDW	5	7	9	11	14	15	22	16	NA
	World	16	17	15	14	18	21	34	24	NA
Soybean oil	UDW	0	0	0	0	0	0	2	5	NA
	World	12	21	32	130	134	145	130	144	NA
Groundnut oil	UDW	66	67	97	73	78	78	74	85	NA
	World	76	85	115	105	103	95	89	99	NA
Coffee	(e)	2,363	2,453	2,193	2,326	2,154	2,003	1,913	1,874	1,804
Tea	(e)	456	630	565	607	565	613	578	589	547

Commodity	Area	1953	1954	1955	1956	1957	1958	1959	1960	1961
Cocoa	(e)	482	743	572	434	441	544	549	520	469
Rubber	(e)	808	793	1,401	1,371	1,132	991	1,394	1,404	1,177
Jute	(e)	176	169	188	161	170	185	159	187	213
Bananas	(e)	271	271	304	311	350	330	333	354	329
Palm kernels	(e)	122	113	96	98	86	99	122	115	NA
Copra	(e)	251	263	226	248	247	250	275	271	NA
UDW subtotal		8,599	9,091	9,249	9,284	9,057	8,745	8,836	8,947	
World total		10,545	11,262	11,180	11,515	12,150	10,962	10,983	11,882	
B. Metals										
Copper ore	UDW	35	42	74	94	56	49	52	935	NA
	World	84	94	128	152	106	74	85	2,035	NA
Copper metal	UDW	425	663	869	1,017	741	588	857	—	NA
	World	948	1,293	1,677	1,998	1,574	1,505	1,705	—	NA
Tin ore	UDW	165	196	179	189	181	109	137	325	NA
	World	165	196	179	189	181	109	137	447	NA
Tin metal	UDW	134	142	146	165	153	98	103	—	NA
	World	274	261	260	280	275	210	274	—	NA
Zinc ore	UDW	30	31	46	65	61	32	39	73	NA
	World	69	63	84	109	98	64	73	263	NA
Zinc metal	UDW	14	22	29	29	33	18	21	—	NA
	World	132	140	166	186	173	124	138	—	NA
Lead ore	UDW	28	29	37	46	45	40	35	81	NA
	World	36	61	81	100	95	71	68	201	NA
Lead metal	UDW	74	79	90	88	83	59	57	—	NA
	World	191	205	221	227	213	163	156	—	NA
UDW subtotal		905	1,204	1,470	1,693	1,353	993	1,301	1,414	NA
World total		1,899	2,313	2,796	3,241	2,715	2,320	2,636	2,946	NA
Total[a] UDW		9,504	10,295	10,719	10,977	10,410	9,738	10,137	10,361	NA
Total[a] World		12,444	13,575	13,976	14,756	14,865	13,282	13,619	14,828	NA

SOURCES: UN, *Yearbook of International Trade Statistics*; IMF, *Intern. Financ. Stat.*; FAO, *Trade Yearbook*; FAO, *State of Food and Agriculture*; FAO, *Monthly Bull. Agr. Econ Stat.*

NOTE: Underdeveloped countries include Latin America, Asia (except Japan and Hong Kong), Near and Middle East, Africa (except South Africa), and Oceania (except Australia and New Zealand).
a Underdeveloped world.

b World totals exclude re-exports and Soviet Bloc exports.
c 1961 figures were not available for these commodities.
d 1961 total is for oranges and lemons.
e Export figures for underdeveloped countries and world total are the same.
f 1960 figures are totals of ore and metals.
g Grand totals include figures for agricultural products and metals combined.

TABLE 6–2: THE ROLE OF SELECTED COMMODITIES IN THE EXPORTS
OF DEVELOPING COUNTRIES, 1953–1954 AND 1960–1961

	1953–1954		1960–1961	
Country and Commodity	Average Export Value ($ million) (1)	Commodities as Per Cent of All Exports (2)	Average Export Value ($ million) (3)	Commodities as Per Cent of All Exports (4)
A. Latin America				
Colombia				
Coffee	521	83.1	320	71.1
Bananas	13	2.0	15	3.3
All exports	627	85.1	450	74.4
Costa Rica				
Coffee	35	44.9	45	51.7
Bananas	33	42.3	23	26.4
All exports	78	87.2	87	78.1
Cuba				
Sugar	453	76.8	468[a]	75.9[a]
All exports	590	—	617[a]	—
Brazil				
Coffee	1,018	65.6	712	53.3
Cocoa	119	7.7	58	4.3
Sugar	17	1.1	62	4.6
Bananas	10	0.6	5	0.4
All exports	1,551	75.0	1,336	62.6
British Guiana				
Bananas	—	—	1	1.3
Sugar	23	47.9	34	42.5
All exports	48	—	80	43.8
Dominican Republic				
Bananas	2	1.8	11	6.8
Sugar	43	38.7	80	49.4
All exports	111	40.5	162	56.2
Ecuador				
Bananas	27	31.0	87	62.6
Cocoa	25	28.7	19	13.7
All exports	87	59.7	139	76.3
El Salvador				
Coffee	85	87.6	76	64.4
All exports	97	—	118	—
Guadalupe				
Bananas	12	40.0	12[a]	34.3[a]
All exports	30	—	35[a]	—
Guatemala				
Coffee	71	76.3	74	63.2
Bananas	12	12.9	18	15.4
All exports	93	89.2	117	78.6

TABLE 6–2—*continued*

Country and Commodity	1953–1954		1960–1961	
	Average Export Value ($ million) (1)	Commodities as Per Cent of All Exports (2)	Average Export Value ($ million) (3)	Commodities as Per Cent of All Exports (4)

A. Latin America—*continued*

Honduras				
Bananas	38	58.5	31	43.1
All exports	65	—	72	—
Jamaica				
Bananas	15	19.2	14	8.5
Sugar	32	41.0	30	18.2
All exports	78	60.2	165	26.7
Mexico				
Coffee	81	14.9	73	9.2
Sugar	9	1.7	65	8.2
All exports	544	16.6	795	17.4
Panama				
Bananas	9	56.3	21	70.0
All exports	16	—	30	—
Peru				
Sugar	34	14.5	56	12.1
All exports	235	—	464	—

B. Africa

Angola				
Coffee	55	48.7	47	36.2
All exports	113	—	130	—
Cameroons				
Bananas	7	8.8	—	—
Coffee	12	15.0	22	22.2
Cocoa	44	55.0	34	34.3
All exports	80	78.8	99	56.5
Congo				
Coffee	36	9.1	4[a]	1.3
All exports	394	—	320[a]	—
Ethiopia				
Coffee	39	60.0	44	55.7
All exports	65	—	79	—
Ghana				
Cocoa	205	79.5	191	65.9
All exports	258	—	290	—

TABLE 6-2—continued

Country and Commodity	1953–1954		1960–1961	
	Average Export Value ($ million) (1)	Commodities as Per Cent of All Exports (2)	Average Export Value ($ million) (3)	Commodities as Per Cent of All Exports (4)
B. Africa—continued				
Ivory Coast				
Bananas	—	—	5	3.1
Coffee	—	—	86	53.1
Cocoa	—	—	38	23.5
All exports	—	—	162	79.7
Kenya				
Tea	8	5.0	15	4.1
All exports	159	—	367	—
Madagascar				
Coffee	40	44.9	25	32.5
All exports	89	—	77	—
Mauritius				
Sugar	54	98.2	57[a]	98.3[a]
All exports	55	—	58[a]	—
Nigeria				
Cocoa	90	23.7	97	21.0
Bananas	8	2.1	10	2.2
All exports	380	25.8	463	23.2
C. Asia				
Ceylon				
Tea	163	48.5	232	67.1
All exports	336	—	346	—
India				
Tea	261	22.6	260	19.1
All exports	1,156	—	1,362	—
Indonesia				
Tea	32	3.8	27	3.3
Coffee	35	4.2	14	1.7
All exports	838	8.0	812	5.0
Philippines				
Sugar	102	25.4	139	26.2
All exports	402	—	530	—
Taiwan				
Sugar	70	63.1	65	35.9
Tea	8	7.2	8	4.4
All exports	111	70.3	181	40.3

SOURCES: FAO, *Trade Yearbook;* UN, *Yearbook of International Trade Statistics;* IMF, *Intern. Financ. Stat.;* trade yearbooks of individual countries.
[a] 1960 only.

importing countries are following policies aimed at self-sufficiency, so that the prospects for long-run improvements in the rice export trade are poor. The total value of underdeveloped countries' sugar exports in 1960 was about $1.2 billion; rice exports accounted for $425 million in foreign exchange for these countries. Burma, Thailand, Vietnam, and Cambodia account for nearly 90 per cent of underdeveloped countries' rice exports.

A third group of commodities competes directly in production and exports with the output of industrialized countries. This group includes tobacco, cotton, citrus fruit, oilseeds, and nonferrous metals (except tin, which is produced exclusively by the USSR and underdeveloped countries).[8]

What Are the Key Commodities?

If we are to design a commodity policy that will support the export earnings of developing countries, we want to find out what commodities are most amenable to effective commodity agreements, and what the magnitude and distribution of the results might be.

We can use several criteria to define the commodities that merit priority for control schemes:

1. The product should be important in the export trade of underdeveloped countries, preferably affecting a large number of exporters. As a sort of corollary, if a few products are important in the export trade of many countries, then effective agreements for those products can have widespread results, and it may be possible to avoid a plethora of agreements. The pages immediately following discuss the impact of selected commodities in some detail.

2. The product should preferably not be important in the export trade of industrialized countries, but should not be dropped from consideration even if it is. If we assume, however, that the primary objective should be to increase the foreign-exchange earnings of poor countries, this criterion would mean lower priority for such products as tobacco and citrus fruit. Naturally, these observations are not intended to exclude international commodity agreements for temperate zone products. Such agreements also have their place in U.S. trade policy, but are simply not discussed in this study. Our central purpose here is to investigate the effects of price-fixing commodity agreements on the trade of less developed countries.

[8] There is also the subgroup of temperate zone crops—meat, wool, grains. Such exports are important chiefly to Argentina and Uruguay, among developing countries.

3. The product should be one whose free-market earnings prospects, over the next ten years or more, seem relatively unfavorable because of sluggish export demand (tea, rice) or rapid supply growth (coffee, cocoa).

4. If output restriction is the method used to maintain earnings (and we are not considering here the alternative approach of free-market prices plus deficiency payments),[9] then the products should have three economic characteristics:

   a. *Inelastic demand over the price range being considered for support.* It is no use trying to support prices of products at levels that encourage important long-run substitution. The result would simply be a permanent loss of markets and revenues. This means that certain products facing competition from synthetics and other substitutes either cannot be supported at all (rubber), or only at relatively small advances above current price (jute, cotton).

   b. *Preferably, prices that can be supported individually, rather than collectively, in a group of related commodities.* Thus, there might be good reason to support oilseed prices; but it would require controls over at least eight types of oilseeds, which would in turn have to be adjusted to trends in animal fat and fish oil production. Again, possible control measures need not be completely excluded in advance, but it is clearly preferable to start with less complex cases.

   c. *Amenability to effective national marketing and production control systems.* In the case of nonferrous metal, for example, with relatively few producers, such controls are comparatively simple to administer. For the tropical agricultural crops discussed here, control is more difficult. It would require effective national marketing boards of the type that have been established in the past in Ghana, Nigeria, and Pakistan.

In light of these considerations, two groups of commodities[10] merit particular attention for commodity agreements:

1. *Noncompeting exports that have no close substitutes:* coffee, tea, cocoa, and bananas (1960 export value of $3.2 billion, compared to $3.9 billion average, 1953–1954).

2. *Products that have no close substitutes, exported preponderantly by developing countries:* sugar and rice (1960 export value of $1.7 billion,

---

[9] See the first section of this chapter.
[10] Excluding tin, which is already under an operating control scheme.

compared to the $1.5 billion average in 1953–1954). These present more complex problems than does the first group, and the fact that rice is mostly purchased by underdeveloped countries may exclude it on other grounds.

Two further groups of lesser priority are

3. *Products that compete with industrial countries' exports:* cotton, oilseeds, and nonferrous metals.

4. *Products that are predominantly exported by industrial countries:* citrus fruit and tobacco.

Grains, meat, wool, dairy products, and paper pulp have only a minor role in developing countries' exports, and should be considered primarily as an issue of industrialized countries' agricultural policies.

Finally, there is a group of industrial raw materials—rubber, jute, sisal—important to developing countries and not produced in industrial countries, that probably would not benefit from commodity agreements aimed at raising prices and revenues. All of these products (accounting for $1.7 billion of 1960 exports) face close competition from synthetics in many uses. They will have to be responsive to market forces (although Pakistan, with its predominant position in the trade, can and does exercise a certain degree of national control over jute exports), and they are unlikely to prosper, although export volumes may increase modestly.

Initially, then, it seems that coffee, tea, cocoa, bananas, and sugar (noncompeting crops with no close substitutes) should receive priority attention. The following paragraphs examine the impact on trade these products have for a number of underdeveloped countries.

The Impact of Key Commodities on the Trade of Developing Countries

All thirty major exporters of coffee, tea, cocoa, bananas, and sugar are located in Latin America, Asia, and Africa. Table 6–3 reveals the importance of the products in the trade of these countries in the 1953–1954 and 1960–1961 periods. Column 1 lists, for each country, the export value of its prime commodities and its total exports in 1953–1954; Col. 2 lists the percentages of total exports that these commodities accounted for. Columns 3 and 4 list the same information for 1960–1961 (when 1961 data were not available, only the 1960 figure was used).

In general, Latin American countries are the most dependent on exports of these commodities. Nine of the fifteen countries listed (Colombia, Costa Rica, Cuba, Brazil, Dominican Republic, El Salvador, Ecuador, Guate-

TABLE 6–3: EFFECT OF COMMODITY AGREEMENTS ON EARNINGS OF INDIVIDUAL COUNTRIES
(Products Considered: Coffee, Tea, Cocoa, Sugar, and Bananas)
(In $ million)

Country	Actual 1961 Earnings (1)	Monopoly Prices 1961 Earnings (2)	Projected 1971 Earnings at 1961 Prices (3)	Projected 1971 Earnings at Monopoly Prices (4)	Percentage Difference between Cols. 3 and 4 (5)
A. Latin America					
Brazil	804	1,009	967	1,367	41
El Salvador	70	87	96	120	25
Costa Rica	61	72	85	101	19
Colombia	323	380	444	521	17
Guatemala	85	97	118	135	14
Mexico	142	159	177	201	14
British Guiana	27	30	30	34	13
West Indies	72	80	80	90	13
Dominican Republic	86	95	101	113	12
Panama	20	22	29	32	10
Honduras	29	31	41	45	10
Ecuador	81	83	117	119	2
Peru	64	62	72	70	−3
B. Africa					
Ethiopia	43	54	59	74	25
Kenya	11	13	13	16	23
Angola	64	77	87	105	21
Ivory Coast	124	150	170	204	20
Cameroons	46	55	63	75	19
Ghana	194	231	262	311	19
Nigeria	95	108	128	146	14
Nyasaland	12	14	15	17	23
Mauritius	45	50	50	56	12
C. Asia					
Indonesia	36	44	45	54	20
Ceylon	234	260	290	322	11
Taiwan	67	64	65	72	11
Fiji	13	15	15	16	7
India	260	278	323	344	7
Philippines	135	133	151	149	−1

NOTE: Assumes no change from relative 1961 market shares.

mala, Panama) depended on one or more of these five commodities for more than half their export earnings.

Several commodity-exporting countries in Latin America—Argentina (grains, meat, wool); Bolivia, Chile, Peru (metals); Paraguay, Uruguay (meat, hides, wool); and Mexico (cotton and diversified exports)—would not be greatly helped by policy aimed at the five key products alone. On the other hand, most of these nations would benefit substantially from effective programs for nonferrous metals and cotton.

In Africa the five commodities are very important in at least eight countries: Ivory Coast, Angola, Ghana, Nigeria, Cameroons, Ethiopia, Madagascar, and Mauritius.[11] Other countries rely on metals (Congo, Rhodesia, Morocco); oilseeds (Nigeria, Dahomey, Sierra Leone, Senegal); cotton (Egypt, Sudan, Uganda); tobacco (Rhodesia); and citrus fruit (Algeria, Israel, Morocco).

In Asia only four of the countries analyzed (Philippines, Taiwan, Ceylon, and India) relied on these crops for a significant part of their export earnings. Of all the regions of the underdeveloped world, Asia is least dependent on trade in these five crops.

The general conclusion from Table 6–3 is that at least 25 countries could benefit substantially from higher prices for cocoa, tea, coffee, sugar, and possibly bananas. The greatest concentration of benefits from operations on these crops would be in Latin America, which exports more than 60 per cent of the world's sugar, 70 per cent of the world's coffee, and 80 per cent of the world's bananas. Cocoa and tea controls would help primarily in Africa (75 per cent of world cocoa exports) and Asia (85 per cent of tea exports).

If such a policy were followed, it would have some effect on the present distribution of economic aid costs. The United States now provides about 60 per cent of free-world international economic aid, but the incidence of payment would differ somewhat from present aid. In 1960 the United States imported about 39 per cent (by value) of these five crops; and the additional costs to the United States of commodity agreements would not be more than 39 per cent of world total additional costs. Table 6–4 reveals the relative U.S. and Western European shares in imports of these commodities. The United States might pay somewhat less than 39 per cent of a total cost increase, because it is already paying premium prices for sugar,

---

[11] Lack of data prevented complete coverage of Africa. There are actually more African countries that depend heavily on trade in these products.

while countries that import free-market sugar would presumably bear a somewhat larger percentage of total cost increases.

TABLE 6–4: U.S. AND EUROPEAN IMPORTS OF
SELECTED COMMODITIES, 1960

Crop	U.S. Imports as Per Cent of World Trade	Western Europe's Imports as Per Cent of World Trade
Coffee	51.3	36.4
Cocoa	28.2	53.0
Sugar	25.6	27.7
Tea	9.2	49.0
Bananas	46.4	38.3

Therefore, in terms of the burden-sharing criteria discussed in Chapters 3 and 5, the United States would be underpaying in this form of economic aid. If we believe that real income is the appropriate progressive tax base, then there might be some argument for such a division of costs to compensate for the slight U.S. overpayment found in the less progressive systems shown in the real-income tax schedules of those chapters. If agreements are limited to coffee and cocoa, the U.S. share of cost increases would be nearly 50 per cent.

Proposals for Commodity Policy

General Principles

In theory, the goal is to establish commodity prices that will bring maximum long-run revenues to producing countries; but in practice, our knowledge of demand elasticities and substitution possibilities is inexact, so that such aims could not be met precisely even if there were no political or organizational obstacles.

Such a policy involves three kinds of measures. In order of priority, they are (1) establishment of effective international commodity agreements; (2) removal by industrial countries of tariffs and consumption taxes on noncompeting products exported by developing areas (coffee, cocoa, bananas); and (3) ultimately, moderate and progressive reduction of protection and subsidy on industrialized countries' production of agricultural commodities that compete directly with developing countries' exports (sugar, oilseeds, cotton).

Commodity agreements based on such goals would presumably include the following principles, where possible:

a. Establishment of export quotas for each exporting country whenever prices are below an agreed minimum. These quotas would be subject to regular revision, to reflect changes among countries in the production situation and in demand conditions.

b. Equal treatment by importers of exports from all parties to the agreement; discrimination by importers against exporters not joining the agreement.

c. Establishment of annual target prices for each crop, designed to meet, insofar as practical, the objective stated above. The annual increase in target price (as reflected in quota changes) should be relatively modest, so as not to disrupt world markets.

d. Establishment of marketing boards or similar groups in exporting countries to assure (*i*) quota enforcement, and (*ii*) setting of domestic prices at levels that will discourage excess supply.

e. After consideration in certain cases, establishment of buffer stocks, either under international control or under national control, subject to internationally agreed-on rules about managing them. These stocks could help stabilize prices at the target levels; they would probably have to include penalty provisions for countries whose products consistently exceeded quota levels. One class of products, such as bananas, is almost prohibitively expensive to store; therefore, buffer stocks must be ruled out. Another group, such as coffee, has already built up such large stocks that there are serious short-term problems in creating a buffer-stock system; with a policy of gradual stock liquidation or with a series of short crops (such as occurred in Brazil in 1963), these problems may turn out to be manageable over the next decade.

f. Organization, in commodity councils, of both exporters and importers. Consideration should be paid to giving consumer countries the right to establish general principles for use of incremental revenues obtained through the agreement. For example, where these revenues take the form of a council tax, the member governments might apply certain conditions to the release of tax funds to individual exporting countries. These conditions would require that exporting governments devote part or all of increased earnings resulting from restrictive features of the agreement to programs of economic development, including measures aimed at diversifying production out of commodities in excess supply.[12]

There are several general points to be made about commodity agreements and their limitations (specific issues associated with regulation of individual commodities are discussed in the next part of this study):

1. Even if the conditions listed above are met, the amount by which they can raise exporters' income may often be small, or even zero. Long-run demand elasticities for some or most uses of the product may be greater than one, for any large increases in price.[13] As noted above, in cases where close substitutes exist, there may be no way to raise prices without reducing revenues.

2. For many commodities, the existence of different product grades and types can create difficulties. If the prices of the various grades move in unison, the difficulties are slight. If not, the system of regulation may have to include provisions for quotas by grade. In this case, for example, countries specializing in particular grades for which demand is favorable, may at times not be subject to export restrictions, while relatively severe quotas might govern grades facing sluggish demand.

3. The export quota system tends to freeze existing production and export patterns. This may hurt the interests of countries whose relative cost position is improving. To the extent that periodic quota revisions can be related to diversification measures, the system can adjust to changing production situations among countries. It might be true, however, that lower cost producers also have the greatest diversification potential, so that quota revisions might not always mean larger exports for low-cost producers.

4. If not all major exporters are included in the system, it is essential that all major importers be members of the agreement. China, for example, is a major exporter of tea, soybean oil, and tin, but need not be included in the agreements for these products, as long as major non-Soviet Bloc importers agree to buy only from other members of the agreement. In a sense, then, such agreements offer the West additional leverage in its economic dealings with the Soviet Bloc.

5. Demand elasticities for most commodities are higher in low-income

[12] None of these proposals are entirely novel. See Tinbergen; and GATT, *Trends in International Trade.*

[13] This assumes that demand curves for some products are characterized by varying elasticity, often becoming more elastic with large increases above normal price.

countries than in wealthy ones. To maximize exporters' revenues, an agreement could set higher prices (relatively smaller quotas) in industrial countries, and lower prices in developing areas. The present coffee agreement makes an effort in this direction by establishing a list of "new markets" without quota restrictions. Provided that an effective policy of controlling re-exports is possible, such a discriminating price policy has advantages for both exporters and importers.

6. New producers, or producers whose output is originally too small to merit inclusion in the agreement, may sharply expand output at the expense of members of the agreement. Presumably, they would have to be included in the agreement; or if they preferred to remain outside, importing members of the agreement would have to discriminate against them.

7. Despite the complexities introduced by international price control schemes, with or without buffer stocks, they are probably more practicable than a system of international deficiency payments. Many countries use deficiency payments, often as a subsidy for high-cost domestic agriculture; they are preferable to price supports in that they encourage consumption through lower market prices. Furthermore, deficiency payments systems can be operated with fewer restrictions on imports than can domestic price control schemes. On the international scene, however, direct subsidies paid by industrialized countries to developing countries would logically be considered an extension of economic aid programs. Because many legislatures oppose direct subsidy payments to their own farmers, they would be even more reluctant to vote direct subsidies to foreign farmers. If they did, they would certainly consider the subsidies as part of the economic aid budget. As noted in Chapter 1, the chances for rapid expansion of economic aid are slight; furthermore, such payments are a vulnerable target when governments decide to reduce budgets. Consequently, the chances of parliamentary approval of subsidy payments as an increment to existing aid are equally slight.

8. Effective production control is essential. It would require a combination of incentives, generally including both farm prices below export prices, and subsidy payments (or guaranteed prices) to farmers who diversify their production. Marketing quotas for individual farmers may also be needed, but cannot be relied on exclusively; positive incentives to shift production are also needed. Because these incentives may cost governments a good deal, the case is even stronger for marketing boards or other

organizations that can effectively channel part or all of increased commodity revenues into diversification schemes.

9. One important merit of such agreements is that they whittle away the advantage now enjoyed by some countries under preferential import schemes.[14] For example, if the world sugar price is raised to the level of the U.S. quota price, or if the world price for African coffee reaches the price paid by France to its former colonies, there is no advantage to selling in the preference market, and economic pressures result, in effect, in a nondiscriminatory trading situation.

Individual Commodities

This section discusses the impact and operation of proposed price-fixing schemes for coffee, cocoa, tea, bananas, and sugar. International agreements are already in effect for coffee and sugar. If they had been adapted to the purposes outlined above, and agreements had been negotiated for cocoa, tea, and bananas, developing countries' 1961 revenues from these crops would have been about $5.05 billion, instead of the actual $4.35 billion. If we accept the projections of the Food and Agriculture Organization (FAO)[15] of 1970 demand for these commodities, receipts in that year may rise from the projected level of $5.8 billion (at 1961 relative prices) to a figure in the neighborhood of $6.8 billion. (See Tables 6–5 and 6–6.) Removal of tariffs and consumption taxes might have meant an additional $475 million in export revenues in 1959. (However, see pp. 168–169 for qualification.)

The validity of projected revenue increases depends on the accuracy of the estimates of price and income elasticities of demand. Statistical and logical difficulties make it virtually impossible to achieve precise estimates of the elasticities. The historical data, however, clearly show that demand for the products considered here is quite inelastic, and that FAO and other estimates used here are probably in the right general range. Furthermore, this proposal specifically avoids any attempt to aim at the maximum monopoly revenues that the estimated demand elasticities might imply. Thus, the assumption here is that the elasticities are actually somewhat higher than statistical estimates indicate; therefore price and revenue

[14] For a contrary view concerning the merits of preferential schemes, see Uri, p. 43. He sees them as analogous to infant industry protection.
[15] "Agricultural Commodities."

targets are somewhat lower. In view of substitution possibilities, and the probable downward bias of demand elasticity estimates, this seemed the most practical choice.[16]

In other words, the elasticity estimates used here are illustrative and conservative. This says, in essence, that if the elasticities are as stated here, then the effect would be as shown. If the actual values are lower (and there is considerable reason to believe they are), the less developed countries' revenues would be higher than shown here.

Table 6–5 compares underdeveloped countries' actual 1961 revenues from exports of the five crops with those they would have received if a conservative monopoly price policy had been in effect. The results would have been most striking for coffee, least significant for bananas.

TABLE 6–5: EFFECT OF MONOPOLY PRICING ON DEVELOPING
COUNTRIES' 1961 EXPORT REVENUES

Crop	1961 Actual Revenue ($ million)	1961 Export Price (U.S. cents/lb)	Demand Elasticity	1961 Monopoly Revenues ($ million)	Monopoly Price (U.S. cents/lb)
Sugar	1,209	3.9	0.5	1,328	5
Coffee	1,804	30.8	0.4	2,195	50
Tea	547	48.6	0.3	641	64
Cocoa	469	21.9	0.4	539	29
Bananas	329	3.9	0.7	339	4.7
Total	4,358			5,042	

NOTE: See Table 6–14 (p. 185) for method of deriving monopoly revenues.

Table 6–6 compares, on the basis of extrapolations from Table 6–2 and the FAO forecasts, 1971 revenues at 1961 prices and at monopoly prices. The relative distribution of gains is about the same, but the spread between the two revenue levels would increase by about $250 million, thanks to increased sales volumes. As noted above, actual benefits could be considerably greater if prices of these commodities continued to fall as they have in recent years. Furthermore, with increases in income over the next decade, price elasticities of demand may fall and higher fixed prices may be feasible.

---

[16] Furthermore, the elasticity estimates used here tend to reflect the response to retail price changes. Unless marketing margins and taxes move proportionately with export price changes for the crop itself, these estimates are conservative.

TABLE 6–6: EFFECT OF MONOPOLY PRICING ON
DEVELOPING COUNTRIES' 1971 EXPORT
REVENUES
(In $ million)

| Crop | 1971 Revenues | |
	At 1961 Prices	At Monopoly Prices
Sugar	1,614	1,772
Coffee	2,472	3,008
Tea	678	801
Cocoa	632	726
Bananas	461	475
Total	5,857	6,782

Table 6–7 shows, for four of these commodities, how removing industrial countries' tariffs and consumption taxes affects developing countries' export earnings. The figures are based on 1959 consumption levels. The effects are small for coffee, tea, and bananas. For sugar, the effects are considerably larger; in some European countries, abolishing tariffs would mean the end of most domestic production. It should be assumed, therefore, that some reduction of sugar duties and abolition of consumption taxes are the most that can be expected. Abolition of these duties and charges for tropical crops is desirable on several counts: (1) It would encourage modest short-run trade expansion. (2) As trade expands with the growth of income and population, these increases would naturally become larger. (3) Such measures to encourage consumption may lead to long-run changes in tastes, particularly in such countries as Germany and Italy, where taxes are high.

TABLE 6–7: EFFECTS OF REMOVING INDUSTRIAL COUNTRIES' DUTIES AND
FISCAL CHARGES ON COFFEE, TEA, BANANAS, AND SUGAR
(In $ million)

Commodity	1959 Increase in Imports if Charges Had Been Removed
Coffee	54.3
Tea	1.5
Bananas	8.2
Sugar	412.5[a]

SOURCE: Tinbergen.
[a] Excludes Germany and Sweden.

The FAO has estimated that by 1970 the effect of removing all taxes and duties on coffee, cocoa, tea, bananas, and citrus fruits in Western Europe would be to increase the value of imports of these products by $180 million (11 per cent) over the 1957–1959 average.[17] As in Tinbergen's estimate, most of the increase would be in coffee imports (57 per cent of total increase), with cocoa (17 per cent) and citrus fruit (21 per cent) accounting for most of the rest. Tinbergen gets a larger increase for 1959 banana imports than does FAO for 1970, presumably because his estimate includes Japan, which has very high charges on bananas (per capita consumption there is still below 1939 levels).

Coffee. By value, coffee is the leading agricultural commodity in world trade. From the 1953–1955 peak to the 1960–1962 trough, the annual worldwide value of coffee exports declined from $2.3 to $1.8 billion. Coffee represents a typical case with tree crops; high prices for the commodity in the early 1950's led to large increases in supply. The weighted average of export prices fell from $1050 per metric ton in 1955–1957 to $680 in 1961.

As a result of the steady price fall after 1954, there were a succession of interim coffee agreements culminating, in 1962, in the negotiation of a five-year agreement aimed at more effective control of exports. The agreement stated each country's quota in quantities of coffee per year. Quota exports for 1963 were set at 99 per cent of the basic quota, a total approximately equal to 1961 exports. However, exports to "new markets" (including Japan, the Sino-Soviet Bloc, and a number of underdeveloped countries) were excluded from the quota, so that 1963 sales to quota countries were probably somewhat larger than in 1961. The sharp rise in coffee prices in 1963 probably reflects a short crop in Brazil and anticipation of the effects of the agreement rather than its direct results. In any event, long-term price prospects are not considered favorable.

Effective control for coffee will be hard to achieve. Brazil and Colombia have a relatively clear interest in output controls; but for the other 35 producing countries, the relation between increased sales and falling revenues is much less direct. A small producer can double his sales without affecting world price significantly.[18] There are other difficulties: (1) Supply and demand conditions for African, Brazilian, Colombian, and Central

---

[17] "Tropical Fruit and Beverages: Duties and Taxes in Western Europe," FAO, *Monthly Bull. Agr. Econ. Stat.*, December 1962, pp. 8–11.

[18] This element is particularly important for Central American producers, who frequently have no storage facilities and are already faced with production in excess of export quotas.

American coffees are different, with the latter two normally selling at a premium (1961 average New York price 44 cents a pound) over the others (Brazilian 36 cents, African 20 cents). (2) European Economic Community preferential duties on African coffees somewhat injure the market position of the surplus Latin American producers.

There are also some favorable elements. Producers are anxious for higher prices and have been willing to sign an agreement (1963) that specifically recognized the need for production control, as well as for export quotas. The present agreement contains most of the elements needed: (1) export quotas that can be changed regularly; (2) a target date for establishing production control plans; (3) a proposal that a stock policy be established, although no details are yet provided; and (4) recognition that foreign-aid programs should be related to the need for diversification.

To move toward stable and higher coffee prices, the following steps would be needed:

1. Manipulation of export quotas to maintain reasonably high prices, for example, 48 cents a pound for Brazilian Santos No. 4 at New York. (These prices were actually exceeded for a time during 1963–1964 as a result of poor crops in Brazil, with little apparent effect on sales volume.)

2. An active production control effort aimed at eliminating the present buildup of stocks.

3. Establishment of buffer-stock schemes to help maintain prices at target levels.

In principle, the manager of an international stock would sell when prices rose above or fell below a quarterly target by more than a certain percentage. Given an effective quota system, buffer sales would have to take place only when there were unexpected decreases in supply.

4. Establishment of marketing boards (these already exist in many countries). They are necessary because as long as world prices fall or remain low, a workable agreement will require that farm prices be lower than export prices.

5. Coordination of Western foreign-aid and trade policies with commodity policy to assure (a) that aid is directed to those purposes consistent with production control and diversification; and (b) that Western markets are progressively opened to participating countries' exports of both primary and manufactured products. In some cases, aid levels may be varied as a device to assure compliance with commodity policy.

A few examples, in Table 6–8, illustrate the effects on various countries of a policy that succeeds in raising prices to the levels proposed above.

TABLE 6–8: COFFEE REVENUES AT 1961 PRICES AND AT MONOPOLY PRICES[a]
(In $ million)

Country	Actual 1961 Revenues	Theoretical 1961 Revenues at Monopoly Prices	Projected 1971 Revenues	
			At 1961 Prices	At Monopoly Prices
Brazil	710	893	852	1,223
Colombia	308	363	422	497
Ivory Coast	84	101	116	138
Mexico	73	91	100	125
El Salvador	70	87	96	120
Guatemala	69	81	95	112
Angola	64	77	87	105
Ethiopia	43	54	59	74
Costa Rica	43	52	59	72
Cameroons	21	24	29	33

[a] Assumes no change from 1961 market shares.

Cocoa. Many of the proposals made above for coffee also apply to cocoa, but there are also some important differences in their situations. First, there is very little pressure of stocks, because the cocoa market normally clears each year; existing stocks are held in consuming countries, and although relatively high compared to postwar averages, probably do not generally exceed long-run normal levels (three to six months' consumption). Second, substitution of other fats for cocoa butter imposes limits on possible long-run price gains. Third, cocoa is produced by fewer countries than coffee is, and is important to the export earnings of only six of them (Ghana, Nigeria, Ivory Coast, Cameroons, Ecuador, and, to a lesser extent, Brazil). Fourth, there is no existing cocoa agreement; 1963 negotiations for an agreement were unsuccessful, foundering on the minimum price issue.[19] Fifth, while it is evident that long-run free-market prospects for coffee are bad, the situation for cocoa is much less clear, because of uncertainty about long-run supply trends. Nevertheless, the balance of evidence points to no steady improvement in prices, which are now somewhat above postwar lows.

[19] In 1964 the producing countries organized a program of supply control. It remains to be seen whether the scheme can be carried out successfully without formal cooperation on the importers' side.

A cocoa agreement should include essentially the same provisions as those stressed for coffee. Price targets will have to be below the high average of the 1950's, because of substitution possibilities. An average export price of 29 cents a pound ($639 a metric ton) seems to be feasible, although it might have to be reconsidered if evidence showed that losses from substitution were outweighing the gains from higher prices. Other points of importance are that (1) stocks would have to be stored in temperate climates—cocoa deteriorates in the tropics; (2) there may be fewer diversification possibilities in Africa than in Latin America, because the economies and administrations are less developed; and (3) for the same reason, production control may be more difficult. Table 6–9 shows the projected effect of 29-cent cocoa on major producers' earnings.

TABLE 6–9: COCOA REVENUES AT 1961 PRICES AND AT MONOPOLY PRICES[a]
(In $ million)

| | | | Projected 1971 Revenues | |
Country	Actual 1961 Revenues	Theoretical 1961 Revenues at Monopoly Prices	At 1961 Prices	At Monopoly Prices
Ghana	194	231	262	311
Nigeria	95	108	128	146
Brazil	46	56	62	76
Ivory Coast	40	49	54	66
Cameroons	25	31	34	42

[a] Assumes no change from 1961 market shares.

Sugar. For three major reasons, far worse difficulties beset commodity agreements for sugar than for any of the other four crops discussed here: (1) Importing countries are also sugar producers, and want to protect their own industries. (2) Cuba (accounting for about half the sugar exports of developing countries) introduces important political complications. (3) About 60 per cent of world trade is already conducted under preference agreements, notably the United States' quota system and the Commonwealth's sugar preference system.

Usually, sugar production in industrialized countries is a relatively high-cost enterprise. Table 6–7, illustrating the effect of removal of tariffs and charges on sugar, provides clear evidence on this count. Because of high costs and because of existing preference systems, immediate adoption of free trade in sugar, regulated only by export quotas to maintain prices, is impracticable. Existing preferential arrangements are unsatisfactory, however, because they arbitrarily discriminate against individual countries.

The Sugar Agreement, now in abeyance because of Cuba's demand for higher quotas, worked reasonably well for that portion of world trade it affected, principally because Cuba was willing to manage its stocks in exchange for the bonus it received in the form of a large U.S. import quota. A renewal of the agreement would have to be based on the guarantee of Soviet Bloc markets for Cuban sugar, because Cuba is evidently unwilling to maintain world prices through its own actions in the future.

The preferential system that now governs most of the world's sugar trade could be eliminated indirectly if the world price of sugar were raised to 5 or 6 cents a pound; at this level, there would be no particular advantage to selling in preferential markets.

Despite the special form of agreement that would be necessary, sugar is well adapted to world commodity agreement, because of the relatively low demand elasticity and the relative unimportance of substitutes. Furthermore, an export price of 5 or 6 cents a pound would not in most cases stimulate importing countries' production, because domestic support prices are typically at least this high already. Some of the world's sugar exports (less than 20 per cent) are made by industrial countries; these consist chiefly of refined sugar that has been imported raw from developing countries. The form of the agreement should, through quotas or other means, assure that industrial countries are given no incentive to increase their refined sugar exports from domestically produced raw sugar.

Table 6–10 shows how the data for various exporting countries would be affected by a 5-cent export price for 1961 and at projected 1971 export levels, in comparison with their actual 1961 revenues and their projected 1971 revenues if prices remained at 1961 levels.

1963–1964 sugar prices stayed at remarkably high levels, as high as 11 cents per pound, reflecting short crops in Cuba and elsewhere. Such high prices cannot persist long, because at these levels, additional high-cost production in temperate zones becomes profitable.[20] Table 6–10 is based on changes from the much lower 1961 prices.

Tea.   Tea is exported by a smaller number of producers than are any of the other crops considered here. Six producers—India, Ceylon, Indo-

---

[20] By mid-1964 prices had receded considerably from the prior year's peaks, and by the end of the year they were once more down to 1961 levels.

nesia, Taiwan, Nyasaland, and Kenya—account for 95 per cent of free-world exports. (If Communist China's exports are included, the six countries' proportion of world trade is about 85 per cent.) As Table 6–11 (p. 176) shows, the tea trade is important only in the economies of India, Ceylon, and Kenya; the annual export value (excluding China) was about $470 million in 1961, somewhat below the average of the 1950's. Europe (principally the United Kingdom) is by far the largest importer, accounting for more than one-half of world trade; the United States, the second largest importer, accounts for less than 10 per cent of world imports. An additional 20 per cent goes to developing countries, principally in Asia and the Middle East.

TABLE 6–10: SUGAR REVENUES AT 1961 PRICES AND AT MONOPOLY PRICES[a]
(In $ million)

			Projected 1971 Revenues	
Country	Actual 1961 Revenues	Theoretical 1961 Revenues at Monopoly Prices	At 1961 Prices	At Monopoly Prices
Dominican Republic	70	77	78	87
Philippines	135	133	151	149
Taiwan	58	64	65	72
Brazil	48	60	53	68
Peru	64	62	72	70
Mexico	69	68	77	76
West Indies	72	80	80	90
British Guiana	27	30	30	34
Mauritius	45	50	50	56

[a] Assumes no change from 1961 market shares.

An international tea agreement was in effect from 1933 to 1955, although its quota provisions were effective only from 1933 to 1939. The agreement was essentially an understanding among producers, with India, Ceylon, Indonesia, British East Africa, and Malaya participating. Producers agreed not to expand plantings and to regulate exports on the basis of 1929–1931 export levels. The agreement was quite successful in that the export price of tea fell much less than that of other tropical products during the depression years. The agreement also succeeded in considerably reducing annual price fluctuations.

In addition to the small number of producers, certain features of tea production and consumption make it particularly amenable to commodity agreements. First, the amount of tea picked in any year can be adjusted to the level of demand; it is essentially a question of picking more or fewer leaves from each plant. Second, a great deal of tea is consumed in producing countries; therefore domestic price policies can be manipulated to some extent to encourage local consumption during periods when export quotas are in effect. This, combined with the fact that tea can be stored on the bush, means that there may be less need for rigid production controls or for buffer stocks. Because of recent increases in consumption, both in producing countries and other low-income areas, there is a case for applying quota restrictions only to the exports to industrial countries. Price and income elasticity of demand in the developing areas is presumably relatively high and per capita consumption has been increasing rapidly. In industrialized countries, income and price elasticities are very low, according to all econometric studies.

In theory, a tea agreement therefore should be based on a two-price system agreed to by producers and consumers, with enforcement of export quotas by a system similar to the coffee agreement. On the whole, there seems to be no clear case now for diversification away from tea, although restrictions on new plantings may prove to be desirable. A tea agreement would therefore resemble a producers' cartel much more than would the other agreements discussed here. All the incremental earnings from higher prices could be channeled into general economic development, rather than into financing of tea producers' production shifts. All these objectives *could* be accomplished by a producers' agreement like the earlier tea agreement; however, exclusion of consumer countries from the agreement would have two important disadvantages: First, it might allow Communist China to cut prices and make inroads into developed countries' markets. Second, because monopoly revenues will probably be most effectively achieved by different export prices to industrial and developing countries, agreement of consumer countries to a system of re-export control is important.

Quality differences are as important for tea as for coffee. Most of the quality tea exported is consumed in the high-income countries. To the extent that quality tea production can be expanded, receipts from high-income countries could increase further; at present it appears that the problem in expanding exports of high-quality tea is the difficulty of increasing production of these grades.

Table 6–11 shows how a monopoly price policy would affect the export earnings of leading tea producers. (These figures are based on the assumption of a single export price; earnings from a two-price system would be somewhat higher.)

TABLE 6–11: TEA REVENUES AT 1961 PRICES AND AT MONOPOLY PRICES[a]
(In $ million)

Country	Actual 1961 Revenues	Theoretical 1961 Revenues at Monopoly Prices	Projected 1971 Revenues	
			At 1961 Prices	At Monopoly Prices
India	260	278	323	344
Ceylon	234	260	290	322
Indonesia	36	44	45	54
Nyasaland	12	14	15	17
Kenya	11	13	13	16

[a] Assumes no change from 1961 market shares.

Bananas.   Export of bananas is very important to the trade of a number of developing countries, mostly in Latin America, and to a lesser degree in some of the West African states. In recent years, world prices have declined notably from the level of the mid-1950's (see Table 6–2). Because of demand characteristics and lack of reliable data, the case for an international banana trade agreement remains to be made; there is, however, a political interest because of the heavy dependence of Central and South American republics on this trade.

Banana exports are less suitable for regulation than other crops for a variety of reasons. Exports have grown rapidly in the past decade. Volume rose from 2.7 million tons in 1953 to 3.9 million in 1961; during the same period, export earnings went up from $270 million to $330 million, despite declining prices. Price weakness might justify export regulation, but our limited knowledge of demand indicates that the average price elasticity of demand is only slightly below one, so that gains from trade restriction would be small. Finally, it is generally believed that production and trade data for bananas are highly unreliable.

Once a reasonably accurate perspective on trends in world trade, prices, and demand structure is obtained, the question of an international agreement over the trade can be examined. A price control agreement would probably have little effect on earnings, however, as the estimates in Table 6–12 suggest, based on existing price, quantity, and elasticity data. An agreement on bananas could obviously not include buffer stocks. It might be based on a contract scheme, with importing governments agreeing to take specified quantities within specified price ranges. It seems premature, however, to discuss such issues in any detail now.

TABLE 6–12: BANANA REVENUES AT 1961 PRICES AND AT MONOPOLY PRICES[a]
(In $ million)

Country	Actual 1961 Revenues	Theoretical 1961 Revenues at Monopoly Prices	Projected 1971 Revenues	
			At 1961 Prices	At Monopoly Prices
Ecuador	81	80	117	114
Honduras	29	30	41	43
Costa Rica	18	19	26	27
Panama	20	21	29	30
Guatemala	16	15	23	22

[a] Assumes no change from 1961 market shares.

The Pros and Cons of Price-fixing Agreements

Using illustrative figures for price and income elasticities of demand, the preceding sections have discussed the possible effects of price-fixing international commodity agreements on the foreign-exchange earnings of less developed countries.

We have seen that they could probably apply to only a few crops, and that the effects, though significant for a few countries, are by no means a panacea for developing countries' exchange problems. Let us now, in concluding our discussion of commodity agreements, summarize the pros and cons.

The following arguments appear to support the case for a monopoly price policy:

1. It increases the flow of resources to less developed countries above the amounts now provided by trade and foreign-aid appropriations. If we accept the contention that foreign-exchange shortages are an important obstacle to development, then such agreements offer certain advantages.

This may be particularly important where national governments are reluctant to increase direct foreign-aid appropriations.

2. More than half the benefits from the four or five commodity schemes initially proposed here would flow to South American countries. These are the nations whose trade positions have suffered most in recent years; and despite the Alliance for Progress, their foreign-exchange problems are still often severe.

3. The adoption of monopoly pricing schemes would erode existing preferential systems for these crops. With world prices set at the levels suggested here, favored exporters would no longer benefit from selling into the U.S. sugar market or into the French markets for tropical crops. Economic pressures would promote establishment of nonpreferential multilateral trade.

4. If the administration of commodity agreements assures a spread between world prices and farm export prices for crops in surplus production, then the marketing profits resulting from this spread can be used to finance programs of agricultural diversification and economic development. It may be an important organizational advantage to tie the financing of diversification programs into the effective administration of the commodity agreement itself.

On the other hand, there are a number of arguments against the introduction of agreements aimed at establishing relatively high prices:

1. They interfere with the operation of free markets, thereby leading to complicated and often ineffective systems of production and export control.

2. This is really an inefficient way to transfer $900 million annually for two reasons: (a) It may go to the wrong countries. (b) Within each country, it may go to the wrong groups, thereby not promoting development notably. The force of the latter argument depends largely on whether an effective system of marketing boards or export taxes can be established, allowing the exporting government to retain its monopoly rents for development purposes.

3. This may be an inequitable way to transfer income. That is, low-income tea producers and low-income sugar consumers in importing countries may be carrying a larger part of the cost than they would if the transfer were made through the importing countries' regular tax systems.

4. It is argued that such agreements are really a form of economic aid,

and a form that gives relatively little control to the aid-granting country. Much of the force of this argument rests on the assumption that commodity agreements cannot control prices and revenues. In fact, the provisions of such agreements as the International Coffee Agreement allow for quarterly revision of quotas, so that the degree of control may be at least as close as in foreign-aid channels.

5. One probable result of such a policy would be that countries not benefiting from these agreements would argue that they deserved more aid by way of compensation. They would probably be correct; the implications are discussed in the final section of this chapter.

If we accept the contentions of Chapter 1—that foreign-exchange shortages are likely to be a serious brake on development, and that neither increases in direct aid nor rising exports of manufactures are likely to fill the gap in the next decade—then it seems at least arguable that the advantages of commodity policy based on monopoly pricing may outweigh the disadvantages.

Even if such agreements are adopted, it should be recognized that they have certain inherent limitations. They can be established for only a handful of commodities, and do nothing for about two-thirds of the commodity exports of less developed countries. The producers of oilseeds, rubber, jute, tobacco, citrus fruits, and probably cotton, copper, lead, and zinc can hope for no relief through these measures.

It can be expected, therefore, that countries not benefiting from the proposed agreements will increase their demands for relief if commodity agreements are established. The response could be a refusal to recognize the validity of their claims, or a direct increase in the aid flow to these countries, or an indirect increase brought about by establishing stabilization schemes aimed at ensuring developing countries against declining export earnings. The section immediately following discusses these schemes.

Finally, it should be reiterated that even the most effective system of commodity agreements is no panacea for developing countries, not even for the ones that rely heavily on the protected commodities. Essentially, we are dealing here with low-productivity industries. The long-run development of these countries would normally require steady increases in productivity, which can best be achieved in the future by developing industry and high-productivity agriculture.

Stabilizing Fluctuations in Export Earnings

There has been a great deal of interest in measures for stabilizing short-period fluctuations in the export earnings of developing countries.[21] International discussions are now underway concerning possible adoption of such schemes, both in the United Nations and the Organization of American States (OAS). This section first briefly discusses the impact of the commodity agreements proposed above on fluctuations in less developed countries' export earnings (see "Proposals for Commodity Policy," p. 162), and second, summarizes possible methods for reducing fluctuations in earnings, including an estimate of their probable impact. This chapter does not try to analyze such methods in detail.

The proposed commodity agreements just mentioned would obviously help stabilize the incomes of exporters who rely heavily on trade in these tropical products, because an effective price-fixing scheme is also an effective measure against fluctuations. Many countries, however, do not rely heavily on exports for which price-fixing agreements are feasible; therefore, once the alternative of direct subsidy payments from rich to poor countries for this purpose is rejected, international attention naturally focuses on an important, although perhaps secondary, form of relief. To the extent that commodity agreements of the type suggested above become effective, the antifluctuation measures become less urgent for a number of countries; they would still, however, offer significant advantages to many developing countries.

As pointed out earlier, nonferrous metal producers in a number of countries, including most of Asia, and oilseed and fiber exporters in Latin America and Africa, will receive little benefit from the schemes proposed above. If commodity agreements were adopted, then most of the transfer under stabilization programs would go to these countries, although we cannot now estimate the actual incidence. Furthermore, the cost of an antifluctuation scheme would be reduced because of the existence of price-fixing commodity agreements. Again, we cannot now estimate the exact amount of such cost savings.

[21] See UN, *Commodity Trade and Economic Development*, New York, 1953, and *International Compensation for Fluctuations in Commodity Trade*, New York, October 1961; GATT, *Trends in International Trade;* Organization of American States, *Finai Report of Experts on the Stabilization of Export Receipts*, Washington, D.C., November 1961.

Such stabilization measures, based on the social insurance principle, are a logical corollary to the system of commodity agreements proposed above. It must be recognized that the system would present certain difficulties. A policy of full compensation would reduce developing countries' incentive to adjust production to world-market conditions; consequently, a system of partial compensation for shortfalls is probably preferable to full compensation. Another way of getting around this difficulty would be to pay compensation on individual commodities. Under such a system, stabilization schemes could be aimed at the exporters of commodities not covered by agreements; but it would still leave a certain share of their trade unprotected, thereby providing incentives to diversify production and increase total export earnings. In this respect, such a system is symmetrical with the situation produced through price-fixing commodity agreements. That is, despite guaranteed coffee earnings, Brazil would still have an incentive to expand exports in other fields. In the same manner, compensatory financing for rubber exports would give Indonesia similar incentives.

The argument for such stabilization measures is evident. When export earnings fluctuate greatly, it is difficult to plan and carry out development programs because of uncertainties in foreign earnings. Furthermore, by affecting domestic income, fluctuations make government tax revenues uncertain. Industrialized countries may also suffer because their capital-goods industry, which is relatively unstable anyway, faces intensified fluctuations in the export sector. National policies aimed at stabilizing export incomes, through marketing boards or other devices, can clearly moderate these effects to a degree, but such measures cannot always be applied, nor by themselves do the whole job.[22]

In general, the international measures proposed to control fluctuations have been of two kinds:

1. Providing the affected countries with greater drawing rights from the International Monetary Fund (IMF), in years when their exports are below a recent average; or, alternatively, as in the OAS proposals, establishing a special fund for stabilizing export receipts, financed largely by industrial countries. In both cases, the advances would be repayable over a period of

[22] There is evidence that fluctuations in export earnings do not affect investment levels, perhaps because investors regard low prices as abnormal and base their plans on average prices. See Michael Michaely, *Concentration in International Trade*, North-Holland Publishing Co., Amsterdam, 1962; and A. I. MacBean, "The Importance of Instability in the Exports of Less Developed Countries," Center for International Affairs, Harvard University, Cambridge, Mass., 1963 (mimeographed).

one to five years. In 1963 the IMF announced the establishment of a "commodity *tranche*" that would allow less developed countries, whose export earnings fall below a recent moving average of earnings, to borrow up to 25 per cent of their IMF quotas with Fund approval. The theoretical combined maximum the underdeveloped countries could borrow would be $800 million.

2. Establishing an exports stabilization fund, based on the social insurance principle, either for single commodities, or for all export earnings. In such schemes, both underdeveloped and developed countries annually contribute a sum determined by their level of GNP or of export earnings. Countries whose export earnings have fallen below recent averages by more than a given percentage are paid from the insurance fund. In essence, this is a form of economic aid, because developed countries are excluded from benefits under most proposals,[23] and because no repayment, or at most partial repayment, would be required.

The first type of proposal has more appeal for industrialized countries, because it costs them less. At most, as in the OAS scheme, they contribute to a revolving fund, and from then on the process is more or less self-sustaining.

The second set of proposals naturally is more attractive to developing countries. Every member pays a premium each year, but all, or virtually all, of the payments go to poor countries. The United Nations report estimates what the annual average cost would have been during the 1950's of a scheme that would compensate countries for a shortfall of total export proceeds below the previous three-year average. Depending on whether payments included a deduction of 2.5 per cent, 5 per cent, or 10 per cent below the three-year earnings average, the annual cost of the scheme during 1953–1959 would have been $932 million, $766 million, and $492 million, respectively, of which 85 per cent would have gone to underdeveloped countries. Of course, if only part of the shortfall had been paid, or if part of the payment were a loan, the annual costs would have been less. Under the UN proposal, more than 60 per cent of the premiums would be paid by developed countries.

Consistent with the viewpoints advanced here, social insurance is more

[23] In any event, their export earnings fluctuate relatively less than those of underdeveloped countries, so their drawings would be far less than their premiums. A 1961 report of the United Nations estimates that three-fourths of developed countries' premiums would go to underwriting developing countries' deficits.

desirable than short-term credit. It increases the transfer to developing countries, and makes for a fairer distribution of industrial countries' contributions. The political issue is whether industrial countries are willing to put up the resources for a social insurance scheme. If the method is accepted in principle, there will be technical difficulties of administration, but these are not insuperable. If payments in the 1960's were the same as in the 1950's, adoption of such a scheme would mean an annual transfer of $482 million from rich to poor countries, if full compensation were paid for shortfalls after a 5 per cent reduction. If the commodity agreements were in effect, the transfer might be about half as great. This relatively modest contribution would not strain industrial countries' resources. If it were simply treated as a substitute for existing foreign aid, however, the advantages would be slight, because foreign-aid programs often consider balance-of-payments issues anyway as part of the allocation process. The principal gain would be to make the system automatic. It should be

TABLE 6–13: RELATIVE SHARES OF CONTRIBUTIONS TO SOCIAL INSURANCE FUND FOR COMPENSATORY FINANCE

Country	Share Basis, 1953–1959	
	GNP (%)	Exports (%)
Australia	1.7	3.0
Austria	0.6	1.3
Belgium	1.5	4.6
Canada	4.2	8.1
Denmark	0.6	1.8
Finland	0.5	1.2
France	6.5	7.6
Germany	6.7	11.5
Italy	3.3	3.5
Japan	3.7	3.8
Netherlands	1.2	4.6
New Zealand	0.4	1.2
Norway	0.5	1.1
Sweden	1.4	3.0
Switzerland	1.0	2.3
U.K.	8.1	14.0
U.S.	58.4	27.8

SOURCE: Computed from UN, *International Compensation for Fluctuations in Commodity Trade*, p. 86.

NOTE: Shares are proportional to 1953–1959 GNP and trade, respectively.

recognized that capital transfers designed to compensate for export price fluctuations may, in effect, be nothing but a complicated rationalization for increasing the flow of aid. This section does not analyze the validity of the arguments set forth above; as we have seen, there is at least some evidence that fluctuations per se do not have much effect on economic growth. Nevertheless, the case for a larger capital transfer from rich to poor countries remains unaffected.

The burden-sharing implications of a social insurance scheme depend on the tax method used to finance the fund. If GNP is the tax basis, and it is probably most appropriate for an aid scheme, then the theoretical results would be in accordance with the schedules shown in the computations of Chapters 3 and 5. If foreign trade is the basis, the effect would be to raise the relative contributions of underdeveloped countries and of the major western European trading nations. Table 6–13 shows the percentage distribution of industrial countries' contributions to such a system under two formulas, one based on 1953–1959 GNP at official exchange rates, the other based on 1953–1959 export earnings.

TABLE 6–14: METHOD FOR COMPUTING DEVELOPING COUNTRIES' 1961 AND 1971 MONOPOLY REVENUES

Com-modity	Price (cents/lb)		Quantity (billion lb)		Revenue (in $ million)			Demand Elasticity	1971 Quantity
	1961 Price	Monopoly Price	1961 Exports	1961 Monopoly Quantity[a]	1961 Revenue	1961 Monopoly Revenue	1971 Monopoly Revenue		
	P	P'	Q	Q'	PQ	$P'Q'$	$P'Q'$	e	Q''
Sugar	0.0394	0.05	30.71	26.56	1,209	1,328	1,772	0.5	1.3350 Q'
Coffee	0.3088	0.50	5.84	4.39	1,804	2,195	3,008	0.4	1.3703 Q'
Tea	0.4864	0.64	1.12	1.01	547	641	801	0.3	1.2395 Q'
Cocoa	0.2190	0.29	2.14	1.86	469	539	726	0.4	1.3475 Q'
Bananas	0.0394	0.047	8.55	7.22	329	339	475	0.7	1.4012 Q'

SOURCES: P and Q from Tables 6–1 and 6–2; P' and e, author's estimates; Q'', based on FAO projection of 1970 demand for food.
[a] Given P, Q, P', and e, since

$$ e = \frac{(Q' - Q)/Q}{(P' - P)/P}, \quad Q' = \left(\frac{P' - P}{P} eQ \right) + Q. $$

7

Aid, Trade, and Burden Sharing: Some Conclusions

This study has covered a wide range of topics: economic growth, foreign trade, capital flows, tax theory, the history of international organizations' financing, the valuation of economic aid, and international commodity policy. This chapter reviews the basic elements and points out how these diverse subjects are related.

In such a study, personal assumptions and value judgments are an inescapable issue. Before we proceed with a review of results, it may be wise to keep three of my own assumptions in mind: (1) Economic aid will continue, and barring dramatic changes in the world situation, Western aid to underdeveloped countries will remain within 25 per cent or so of current levels over the next few years. (2) A substantial increase in the aid flow seems desirable, even though its basis in developed countries' self-interest cannot be demonstrated conclusively. (3) In burden sharing, mildly progressive international taxation, described above as an uncertain ideal, is preferable to present methods. Despite its obvious irrelevance to equity in personal taxation, it accords with our ideas of fairness; and mild progressiveness assures that in accordance with the benefit principle everybody will pay something.

To explain why the burden-sharing issue arises in economic aid, it is necessary to explain the sources of demand for the supply of aid. The demand for aid was examined in Chapters 1 and 2. Underdeveloped countries want aid for a variety of reasons, but the basic justification is that increased foreign-exchange availability is often a necessary condition for economic growth at politically acceptable rates. None of the other sources of foreign exchange—export of goods and services, private investment, and import substitution—are likely to compensate fully for foreign-exchange shortages. The historical evidence shows that economic growth is virtually always associated with growth of imports, and very often with persistent trade deficits. Underdeveloped countries' possibilities for growth of exports and of private investment are circumscribed. Import substitution—already pushed to extremes in many countries—itself creates substantial import requirements. The demand for foreign aid therefore appears as the natural successor to the bond issues that financed national development in the nineteenth century.

From another and more abstract viewpoint, of course, the requirement is not for more foreign exchange, or even for an import surplus, but for a higher rate of savings and investment, however financed. In balance-of-payments terms, an import surplus is equivalent to a capital inflow; and the so-called import gap (desired imports minus exports) is equivalent to the savings gap (desired investment minus savings). In a sense, both are aspects of the balance-of-payments problem; in practice, however, our estimates of foreign-aid requirements will differ widely, according to whether we assume that trade will or will not tend to be persistently in deficit.

Chapters 1 and 2 presented several projections of underdeveloped countries' foreign-aid requirements based on these alternative assumptions. Projections based on the first assumption (shortages of foreign exchange) of course produce higher forecasts of aid requirements at any given growth rate than do those based on the assumption that trade will be in balance. Chapter 2 argues that the first assumption is more realistic in policy terms (most underdeveloped countries are unlikely to maintain external balance), and concludes that over the next decade, minimum "acceptable" growth rates will require a minimum increase in *net* annual capital inflow of about $5 billion annually above 1962 levels.

Naturally, any such estimate simply offers an order of magnitude; efforts at precision are necessarily misleading. Nor are we primarily concerned here with what the actual magnitudes may be. The relevant issue for us is whether the demand for aid is likely to continue, given growth rates that the industrial countries might endorse. All the estimates discussed above indicate that the demand for some level of foreign aid—

particularly in countries with poor prospects of trade expansion—is on solid ground once we do accept their growth targets.

On the supply side, however, the ground is much less solid. There is no clearly demonstrable relation between Western economic aid and Western security, broadly defined. Some "economic aid" is merely pay for political services rendered, and as such must be examined on its merits, case by case. The larger part, however, is presumably directed to promoting faster economic growth, and it is not at all clear what this has to do with Western national interest. Ultimately, the justification must be that economic growth will help produce a world of diverse and independent states, and that the West is more likely to prosper and to remain free if it is surrounded by independent states. The possibility that some of these independent states may be hostile must, of course, be admitted. There is no necessary correlation between economic growth and friendliness toward the West; there is simply a presumption that states that are growing and changing are unlikely to band together into a monolithic anti-Western bloc, because economic growth probably eases social tensions in the long run, even though it often incites them in the short run.

Finally, it should be noted that this kind of sought-for security is something different from a narrowly defined view of military security, even though economic aid payments theoretically could be evaluated on a military cost-benefit basis. There is little evidence that such a calculus is actually performed; even if it were, the broader security motives discussed above could not be evaluated. It seems likely that over time, the strictly military motives of aid (bases, communications facilities, etc.) will decline in importance, and the less measurable motives will become more dominant.

In addition to the broad "security" motive for offering aid, there are also humanitarian, commercial, and other motives. These presumably dominate when aid levels are relatively small (Scandinavia), or when aid is offered on commercial terms (Germany, Japan); and in any event, they play a part in all countries' aid. In a sense, however, they have nothing to do with the burden-sharing issue, which is primarily concerned with ability to pay in regard to shared benefits. The commercial benefits of one country's aid may be shared by others, but in the present state of our knowledge it is impossible to measure the benefits—or damages, for that matter—that other countries receive. The sharing of humanitarian benefits may exist, but it is impossible to tax a country on the basis of its citizens' increased sense of well-being derived from the sight of another nation's aid expenditures. Therefore, the fundamental rationale for offering economic aid and for sharing its costs must rest on grounds of security as very broadly defined above. Nonetheless, it must be admitted that much of this rationale stems from the rather vague sentiment that economic growth is a good thing.[1] This is a natural enough expression of Western values, but like all values it cannot be used to demonstrate rigorously that a particular course of action will achieve ultimate ends.

If we agree that economic aid benefits any donor, we have a reason for offering aid; if we agree that one donor's aid benefits all developed countries, we have a reason for sharing the costs of aid. This raises two of the basic questions for burden sharing: (1) What is aid? (2) How should the costs of aid be shared?

From the donor's viewpoint, aid clearly includes grants, loans made at less than market rates of interest, and purchases of goods at higher than market prices. From the recipient's viewpoint, it includes these, and may also include private investment and loans at commercial rates of interest, because capital rationing may make these flows cheaper to the recipient than any alternative source of funds. Furthermore, from the underdeveloped countries' viewpoint, liberal commercial policies that increase the value of trade between developed and underdeveloped countries may also be a form of aid, because they increase their supply of resources at a cost less than that of the alternative domestic production. Thus, a removal of U.S. restrictions on petroleum imports, or of European taxes on tropical products, would clearly increase the economic welfare of underdeveloped countries.

As I have often stated, however, Chapters 3 to 6 are primarily concerned with burden-sharing schemes (the supply side of aid); and liberalization of commercial policies imposes no net costs on industrial countries. The discussion was therefore limited to elements that involve real costs to donors.

Once we have defined aid, we come to the second question: How should

[1] There has also been an effort to link aid and military expenditures as joint contributions to Western security. The United States argues that it pays, through its combined defense and aid expenditures, a disproportionately large part of the costs of Western security. Accordingly, it contends that other countries should at least do more in aid, if they are unwilling to spend more in defense. Although there is obviously a relation between the two, it should be clear from the foregoing that the relation is tenuous. European countries have always rejected the argument.

its costs be shared? This led in Chapter 3 to a discussion of how cost-sharing arrangements might work in theory, using criteria of adequacy, economy, and equity. In general, the equity issue, which is the heart of the burden-sharing problem, does not admit a theoretical solution; therefore, as Chapter 4's discussion of past burden-sharing experiences brought out, agreement on cost-sharing formulas will usually be limited to cases in which sums are relatively small. Even then, the more powerful contributors will ordinarily use their leverage to reduce their contributions below the level indicated by ability-to-pay criteria.

The discussion of these criteria established the points that real income is a better indicator of ability to pay than is income valued in a common currency at official exchange rates, and that present value is a better method of comparing aid costs than is nominal value. Using a number of different tax systems, we computed theoretical shares for NATO military expenditures and OECD members' foreign-aid expenditures. In general, by exchange-rate or real-income equivalents, the United States is overpaying in NATO costs and is not overpaying in economic aid, at least by progressive tax formulas. The NATO overpayment, however slight, more than compensates for U.S. underpayment in all other joint international ventures. The principle of lumping all international ventures, however, can be justified more as a bargaining device than as an application of logical principles.

In examining economic aid (Chapter 5), we saw that existing methods of valuing aid are unsatisfactory, and that under a more meaningful definition there is a sharp drop in the real cost of aid as now reported to OECD. The overstatement is probably from 70 to 100 per cent in the aggregate, although the computations of Chapter 5, which could not include an appropriate discount for all tied aid, show a somewhat smaller overstatement (42 to 70 per cent in 1962, depending on valuation of PL 480 aid and interest rates used for discounting loans).

Using a present-value basis for estimating aid values emphasizes the point of Chapters 1 and 2: The real flow of aid, although increasing until 1964, is still rather small in relation to minimum needs, defined as an annual per capita growth rate of 2.5 to 3.5 per cent. Consequently, Chapter 6 examined how commodity agreements and compensatory payments for export fluctuations could increase the total aid flow. The former might produce an annual real increase of about $900 million in untied grant aid, using a system of export controls to maintain prices. A system of compensatory payments for fluctuations, on a grant basis, could increase the flow by several hundred million dollars more, if the donor countries did not consider it simply a substitute for aid.

We are thus left with the following conclusions:

1. If we accept certain propositions about growth rates, there is a good case for demanding increased foreign aid as a condition that is often necessary but usually not sufficient for growth.

2. Aid donors give aid because they expect benefits, even though the means-to-ends relationship is not at all clear, at least for what is probably the major expected benefit—the long-run development of free societies in the West.

3. The burden-sharing issue therefore arises primarily over the equitable sharing of costs. Thus, by analogy to domestic taxation, ability to pay becomes the chief criterion.

4. In practice, this criterion has been increasingly accepted in international organizations, although never strictly observed (while benefit criteria are less often advanced). Whenever sums are large or politically sensitive (NATO, DAC), nations dispense with even ostensible adherence to the ability-to-pay criterion, although it continues to be a point of discussion.

5. The actual flow of foreign aid after adjusting for present value of loans and market value of tied aid is far smaller than the data imply. By ability-to-pay criteria, all donor countries except France, Belgium, and the United States are relatively underpaying. Furthermore, by the adequacy-of-effort criterion, the total flow is probably less than half the amount needed, by the standards discussed in Chapters 1 and 2.

6. Therefore, additional sources of aid are needed. The two methods discussed in Chapter 6, combined, might add $1.5 billion to the total.

7. This still leaves the annual flow at least $3.5 billion short in grant equivalent annually, if we accept a current $5 billion import gap for illustrative purposes. The present annual grant equivalent is probably about $4 billion on a commitment basis ($3 billion or so on a flow-of-funds basis). The minimum requirement today for meeting the necessary foreign-exchange inflow, *at the growth rates cited above,* may be of the order of $9 billion annually (grant equivalent).

In the light of these conclusions, where can the additional capital come from and how should the costs be shared? Clearly, if it comes from trade and investment, the sums will have to be much larger than the $3.5 billion implied. In the case of trade, some of the increase in imports is an input for exports, so that the net increase in foreign exchange available for development is less than the trade figures show. Furthermore, resources used to produce exports may simply be substituting for pre-existing domestic production, according to comparative advantage; thus, although national product now buys a more valuable basket of goods, its value has increased by less than the amount of the increase in imports.

By the same token, unless foreign private investment is (a) based entirely on imported resources and (b) involves no return flow of income to the investor, a much larger amount will be required to achieve the equivalent growth of a $3.5 billion grant. Naturally, this abstracts from the important advantages forthcoming from trade and private investment (development of technique, managerial ability, imposition of efficiency by market pressures, etc.).

Even if aid did increase substantially, the case for increasing the value of trade and private investment remains undisturbed in terms of both efficiency and growth criteria. But the prospects for a short-run doubling of aid are slight, although much could be accomplished by shifting from loans to grants. Therefore, the case for liberal commercial policies and encouragement of private investment (if income repatriation levels are not excessive) is more urgent.

The kinds of commercial policy measures that could be taken have been discussed at length elsewhere.[2] As pointed out in Chapter 1, they are unlikely, even if adopted, to increase trade and investment enough over the next decade to meet the modest need specified here; but they would be particularly useful in promoting industrial growth.

We are thus brought back once more to the aid gap and how the bill should be footed. Generally speaking, the discussion of Chapter 3 leads to the conclusion that aid increases should be paid by the developed countries on the basis of a mildly progressive tax on real income. The computations of Tables 3–17 and 5–15 show the range. A more precise definition of the amounts required, and of theoretically appropriate shares, awaits both an improvement in existing real-income analysis and a detailed study of developing countries' needs along the lines initiated by Rosenstein-Rodan. In the meantime, proportional taxation in a common unit of account, and a doubling in grant equivalent of the present annual aid commitment, give

[2] Tinbergen; UN, *World Economic Survey 1962.*

rough approximations of minimum requirements under adequacy and equity criteria.

Improvements in the effectiveness of aid giving, by placing greater reliance on such experienced independent institutions as the International Development Association, could help cover part of the gap. But even if we adopt that recourse along with more liberal aid terms, changes in commodity policy, commercial policy, and foreign investment promotion, it is difficult to believe that the goals can be met in the short run without more aid. Over the next decade at least, acceptable aggregate growth rates in most underdeveloped countries will not come about unless there is a substantial increase in direct aid.

As Chapter 3 implies, it is impossible to say exactly what the consequences of the current aid gap will be if it continues, but they are unlikely to favor Western interests.

Bibliography

BOOKS AND MONOGRAPHS

ADAMS, N., "Economic Growth and the Structure of Foreign Trade," unpublished Ph.D. thesis, Harvard University, Cambridge, Mass., 1962.

AVRAMOVIC, D. G. R., and R. GULHATI, *Debt Servicing Capacity and Postwar Growth in International Indebtedness*, Johns Hopkins Press, Baltimore, Md., 1958.

————, *Debt Servicing Problems of Low Income Countries*, The Johns Hopkins Press, for The International Bank for Reconstruction and Development, Baltimore, Md., 1960.

BALASSA, BELA A., *Trade Prospects for Developing Countries*, Richard D. Irwin, Homewood, Ill., 1964.

BEYEN, J. W., *Money in a Maelstrom*, The Macmillan Company, New York, 1949.

BRANDOW, G. E., *Interrelations among Demands for Farm Products and Implications for Control of Market Supply*, Agricultural Experiment Station Bulletin 680, College of Agriculture, Pennsylvania State University, University Park, Pa., August 1961.

CAVES, R. E., *Trade and Economic Structure*, Harvard University Press, Cambridge, Mass., 1960.

————, and R. H. HOLTON, *The Canadian Economy*, Harvard University Press, Cambridge, Mass., 1959.

COOPER, RICHARD, *A Note on Foreign Assistance and the Capital Requirements for Development*, The RAND Corporation, Santa Monica, Calif., RM-4291-AID, January 1965.

COPPOCK, JOSEPH, *International Economic Instability*, McGraw-Hill Book Company, Inc., New York, 1962.

ECKSTEIN, OTTO, "A Survey of the Theory of Public Expenditure," in National Bureau of Economic Research, *Public Finances: Needs, Sources, and Utilization*, Princeton University Press, Princeton, N.J., 1961.

ELLIS, H. S. (ed.), *Economic Development for Latin America*, St. Martin's Press, New York, 1961.

GARDNER, R. N., *Sterling-Dollar Diplomacy*, Clarendon Press, Oxford, 1956.

GILBERT, M., and ASSOCIATES, *Comparative National Products and Price Levels*, Organization for European Economic Cooperation, Paris, 1957.

GILBERT, M., and IRVING B. KRAVIS, *An International Comparison of National Products and the Purchasing Power of Currencies*, Organization for European Economic Cooperation, Paris, 1954.

HABERLER, GOTTFRIED, *International Trade and Economic Development*, National Bank of Egypt, Cairo, 1959.

——, "Terms of Trade and Economic Development," in H. S. Ellis (ed.), *Economic Development for Latin America*, St. Martin's Press, New York, 1961.

HARROD, R. F., *The Life of John Maynard Keynes*, The Macmillan Company, New York, 1951.

HIRSCHMAN, ALBERT O., *The Strategy of Economic Development*, Yale University Press, New Haven, Conn., 1958.

HITCH, CHARLES J., and ROLAND N. MCKEAN, *The Economics of Defense in the Nuclear Age*, Harvard University Press, Cambridge, Mass., 1960.

JOHNSON, H. G., *International Trade and Economic Growth*, George Allen and Unwin, London, 1958.

KINDLEBERGER, C. P., *International Trade and the National Economy*, Yale University Press, New Haven, Conn., 1962.

KUZNETS, SIMON, *Six Lectures on Economic Growth*, The Free Press, Glencoe, Ill., 1959.

MACBEAN, A. I., "The Importance of Instability in the Exports of Less Developed Countries," Center for International Affairs, Harvard University, Cambridge, Mass., 1963 (mimeographed).

MALLON, RICHARD, "Economic Development and Foreign Trade of Pakistan," unpublished Ph.D. thesis, Harvard University, Cambridge, Mass., June 1963.

MASON, E. S., *Foreign Aid and Foreign Policy*, Harper and Row, New York, 1964.

MEIER, GERALD M., *International Trade and Development*, Harper and Row, New York, 1963.

MEINKEN, K. W., *The Demand and Price Structure for Wheat*, Technical Bulletin 1136, U.S. Department of Agriculture, 1956.

MICHAELY, MICHAEL, *Concentration in International Trade*, North-Holland Publishing Co., Amsterdam, 1962.

MUSGRAVE, R. A., *The Theory of Public Finance*, McGraw-Hill Book Company, Inc., New York, 1959.

MYERS, DENYS P., *Handbook of the League of Nations*, New York, 1935.

NEALE, ALAN D., *The Flow of Resources from Rich to Poor*, Occasional Papers in International Affairs, No. 2, Center for International Affairs, Harvard University, Cambridge, Mass., November 1961.

NETHERLANDS ECONOMIC INSTITUTE, "The European Community and Underdeveloped Countries," Netherlands Economic Institute, Rotterdam, May 1959 (mimeographed).

NURKSE, RAGNAR, *Equilibrium and Growth in the World Economy*, Harvard University Press, Cambridge, Mass., 1961.

NURSKE, RAGNAR, *Patterns of Trade and Development*, Almquist and Wiksell, Stockholm, 1959.

——, *Problems of Capital Formation in Underdeveloped Countries*, Basil Blackwell, Oxford, 1953.

OHLIN, GORAN, *Reappraisals of Foreign Aid Policies*, OECD Development Center, Paris, December 1964.

OLSON, MANCUR, JR., and R. ZECKHAUSER, *An Economic Theory of Alliances*, The RAND Corporation, Santa Monica, Calif., P–2992, October 1964.

PINCUS, JOHN A., *Commodity Policy and Economic Development*, The RAND Corporation, Santa Monica, Calif., RM–3887–ISA, October 1963.

SCHELLING, T. C., "International Cost-Sharing Arrangements," *Essays in International Finance*, No. 24, Department of Economics, Princeton University, Princeton, N.J., 1955.

SINGER, J. D., *Financing International Organization: The United Nations Budget Process*, Martinus Nijhoff, The Hague, 1961.

TINBERGEN, JAN, *Shaping the World Economy*, The Twentieth Century Fund, New York, 1962.

URI, PIERRE, *Partnership for Progress*, Harper and Row, New York, 1963.

ARTICLES AND PERIODICALS

ALTMAN, OSCAR L., "Quotas in the International Monetary Fund," *International Monetary Fund Staff Papers*, Vol. 5, No. 2, August 1956, pp. 129–150.

BALDWIN, R. E., "The Commodity Composition of Trade: Selected Industrial Countries, 1900–1954," *Review of Economics and Statistics*, Vol. 40, No. 1, February 1958 (Supplement), pp. 50–71.

——, "Secular Movements in the Terms of Trade," *American Economic Review, Papers and Proceedings*, Vol. 45, No. 2, May 1955, pp. 259–269.

BERNSTEIN, E. M., and I. G. PATEL, "Inflation in Relation to Economic Development," *International Monetary Fund Staff Papers*, Vol. 2, 1951–1952, pp. 363–398.

BERRILL, K. E., "International Trade and the Rate of Economic Growth," *Economic History Review*, Vol. 12, No. 3, April 1960, pp. 351–359.

BETOUT-MOSSÉ, E., "Sur quelques problèmes posés par l'aide aux pays sous-développés," *Revue économique*, No. 4, July 1962, pp. 590–628.

BHAGWATI, J., "International Trade and Economic Expansion," *American Economic Review*, Vol. 48, No. 5, December 1958, pp. 941–953.

BISHOP, G. A., "The Tax Burden by Income Class, 1956–58," *National Tax Journal*, March 1961.

BUTLER, W. F., "Trade and the Less Developed Areas," *Foreign Affairs*, Vol. 41, No. 2, January 1963, pp. 372–383.

CAIRNCROSS, A. K., "International Trade and Economic Development," *Kyklos*, Vol. 13, No. 4, 1960.

CHENERY, H. B., "Comparative Advantage and Development Policy," *American Economic Review*, Vol. 51, No. 1, March 1961, pp. 18–51.

———, "Development Policies for Southern Italy," *Quarterly Journal of Economics*, Vol. 76, No. 4, November 1962, pp. 515–547.

———, "Patterns of Industrial Growth," *American Economic Review*, Vol. 50, No. 4, September 1960, pp. 624–654.

DEUTSCH, K. W., and A. ECKSTEIN, "National Industrialization and the Declining Share of the International Economic Sector," *World Politics*, Vol. 13, No. 2, January 1961, pp. 267–299.

DORRANCE, G. S., "The Effect of Inflation on Economic Development," *International Monetary Fund Staff Papers*, Vol. 10, No. 1, March 1963, pp. 1–47.

FLEMING, J. M., and G. LOVASY, "Fund Policies and Procedures in Relation to the Compensatory Financing of Commodity Fluctuations," *International Monetary Staff Papers*, Vol. 8, No. 1, November 1960, pp. 1–76.

GORDON, L., "Economic Aspects of Coalition Diplomacy: The NATO Experience," *International Organization*, Vol. 10, 1956, pp. 529–543.

HOAG, M. W., "Economic Problems of Alliance," *Journal of Political Economy*, Vol. 65, No. 1, December 1957, pp. 522–534.

HOWELL, L. D., "Benefits versus Costs of Price Supports," *Quarterly Journal of Economics*, Vol. 68, No. 1, February 1954, pp. 115–130.

HUGHES, J. R. T., "Foreign Trade and Balanced Growth: The Historical Framework," *American Economic Review*, Vol. 49, No. 2, May 1959, pp. 330–337.

JOHNSON, H. G., "Economic Expansion and International Trade," *The Manchester School of Economic and Social Studies*, Vol. 23, No. 2, May 1955, pp. 95–112.

KINDLEBERGER, C. P., "The Terms of Trade and Economic Development," *Review of Economics and Statistics*, Vol. 40, No. 1, February 1958 (Supplement), pp. 72–85.

KRAVIS, IRVING B., and M. W. S. DAVENPORT, "The Political Arithmetic of International Burden Sharing," *Journal of Political Economy*, Vol. 71, No. 4, August 1963, pp. 309–330.

KUZNETS, SIMON, "Quantitative Aspects of the Economic Growth of Nations: II. Industrial Distribution of National Products and Labour Force," *Economic Development and Cultural Change*, Vol. 5, No. 4, July 1957 (Supplement)

———, "V. Capital Formation Proportions: International Comparisons for Recent Years," *ibid.*, Vol. 8, No. 4, July 1960 (Supplement), pp. 1–96.

———, "VI. Long-term Trends in Capital Formation Proportions," *ibid.*, Vol. 9, No. 4, July 1961 (Supplement), pp. 1–124.

LEWIS, W. A., "Economic Development with Unlimited Supplies of Labour," *The Manchester School of Economic and Social Studies*, Vol. 22, No. 2, May 1954, pp. 139–191.

MACDOUGALL, G. D. A., "The Benefits and Costs of Private Investment from Abroad: A Theoretical Approach," *Economic Record*, Vol. 36, No. 73, March 1960, pp. 13–35.

———, "India's Balance of Payments," *Bulletin of the Oxford Institute of Statistics*, Vol. 23, May 1961, pp. 154–177.

MAIZELS, A., "Effects of Industrialization on Exports of Primary-Producing Countries," *Kyklos*, Vol. 14, No. 1, 1961, pp. 18–46.

MASON, E. S., "The Equitable Sharing of Military and Economic Aid Burdens," *Proceedings of the Academy of Political Science*, (Columbia University), Vol. 27, No. 3, May 1963, pp. 62–76.

MEHTA, F., "The Effect of Adverse Income Terms of Trade on the Secular Growth of Underdeveloped Countries," *Indian Economic Journal*, Vol. 4, No. 1, July 1956, pp. 9–21.

MORGAN, T., "The Long-run Terms of Trade between Agriculture and Manufacturing," *Economic Development and Cultural Change*, Vol. 8, No. 1, October 1959, pp. 1–23.

MYINT, H., "The 'Classical Theory' of International Trade and the Underdeveloped Countries," *Economic Journal*, Vol. 68, No. 270, June 1958, pp. 317–337.

———, "An Interpretation of Economic Backwardness," *Oxford Economic Papers*, Vol. 6, No. 2, June 1954, pp. 132–163.

NEEDLEMAN, L., "The Burden of Taxation: An International Comparison," *National Institute Economic Review*, No. 14, September 1961, pp. 55–61.

PATEL, S. J., "Export Prospects and Economic Growth: India," *Economic Journal*, Vol. 69, September 1959, pp. 490–506.

PINCUS, JOHN A., "The Cost of Foreign Aid," *Review of Economics and Statistics*, Vol. 45, No. 4, November 1963.

———, "What Policy for Commodities?" *Foreign Affairs*, Vol. 42, January 1964.

PREBISCH, R., "Commercial Policy in Underdeveloped Countries," *American Economic Review, Papers and Proceedings*, Vol. 49, No. 2, May 1959, pp. 251–269.

RAJ, J. N., and A. K. SEN, "Alternative Patterns of Export Growth under Conditions of Stagnant Export Earnings," *Oxford Economic Papers*, Vol. 13, No. 1, February 1961, pp. 43–52.

ROSENSTEIN-RODAN, P. N., "International Aid for Underdeveloped Countries," *Review of Economics and Statistics*, Vol. 43, No. 2, May 1961, pp. 107–138.

SCHMIDT, WILSON, "The Economics of Charity: Loans vs. Grants," *Journal of Political Economy*, Vol. 71, August 1964, pp. 387–395.

SCHULTZ, T. W., "Value of U.S. Farm Surpluses to Underdeveloped Countries," *Journal of Farm Economics*, Vol. 42, December 1960, p. 1020.

SEERS, D., "A Theory of Inflation and Growth in Underdeveloped Economies Based on the Experience of Latin America," *Oxford Economic Papers*, Vol. 14, No. 2, June 1962, pp. 173–195.

SEGRE, CLAUDIO, "Problems of Foreign Indebtedness of Developing Countries,"

Banca Nazionale del Lavoro Quarterly Review, No. 62, September 1962, pp. 269–285.

SIMONET, P. A., "L'Aide au 'Tiers monde': Efforts de conception et procédés d'évaluation," *Développement et civilisations*, No. 14, March 1963, pp. 65–78.

SINGER, H. W., "Comment on 'The Terms of Trade and Economic Development'," *Review of Economics and Statistics*, Vol. 40, No. 1, February 1958 (Supplement), pp. 85–88.

———, "The Distribution of Gains between Investing and Borrowing Countries," *Amer. Economic Review, Papers and Proceedings*, Vol. 40, No. 2, May 1950, pp. 473–485.

———, "Trends in Economic Thought on Underdevelopment," *Social Research*, Vol. 28, No. 4, Winter 1961, pp. 387–414.

SINGER, J. D., "The Finances of the League of Nations," *International Organization*, Vol. 13, No. 2, 1959, pp. 255–273.

SUMBERG, T. A., "Financing International Institutions," *Social Research*, September 1946, pp. 276–306.

SWERLING, BORIS C., "Some Interrelationships between Agricultural Trade and Economic Development," *Kyklos*, Vol. 14, No. 3, 1961, pp. 364–395.

WOLF, CHARLES, JR., "Some Aspects of the 'Value' of Less Developed Countries to the United States," *World Politics*, Vol. 15, No. 4, July 1963, pp. 623–635.

PUBLIC DOCUMENTS

Committee To Strengthen the Security of the Free World, *The Scope and Distribution of United States Military and Economic Assistance Programs*, Department of State, Washington, D.C., March 20, 1963.

Food and Agriculture Organization, "Agricultural Commodities: Projections for 1970," Doc. E/CN 13/48 CCP 63/5, Special Supplement to *FAO Commodity Review 1962*, Rome, 1962.

———, *Monthly Bulletin of Agricultural Economics and Statistics*.

———, *The State of Food and Agriculture*, Rome. Annual.

———, *Trade Yearbook*, Rome. Annual.

General Agreement on Tariffs and Trade, Special Group on Trade in Tropical Products, "Report on Meeting of Subgroup, March 18–26, 1963," Geneva, 1963 (mimeographed).

———, *Trends in International Trade*, Geneva. Annual.

International Bank for Reconstruction and Development, Economic Staff, "Imports and Economic Growth," Washington, D.C., January 3, 1963 (mimeographed).

———, *The World Bank, IFC, and IDA Policies and Operations*, Washington, D.C., April 1962.

International Monetary Fund, *International Financial Statistics*, Washington, D.C. Monthly.

League of Nations, *Industrialization and Foreign Trade*, Geneva, 1945.

Organization for Economic Cooperation and Development, *Development Assistance Efforts and Policies*, Paris. Annual.

———, *The Flow of Financial Resources to Countries in Course of Economic Development 1956–1959*, Paris, 1961.

———, *The Flow of Financial Resources to Countries in Course of Economic Development in 1960*, Paris, February 1962.

———, *The Flow of Financial Resources to Developing Countries in 1961*, Paris, July 1963.

———, *General Statistics*, Paris. Bimonthly.

Organization of American States, *Final Report of Experts on the Stabilization of Export Receipts*, Washington, D.C., November 1961.

Proceedings and Documents of the United Nations Monetary and Financial Conference, Bretton Woods, U.S. Department of State, Washington, D.C., 1948. 2 vols.

Report of the President's Committee To Study the Military Assistance Program, Government Printing Office, Washington, D.C., 1959.

United Nations, *Commodity Trade and Economic Development*, New York, 1953.

———, *Instability in Export Markets of Underdeveloped Countries*, New York, 1952.

———, *International Compensation for Fluctuations in Commodity Trade*, New York, October 1961.

———, *International Flow of Long-Term Capital and Official Donations, 1959–1961*, New York, 1963.

———, *Report of the Committee on Contributions*, General Assembly Document A/80, New York, October 11, 1946.

———, *Statistical Yearbook*, New York, Annual.

———, *World Economic Survey 1958*, New York, 1959.

———, *World Economic Survey 1959*, New York, 1960.

———, *World Economic Survey 1962*, New York, 1963.

———, Economic and Social Council, "Prospective Demand for Non-Agricultural Commodities: Problems of Definition and Methodology," Document E/3629 E/CN. 13/49, New York, May 23, 1962 (mimeographed).

———, Economic Commission for Europe (ECE), *Economic Survey of Europe in 1960*, Geneva, 1961.

———, Economic Commission for Latin America, *The Economic Development of Latin America and Its Principal Problems*, Lake Success, 1950.

———, ———, *Economic Survey of Latin America 1956*, New York, 1957.

———, Statistical Office, *Monthly Bulletin of Statistics*.

———, ———, *Yearbook of International Trade Statistics*, New York. Annual.

———, ———, *Yearbook of National Income Accounts*, New York. Annual.

U.S. Congress, House of Representatives, *Semiannual Report on Activities Carried on under Public Law 480*, Government Printing Office, Washington, D.C.

————, Joint Economic Committee, *Outlook for United States Balance of Payments*, Hearings before the Subcommittee on International Exchange and Payments, December 12, 13, and 14, 1962, Government Printing Office, Washington, D.C., 1963.

U.S. Department of Agriculture, *Agricultural Marketing Service Reports*.

Index

GNP, t75, t77, t78, t79, t82, t135, t136, t137, t139
GNP contribution, t81
industrialization, 19
international contributions, t93, t101
NATO contributions, t107, t108
per capita GNP, t87, t91
purchasing-power equivalents, t88, t91
transfers in aid, t119
unemployment in, 70, t77, t78, t79
Netherlands Economic Institute, 38
New Zealand
exports insurance fund, t183
import volume, 11
manufactured exports, 19
UN contributions, 96
Nigeria
cocoa exports, 171
cocoa revenues, t172
and commodity agreements, 161
earnings from commodities, t160
exports values, t156
GNP and import growth, t10
production control systems, 158
North Atlantic Treaty Organization (*See* NATO)
Norway
aid shares, 143
contributions formula, t78
DAC aid shares, t80, t133, t134, t135
defense expenditures, t77
discounted value of loans, t136, t137, t138
exchange-rate equivalent, t75, t76
exports insurance fund, t183
GNP, t75, t77, t78, t79, t135, t136, t137
GNP contribution, t81
international contributions, t93, t101
NATO contributions, t107, t108
per capita GNP, t87, t91
purchasing-power equivalents, t88, t91
real cost of aid, 142
unemployment in, 70, t77, t78, t79
Nuclear first-strike capacity, 56
Nuclear missiles, 41, 43
Nurske, Ragner, 2, 6, 11, 12
Nyasaland
earnings from commodities, t160
tea exports, 174
tea revenues, t176

OAS (*See* Organization of American States)
Oceania, GNP contribution, t81

OECD (Organization for Economic Cooperation and Development), 51
burden sharing, 50
burden-sharing formulas, 51–91 *passim*
capital flow estimates, 32
contributions to, t93
cost sharing, 111
real cost of aid, 190
OEEC (Organization for European Economic Cooperation), proportional contributions, 60
Oils
export supply, 16
PL 480 shipments, t144, t145
tariffs on, 19
(*See also* Coconut oil; Cottonseed oil; Groundnut oil; Linseed oil; Oilseeds; Olive oil; Palm kernel oil; Palm oil; Soybean oil)
Oilseeds
and commodity agreements, 159, 161, 163, 180
price supports, 158
tariffs on, 19
in world trade, 157, 179
Olive oil, in world trade, t152
Oranges, in world trade, t152
Organization of American States, exports stabilization, 180
Organization for Economic Cooperation and Development (*See* OECD)
Organization for European Economic Cooperation (*See* OEEC)

Pakistan
import substitution, 18
industrialization in, 19
jute exports, 159
production control systems, 158
Palm kernel oil, in world trade, t152
Palm kernels, in world trade, t153
Palm oil, in world trade, t152
Panama
banana revenues, t177
and commodity agreements, 161
earnings from commodities, t160
exports values, t155
GNP growth, t10
import growth, t10
Paper pulp, and commodity agreements, 159
Paraguay, and commodity agreements, 161
Pareto optimum, 58(n)

SELECTED RAND BOOKS

BAUM, WARREN C., *The French Economy and the State*, Princeton, N. J., Princeton University Press, 1958.

BRODIE, BERNARD, *Strategy in the Missile Age*, Princeton, N. J., Princeton University Press, 1959.

DINERSTEIN, HERBERT S., *War and the Soviet Union: Nuclear Weapons and the Revolution in Soviet Military and Political Thinking*, New York, Praeger, 1959.

DOLE, STEPHEN, and ISAAC ASIMOV, *Planets for Man*, New York, Random House, 1964.

DORFMAN, ROBERT, PAUL A. SAMUELSON, ROBERT M. SOLOW, *Linear Programming and Economic Analysis*, New York, McGraw-Hill Book Company, Inc., 1958.

HALPERN, MANFRED, *The Politics of Social Change in the Middle East and North Africa*, Princeton, N. J., Princeton University Press, 1963.

HIRSHLEIFER, JACK, JAMES C. DEHAVEN, and JEROME W. MILLIMAN, *Water Supply: Economics, Technology, and Policy*, Chicago, The University of Chicago Press, 1960.

HITCH, CHARLES J., and ROLAND MCKEAN, *The Economics of Defense in the Nuclear Age*, Cambridge, Harvard University Press, 1960.

HSIEH, ALICE L., *Communist China's Strategy in the Nuclear Era*, Englewood Cliffs, N. J., Prentice-Hall, Inc., 1962.

JOHNSON, JOHN J., (ed.), *The Role of the Military in Underdeveloped Countries*, Princeton, N. J., Princeton University Press, 1962.

JOHNSTONE, WILLIAM C., *Burma's Foreign Policy: A Study in Neutralism*, Cambridge, Harvard University Press, 1963.

LIU, TA-CHUNG, and KUNG-CHIA YEH, *The Economy of the Chinese Mainland: National Income and Economic Development, 1933–1959*, Princeton, N. J., Princeton University Press, 1965.

LUBELL, HAROLD, *Middle East Oil Crises and Western Europe's Energy Supplies*, Baltimore, The Johns Hopkins Press, 1963.

MCKEAN, ROLAND N., *Efficiency in Government through Systems Analysis: With Emphasis on Water Resource Development*, New York, John Wiley & Sons, Inc., 1958.

MEYER, J. R., J. F. KAIN, and M. WOHL, *The Urban Transportation Problem*, Cambridge, Harvard University Press, 1965.

QUADE, E. S. (ed.), *Analysis for Military Decisions*, Chicago, Rand McNally & Company; Amsterdam, North-Holland Publishing Company, 1964.

RUSH, MYRON, *Political Succession in the USSR*, New York, Columbia University Press, 1965.

SPEIER, HANS, *Divided Berlin: The Anatomy of Soviet Political Blackmail*, New York, Praeger, 1961.

WHITING, ALLEN S., *China Crosses the Yalu: The Decision To Enter the Korean War*, New York, The Macmillan Company, 1960.

WILLIAMS, J. D., *The Compleat Strategyst: Being a Primer on the Theory of Games of Strategy*, New York, McGraw-Hill Book Company, Inc., 1954.

WOLF, CHARLES, JR., *Foreign Aid: Theory and Practice in Southern Asia*, Princeton, N. J., Princeton University Press, 1960.

WOLFE, THOMAS, *Soviet Strategy at the Crossroads*, Cambridge, Harvard University Press, 1964.